CHANGE MANAGEMENT

CHANGE MANAGEMENT

Altering Mindsets in a Global Context

V. Nilakant
and
S. Ramnarayan

Response Books
A division of Sage Publications
New Delhi/Thousand Oaks/London

Copyright © V. Nilakant and S. Ramnarayan, 2006

All rights reserved. No part of this book may be reproduced or utilised in any form or by any means, electronic or mechanical, including photocopying, recording or by any information storage or retrieval system, without permission in writing from the publisher.

First published in 2006 by

Response Books
A division of Sage Publications India Pvt Ltd
B-42, Panchsheel Enclave
New Delhi 110 017

Sage Publications Inc	**Sage Publications Ltd**
2455 Teller Road	1 Oliver's Yard
Thousand Oaks	55 City Road
California 91320	London EC1Y 1SP

Published by Tejeshwar Singh for Response Books, typeset in 10.5/12.5 pts. Optima by Innovative Processors, New Delhi, and printed at Chaman Enterprises, New Delhi.

Library of Congress Cataloging-in-Publication Data

Nilakant, V., 1952–
    Change management: altering mindsets in a global context/V. Nilakant and S. Ramnarayan.
    p. cm.
    Includes index.
    1. Organizational change—India. 2. Organizational change—Asia. 3. Organizational change. I. Ramnarayan, S. II. Title.
HD58.8.N553   2006   658.4′06095—dc22   2005035067

ISBN: 0-7619-3468-5 (US-PB)   81-7829-622-5 (India-PB)

Production Team: Anupama Purohit, R.A.M. Brown and Santosh Rawat

Contents

List of Tables	6
List of Figures	7
List of Boxes	9
Foreword	11
Preface	13
Chapter 1. The Change Management Model	17
Chapter 2. Appreciating Change: Industry Analysis	56
Chapter 3. Appreciating Change: Mental and Business Models	98
Chapter 4. Mobilising Support	134
Chapter 5. Executing Change	189
Chapter 6. Building Change Capability	248
Chapter 7. Leadership and Change	307
Index	343
About the Authors	356

List of Tables

1.1	Change Need Analysis	34
2.1	Percentage Changes in Births and Deaths 1988–1998	60
2.2	Transition of Firms 1995–1998	61
2.3	Competence-enhancing and Competence-destroying Innovations in Three Industries in the United States	77
3.1	Evaluating a Business Model	128
4.1	Four Approaches to Change	138
4.2	Six Principles of Persuasion and Related Change Management Tactics	158
4.3	Core Tasks for Mobilising Support	165
4.4	Techniques for Framing	170
6.1	Accelerating Decisions in High-uncertainty Environments	258
6.2	Distinguishing Features of Purposeful and Distracted Managers	263
6.3	Factors that Lead to Recognition and Ownership of Problem	272
6.4	Components of Capability Building	297
7.1	AI Interview Guide	315
7.2	AI Summary Sheet	316

List of Figures

1.1	Change Management Model	30
1.2	Four Leadership Roles in Change Management	51
2.1	Distribution of Organisations by Size in New Zealand in 1996	60
2.2	Real GDP Growth: US with Recession	62
2.3	US Economy: Real GDP Growth Rate Across Time	63
2.4	Indian Economy: Real GDP Growth Rate Across Time	63
2.5	Growth in Industrial Production SSI Sector at 1993–94 prices	64
2.6	US Economy: Capacity Build-up and GDP Growth Rate	66
2.7	US Economy: Capacity Build-up and Producer Prices	67
2.8	Life Cycle Stages of Industry Evolution	71
2.9	Factors Shaping the Change Agenda	94
3.1	Managing Change: Impact and Magnitude Grid	101
3.2	Dominant Model in the PC Industry	125
3.3	Dell Direct Model	125
4.1	Sample Commitment Chart	168

8 Change Management

5.1	Four Types of Change	192
5.2	Factors Contributing to Non-Collaboration	217
5.3	Effect of Purpose and Processes on People	234
6.1	The Focus–Energy Matrix	261
6.2	Components of Capability	301

List of Boxes

2.1	Cost Advantages from Flexibility in Plant Capacity	69
2.2	Market Knowledge as Source of Responsiveness and Pricing Power	70
2.3	Digital Music and iPod Phenomenon	82
2.4	Strategic Change in Mobile Phone Industry	83
3.1	Senge's Five Disciplines	112
3.2	The Two Column Approach to Uncover Defensive Routines	117
4.1	Getting Oscar to Eat Lunch	142
4.2	When 'Push' Strategy Pushed the Issues Underground	145
4.3	Communicating to Delhi Residents and Gaining their Support	160
4.4	Malaysian Carpet Company	161
4.5	Crisis and Credibility	163
4.6	Balancing Consideration and Closure in Decision-Making	174
4.7	Unclogging the Communication and Involvement Channels	176
4.8	Resolving a Tangle during Presidential Campaign	181
5.1	Reinforcing Commercial Focus in Day-to-Day Interactions	221

10 Change Management

5.2	Unlearning Mindset of 'Beneficiary' and Learning to be 'Entrepreneur'	222
5.3	New Behaviours Resulting from *Manthan*	235
5.4	Summary of Points for 'Strengthening Action Plan' and 'Evolving Communication Plan'	236
5.5	Deconstructing the Goal of 'Reduction in Purchase Costs' at Nissan	240
6.1	Sample of Performance Achievements Resulting from ASPIRE	250
6.2	What Factors Contribute to Self-Efficacy?	257
6.3	How Mindset Inhibited Learning at J & J	278
6.4	Transfer of Best Practices at GE	281
6.5	Seven Elements in Questioning	285
6.6	Hearing the Unheard	285

Foreword

TODAY INDIA stands at significant crossroads of development and growth. In the last 20 years the country has witnessed sustained economic growth that has brought, in its wake, increased prosperity and a sense of confidence to many of its citizens. Thanks to the revolution that began with information technology, India has emerged as a key player in the global economy. Indian companies are poised for global expansion through foreign direct investments. India is emerging as a major hub for manufacturing and export of automobile parts and accessories, textiles, pharmaceuticals, leather goods and machine tools. Indian companies are now major players in a global market.

Although, as Indians, we can be proud of the tremendous progress we have made, we still have a long way to go. When India became independent in 1947, we set ourselves the mission of eradicating poverty, ignorance and disease that had kept us backward. That mission remains to be accomplished. We need to grow at the rate of eight percent or more annually over the next ten to 15 years. Specifically, we need to modernise our infrastructure in a radical way. We need massive investments in education to build the human capital that will fuel our progress. We need substantial changes in primary and secondary education. We also need huge improvements in healthcare, particularly in the areas of primary and rural healthcare.

All this will require an enhancement of our ability to execute decisions and implement changes. We need new ways of thinking, working, engaging and interacting to build organisations that will help us achieve our goals. Both public and private organisations need to learn new ways of engaging with people and communities in the management of change. The framework of managing growth and change in a dynamic environment presented in this book draws on current research in the social sciences and combines research findings with the practical experience of the authors. The illustrative cases drawn from different sectors and industries highlight the specific leadership challenges of paying attention to mental models both outside and inside the organisation; gaining support for the idea of change; creating right structures, processes and coordination mechanisms for effective execution; and getting people to believe in their own ability to master challenges.

The authors of this book were involved in change management programmes conducted for ministers in the Indian government and civil service officers, with whom I was closely associated under the leadership of Shri Rajiv Gandhi in the 80s. Their ideas on change management were initially developed when they worked with the Tata group of companies at the Tata Management Training Centre, Pune. The authors have vast experience in working with private and governmental organisations in India and abroad. They do not offer a formula or a do-it-yourself kit for bringing about change. They remind us that growth, development and change require shifts in our mindsets and mental models. More importantly, sustained progress demands that we commit ourselves to making tough choices and implementing them.

Systematic frameworks such as the one offered in this book can significantly benefit managers and others struggling to cope with the challenges of change. We need all the knowledge and insights that we can get to achieve the demanding goals that we have set for ourselves. I am confident that this book will be an important contribution to our knowledge of how to manage change in increasingly demanding times.

P. Chidambaram
Finance Minister
Government of India

Preface

THIS BOOK was originally conceived as the second edition of our previous book *Managing Organisational Change*, written in the aftermath of liberalisation initiated by the Indian government in 1991 and published in 1998. Based on primary data from about fifty Indian organisations in a variety of industries, it examined the challenges of growth in an emerging, liberalised competitive environment. We viewed organisational change as comprising three generic processes of growth, transformation and decline. We suggested that these three processes differ from one another in certain crucial respects and, therefore, required different approaches to manage the same. We argued that it was important for managers to know which generic process they are managing in order to be effective. We presented a model of the levers of change that provided an *integrated approach* to the management of change. Our generic model specifically focused on eight tangible levers of change: *values-based leadership, strategy, structure, human resource practices, technology, marketing, quality, and costs*. While the model was illustrated with examples from the best of Indian and international practices, the book emphasised both *what* organisations need to change and *how* they should go about it. It suggested that the effective management of change involves managing *intangibles*, particularly positive values such as selflessness, justice, compassion, tolerance, respect and integrity.

Our previous book was not only about how to manage change, but it also sought to celebrate the success of Indian organisations in a competitive environment. We noted that India was poised on the threshold of a major transformation. Following the liberalisation of the Indian economy in 1991, Indian businesses were exposed to the realities of both domestic and global competition. Many expected indigenous businesses to struggle for survival in the wake of deregulation and increased competition. However, we argued that Indian organisations' response to these changes had been positive and vigorous; presenting lessons from their experiences of managing change. We believed that these lessons were universal and important for those managing organisational change in any part of the world.

Soon as we began to work on a second edition of *Managing Organisational Change,* it became apparent that the book needed more than just a revision. Both, India and Indian organisations had come a long way since that book was published. For instance, Infosys, one of the cases that we had discussed in our previous book, is now a global player with a turnaround exceeding a billion dollars. The Indian software industry has grown rapidly since early 90s, at an average compounded annual growth rate of around 40 per cent. Today, it is a global industry catering primarily to markets in North America and Europe. The World Bank rates India as a leading outsourcing destination for software services. Our ideas on change management were initially developed when we worked with the Tata group of companies at the Tata Management Training Centre in Pune, India. Currently, the turnover of the Tata group of companies is equivalent to about 3 per cent of India's GDP. With a touch of pride, we note that some of these companies have achieved global excellence in their areas of operation. In its 2005 ranking, the World Steel Dynamics rates Tata Steel as the world's best steel company. Tata Consultancy Services, India's largest IT services company operates in 33 countries and has a turnover of more than a billion dollars. Tata Motors' silver prototype of a sports utility/saloon crossover vehicle was one of the stars of the recent Geneva motor show. In our previous book we noted that according to a World Bank forecast, by 2025, India would be the world's fifth-largest economy. Today many expect it to be the third largest by that period.

In spite of its tremendous achievement since 1991, we believe that India has a long way to go before it can claim to be a credible global power. Our vision of India is a country with 100 per cent literacy, in which every village has a road, drinking water and electricity; where all its citizens have access to good health care and whose children have had at least ten years of basic education. We also believe that this is feasible by 2020. To achieve this vision, Indian organisations would be required to manage change in a challenging environment. In this book, we present a model to address this challenge of change.

While *Change Management* builds on the ideas from our previous book, it is different in two significant ways. First, it is less about India and more about change management in a global context. We discuss global best practices in various facets of change management. Second, the model of change management that we present in this book is based not on case studies but on current research and ideas in change management.

In our model of change management, we identify four core tasks that are crucial to the success of any change initiative in organisations. These are: appreciating change, mobilising support for change, executing change and building change capability. We contend that change initiatives that fail to achieve their objectives do so because they fail to effectively manage one or more of these. While the model is based on theory and research, it also offers a practical approach to managing change. In particular, we caution managers against action without reflection, energy without focus and competitiveness without compassion. We suggest that effective management of change is about balance – between short-term and long-term, profits and people, overview and detail, continuity and transformation, reality and imagination, hard-nosed business savvy and soft-hearted dreams, and between what is feasible and what is desirable. We argue that organisational change is inherently complex and warn against adopting simplistic recipes. We have presented our model to several groups of managers. The positive responses we have received indicate that the model is relevant, valid and practical.

The most significant message we would like to offer through this book is that organisational change is not about restructuring, reorganising, merging or downsizing. It is not about six sigma, total quality management or lean production. Fundamentally it is all about changing the ways in which people *think* and *act* in an organisation. It is about altering mental models and mindsets. We believe this to be core task of change managers and leaders; and suggest practical ways in which this can be brought about in organisations. We believe that managing change in organisation is about: (a) tuning to the external environment and people's mindsets inside the organisation, (b) influencing and persuading people and strengthening communication, (c) architecting change through cross-functional collaboration and challenging goals, and (d) creating positive contexts that enable people to: have faith in their own capabilities, experiment, take risks and learn.

We are grateful to the Honourable Union Finance Minister, Government of India, Shri P. Chidambaram, for contributing the 'Foreword' for this book. We have had the privilege of knowing him since he involved us in designing and conducting a series of change management workshops for ministers and senior civil service officers in the mid-1980s. We were keen to have him write this 'Foreword' as it provides affirmation and continuity for an inquiry into change management issues that commenced in 1984, when we became involved with the change initiatives that began in India during the same period.

A number of people in India and New Zealand have contributed to the completion of this book. Besides the many organisational leaders who were generous in sharing with us their experiences, ideas and insights; we are particularly grateful to: Chapal Mehra, Response Books, for his patience and persistence in nudging us towards completion; Prof. Anil Sood for generously devoting his time and energy to go through the manuscript and providing critical inputs; Dr. P. K. Mohanty, Director General of the Centre for Good Governance, India, for being a source of constant inspiration and encouragement during the book-writing project, Kiran Kumar for providing high quality research help; and Jo Jordan, Peter Cammock, Ian Brooks, David Ripley, Bob Hamilton, Irene Edgar and Irene Joseph in New Zealand for their unstinting support.

V. Nilakant   **S. Ramnarayan**

CHAPTER 1

The Change Management Model

OVERVIEW

In our change management model presented in this chapter, we build on Kurt Lewin's fundamental contributions to change management and discuss the assumptions, philosophy and values underlying our model of managing change. We present our model that views change management as a complex task comprising four core activities: appreciating change, mobilising support, executing change and building change capability. We discuss the four leadership roles that are crucial in change management.

CHALLENGES OF CHANGE

Today, both business and non-business organisations confront a world that is challenging in many ways. Managers face three challenges in particular.

First, there is increased competition for an organisation's resources. Business firms today face increasing competition in their markets and for their inputs. Non-business organisations face competition for their funds.

Second, these organisations have to compete in a world that is constantly changing. Globalisation, technological changes and unanticipated events have rendered the world uncertain and unpredictable. Over the years, globalisation has resulted in greater degree of inter-connectedness between markets, economies and countries. This means events in other parts of the world have the potential to affect an organisation's resources. Revolutions in information and communication technologies have the potential to enhance or destroy an organisation's core capabilities. In addition, there are unanticipated events such as wars, epidemics and global terrorism that can come as nasty shocks.

Third, it is increasingly difficult to predict what will happen in an organisation's environment. In a globalised marketplace, competition may arise from anywhere. The future impact of a new technology may be hard to predict. Customer preferences and community standards may shift in unexpected ways. New legislation that impacts on business and non-business organisations may be introduced. In addition to these external uncertainties, there are internal uncertainties. Typically, these are related to people. It may be difficult to predict how people in the organisation would react to change. Key people in the organisation may leave for better pay, career, lifestyle or working conditions. There may be political or power struggles resulting from key individuals jockeying for power. All in all, in today's world, both external and internal uncertainties have turned a manager's job both challenging and difficult.

The only certainty in a changing world is that you can't escape change! Change management is a relatively new discipline that focuses on why and how organisations change. Based on theory and research, it offers practical advice to managers who are confronted with change. Over the years, the discipline of change management has evolved from a set of practical, descriptive and prescriptive tools to models and frameworks based on theory and empirical research. Recent research in the related disciplines of organisational behaviour and organisation theory provides a sophisticated understanding of change issues and how to manage them. More importantly, research in organisation theory has also highlighted the cost and risks associated with change. We know, for instance, why managing change in large, complex organisations is more difficult and risky.

A major finding in change management research is that most organisations do not manage change well. Less than 30 per cent of organisations that implement large-scale change are successful.[1] Even in smaller organisational changes such as implementing new information systems, less than 20 per cent of information technology projects are successful.[2] In a competitive business environment, the ability to manage change effectively can translate into increased market share, revenue and profits. Therefore, it is not surprising that change management and leadership have emerged as the two critical areas in management in recent years. We propose that it is possible to design change programmes, which not only have better chances of success, but are also unlikely to hurt people inside the organisation.

RE-INVENTING KURT LEWIN

CONTRIBUTION OF KURT LEWIN

An individual called Kurt Lewin first articulated the science of change in human systems.[3] His seminal work is the foundation for our model of change management. We have developed our model of change management by combining Lewin's ideas with current concepts in organisation theory. In other words, we have sought to re-invent Kurt Lewin for managing change in the current global environment. Two ideas of Kurt Lewin that underlie all contemporary approaches to managing change are his change model and his concept of action research. We'll begin by examining Lewin's change model in this section and discuss his concept of action research in the next. Lewin's ideas are the basis of the first assumption in our change model.

According to Lewin, in any individual, group or organisation there are two competing forces in operation. These are the forces of stability that aim to maintain the human system in the status quo and the forces of change that push the system towards change. In most human systems, these two forces are evenly balanced—leading to what is known as a *quasi-stationary equilibrium*. This maintains the system in the status quo. Therefore for change to happen, either the forces of change need to be strengthened or the forces of stability need to be weakened.

Lewin argued that enhancing the forces of change would lead to a corresponding increase in the forces of stability. Therefore, weakening or reducing the forces of stability can more effectively bring about change. This step of weakening the forces of stability is referred to as *unfreezing* in his change model. After a system is unfrozen, the existing forces of change will ensure that the system *moves* towards a new state. Once the system has moved into a new state, it is *refrozen* in that state by the adoption of new habits, structures or culture.

In Lewin's change model, forces of stability and change are both within the organisation. In other words, the seeds of change are present in every organisation. The primary task of change management is to discover these forces of change and create conditions suitable for these forces to push the organisation towards a new state. Therefore, the first assumption underlying our model of change management is that *solutions to an organisation's problem cannot be found outside the organisation. An organisation possesses the potential and the capability to solve its own problems.*

Following Lewin, we contend that change can be brought about most effectively by weakening an organisation's forces of stability. If we want to weaken these forces of stability, we need to first understand the dynamics of these forces of stability. What are the forces of stability in an organisation? Modern organisation theory provides a clue to this question with its concept of *routines*. This concept is a fundamental building block of our model and needs to be explained before we present our model of change management.

ORGANISATIONAL ROUTINES AND MENTAL MODELS

Our approach to change management is based on the idea of *organisational routines*. This idea of a routine is the basis of the second assumption in our change management model. We know what we mean when we use the term *organisation*. Organisations produce and distribute the goods and services that we consume everyday. Right from birth to death, our life is mediated by a variety of organisations. Among other things, organisations educate us, provide us food, clothing and housing, employ us, lend us money, tend to us when we are sick, transport us, arrange our vacation and provide us entertainment. They are so ever-present that we take them for granted. While we might be able to talk about organisations and identify and name them, most of us would be at a loss if asked to *define* an organisation. What *is* an organisation?

In simple terms, an organisation helps us to accomplish tasks that are beyond the capacity of a single individual. In other words, an organisation is a remarkable social tool created by human beings to transcend individual limitations. When individuals work together collectively to achieve common goals, they are able to accomplish tasks that are way beyond the capacity of any single individual. The common adage 'united we stand, divided we fall' captures this remarkable truth about organisations. Thus, when individuals work together to achieve common goals, they become *organised*.

What does it mean when we say that individuals or more correctly their activities are organised? It means that individuals do not act as they please—in other words, their behaviour is not idiosyncratic; it is governed by certain commonly understood rules.

For example: when you drive on the road you have to be aware of the traffic rules/road code of the country in which you are driving, which specify which side of the road you can drive on. Then there are rules regarding how fast you can go, how you may or may not overtake and rules that specify what to do when you are at an intersection. Many of these rules are written down and elaborate; but we don't need to have read them to understand. Universally, if the traffic light turns red at an intersection we know that we must stop. If you are caught violating these rules, it can result in punishment.

Similarly, most countries have a penal code that specifies the kind of behaviour that is unacceptable in that country. Not all our behaviour is according to written rules. There are also unwritten rules in the form of norms and conventions that govern our behaviour. We stand in queues in supermarkets, are usually polite to strangers and normally dress according to prevailing customs and fashions.

Think about this carefully and you realise that most of our behaviour is actually organised in such a manner that it takes place according to a set of written or unwritten rules. When activities and behaviour become organised, they become repetitive and predictable. In other words, they become routine. Daily life in a modern society is routine. We get up in the morning and go to sleep at night around the same time each day. We eat breakfast in the morning, lunch around noon and dinner at night. Everyday, we interact with almost the same people. Even when we encounter strangers, our behaviour is governed by commonly accepted conventions and etiquette.

Most importantly, when we behave or act in conformity to unwritten or written rules or conventions, we reinforce those rules or conventions. If we refer to these written and unwritten rules as *structure,* then actions and behaviour that are shaped by the structure also reproduce the structure. This significant insight is provided by Anthony Giddens, the well-known sociologist, who says that structure is both the medium and an unintended outcome of social practices. He refers to this as the 'duality of structure.'

According to Giddens, structure provides us with a sense of security. People and activities become familiar and predictable. If we were to live in a world where everything is unfamiliar and unpredictable, we would experience very high levels of anxiety. Therefore, structure reduces our anxiety to manageable levels and gives us what Giddens refers to as 'ontological security.' In other words, we feel at home with ourselves and with the world. In sociological jargon, according to Giddens[4]:

Ordinary day-to-day life—in greater or lesser degree according to context and the vagaries of individual personality—involves an ontological security expressing an autonomy of bodily control within predictable routines.

Any disruption to these routines fills most of us with anxiety. Does this mean that our behaviour and actions are tightly controlled by routines? Not at all. We may, for instance, consciously or unconsciously violate some of these routines. If others follow us and also start violating the same routine then the routine itself is no longer viable and has undergone change. Thus, individuals acting collectively can also change the rules or codes that have governed their behaviour.

In this book, we shall use the terms rules, codes and routines to mean the same thing. These are like formulae that people carry in their heads to perform their jobs and interact with people. The remarkable contributions of Giddens elaborated in his book *The Constitution of Society,* as the theory of structuration, give us two important insights: (i) Individual actions and behaviour are shaped by a set of written and unwritten rules or codes that we call structure. (ii) When individuals act in conformity with the codes, they reinforce and reproduce the codes or the structure. When they collectively violate the codes, they change the codes or the structure.

How do these insights help us in understanding organisational change? The term organisation, as used in this book, refers to a business firm or a non-business enterprise set up to provide specific goods and services. Most of us associate the word organisation with a building, place or location. We also associate the word with a collection of people. However, any collection of people does not make up an organisation. For instance, we do not think of spectators in a cricket or rugby match as an organisation. In addition, people who are part of an organisation do not necessarily have to be in one location, place or building.

A collection of individuals needs to have three aspects to be called an organisation[5]: (i) The group or collection of people must be *goal-directed*. An organisation exists for a purpose and people inside the organisation engage in activities to help achieve that purpose. An organisation may have more than one goal but essentially an organisation exists to achieve those goals. (ii) An organisation must have *boundaries*—it should be possible to distinguish between people who belong to the organisation and those who are not part of the organisation. A feature of organisations is that they continually maintain these boundaries. If an organisation is unable to maintain its boundaries, it cannot survive. (iii) People inside the organisation must be connected by a pattern of interactions that are governed by written and unwritten rules. Thus, the pattern of interactions is not random. Interactions occur as a result of tasks or activities that individuals perform to achieve the organisation's goals. These individual activities need to occur in a coordinated manner for the organisations to be effective. The structure facilitates the coordination of these individual activities. The activities of people in an organisation are governed by a system of rules, regulations, procedures, conventions, norms, habit and tradition.

Many organisations have elaborate operating manuals or standard operating procedures that specify how each activity should be carried out in the organisation. Some do not have any written rules but have well-established habits and traditions that govern its activities. We refer to these formal and informal rules as routines. The formal aspect of routines specifies the *architecture* or configuration of an organisation. Architecture includes factors such as the levels of hierarchy (who controls whom?), pattern of authority (who makes the decisions and how are decisions made?), job descriptions and titles (also known as specialisation), grouping of activities (departmentalisation), rules and procedures for performing individual tasks (standard operating procedures), recruitment and compensation policies and so on.

Architecture specifies the way in which activities *should* be carried out in the organisation. It is important to note that there are several elements to architecture such as hierarchy, authority, specialisation, departmentalisation and standard operating procedures. There are choices for each of these elements. For instance, an organisation may have a tall hierarchy (many vertical levels) compared to one that has a flat hierarchy (few vertical levels). One organisation may have elaborate rules and procedures while another may have few rules and procedures. In one organisation, critical decisions may be made by a single individual while in another one a team or group may make similar decisions. Thus, every organisation has a variety of architectural choices for achieving its goals. In reality, however, most organisations have similar architectural features. Why is this so? The answer to this puzzle lies in the informal aspect of structure.

The informal aspect of routines refers to unwritten, tacit rules that govern how activities are *actually* carried out in the organisation. We refer to these unwritten tacit rules as the *culture* of the organisation. Culture is made up of both internal and external codes. Internal codes are made up of habits and traditions. These habits and traditions also represent people's expectations about how activities and work should be performed in the organisation. They may rule out some architectural choices if these go against the habits, traditions and expectations. External codes may be in the form of legislation, community standards, community expectations and norms of professional conduct. Once again, these codes represent community expectations of how activities should be patterned and how tasks are to be carried out in the organisation. If an organisation violates these external codes, it is likely to face an eventual loss in its valuation. Both internal and external cultural codes restrict the architectural choices available to a firm or enterprise. Therefore, in reality, organisations have relatively few architectural choices.

The term organisational change implies changes in the following: (a) goals, (b) boundaries or (c) pattern of activities of an organisation. Since these three aspects are interconnected, changes in one of the aspects may also change the other two aspects. Typically, changing the goals of an organisation will change its boundaries and its pattern of activities but changes in pattern of activities and/or boundaries need not lead to change in goals. In other words, no matter how changes are initiated in an organisation they will inevitably involve a change in the pattern of activities or the routines of the organisation.

This leads to our second assumption, which states *that organisational change involves changing routines in an organisation. These routines are embedded in people's head as mindsets or mental models. These mindsets or mental models are made up of assumptions, values and beliefs. More importantly, they contain formulae or codes to guide behaviour in specific situations. Since routines create and sustain stability in an organisation, change management is largely about changing people's mindsets.* This brings us to an important question: How can people's mindsets be changed?

CHANGING MENTAL MODELS OR MINDSETS

If we assume that routines drive organisations towards stability, and further assume that routines are embedded in mental models or mindsets that people carry, then change involves altering these mental models. Following Lewin, we only want to change those mental models or routines that sustain and maintain an organisation in the status quo. This would reduce the forces of stability and the existing forces of change will move the organisation forward. Changing an individual's mental model involves inducing the individual to give up some of his or her beliefs, assumptions and values. This is a part of the process of learning. In this sense, learning and change are synonymous—i.e. they refer to the same phenomenon. Therefore, in order to understand how mental models can be changed, we need to understand how people learn and unlearn.

Edgar Schein, in the Massachusetts Institute of Technology (MIT) in the United States, has made a significant contribution to our understanding of learning and change.[6] Building on Kurt Lewin's ideas, he argues that change in individuals involves two opposing forces.

Schein refers to one of these as *learning anxiety*. According to him, the prospect of learning something new itself produces anxiety. Individuals are reluctant to learn anything new because they may appear incompetent to others or may feel rejected by those they value and may risk losing their identity. Learning anxiety causes resistance to change. In other words, learning anxiety is a force against change in an organisation. In Lewin's change model discussed above, learning anxiety is a force of stability.

However, individuals are exposed to another kind of anxiety in times of change: *survival anxiety*. According to Schein, this is the feeling that—unless we learn something new—we are going to be out of business or we shall fail to achieve some important goals. For change to take place, survival anxiety has to be greater than learning anxiety. Schein's ideas are the basis of the third assumption in our change management model.

Following Lewin, Schein argues that reducing learning anxiety—rather than increasing survival anxiety—can more effectively bring about change. This involves creating a climate of psychological safety so that individuals feel comfortable in changing their mental models and ways of thinking. Individuals need to be persuaded to give up their old mental models so that they can embrace new ways of thinking. This persuasion can take place in a variety of ways.

Schein warns against *coercive persuasion,* which occurs when individuals are forced to change because not-changing is associated with severe physical or psychological punishment; This may occur in business organisations; where employees may be threatened with prospects of job losses if they do not learn and change. While coercive persuasion can lead to learning and change, it robs individuals of their choice to change. This is contrary to the fundamental values of a civil society that is based on the principles of democracy and participation. Therefore we present our third assumption, that *our model of change management is premised on the assumption of free choice. We propose that change is most effective when it is based on free choice and is brought about without coercing individuals.*

If we rule out coercion or pressure, how can we induce individuals to give up their mental models and embrace new ways of thinking? We cannot induce someone to give up their mental models before understanding their ways of thinking and their mental models. Meaning, we need to engage in a process of inquiry in order to change an individual's mental model. This becomes particularly important in an organisational context when we need to understand and change the dominant mental model in the organisation. Our first assumption leads us to the conclusion that one cannot change someone else's mental model. Then how can someone's mental model *be* changed? It is here that Lewin's second contribution assumes significance; the concept of action research.

ACTION RESEARCH AND DIALOGUE

Lewin's concept of action research was that a human system—whether individual, group or in an organisation—can only be changed by engaging the human system in its own change.

Therefore Lewin's action research emphasised involvement and participation. He contended that involvement and participation of individuals facilitated their change; arguing that inquiry and change in social systems could not be viewed as discrete activities. His famous dictum was: *if you want to understand something, try to change it.*

In Lewin's original conception of action research, the agenda for change was set and driven by the researcher. But our third assumption of free choice precludes the setting of change agenda by someone external to the human system. Therefore, we expect change to happen when individuals reflect on their own mental models and choose to change them on their own free will, with the help and support of a change manager or leader.

The role of a change leader is to create conditions that will facilitate reflection, inquiry and change of mental models. The primary tasks of a change leader are to engage and connect with people in an organisation and persuade them to change their dominant mental model. This will require them to reflect and inquire into their mental model, and choose to either retain or discard it.

How can change leaders facilitate reflection and inquiry into mental models? Schein provides the answer to this question, by proposing the notion of *dialogue* to make people aware of their mental models and thinking. According to him,

> *Most communication and human relations workshops emphasize active listening, by which is meant that one should pay attention to all the communication channels—the spoken words, the body language, tone of voice, and emotional content. One should learn to focus initially on what the other person is saying rather than on one's own intended response. In contrast, dialogue focuses on getting in touch with underlying assumptions (especially our own assumptions) that automatically determine when we choose to speak and what we choose to say. Dialogue is focused more on the thinking process and how our perceptions and cognitions are shaped by our past experiences. The assumption here is that if we become more conscious of how our thought process works, we will think better, collectively, and communicate better.*

The Change Management Model

An important goal of dialogue is to enable the group to reach a higher level of consciousness and creativity through the gradual creation of a shared set of meanings and a 'common' thinking process.

We build on this notion of dialogue to argue that change takes place through the medium of *conversations*. However, these conversations need to be different from what takes place ordinarily in most organisations when people talk to one another, and must be based on a different set of rules. In summary, our change management model is based on the following premises:

- Solutions to an organisation's problem cannot be found outside the organisation. An organisation possesses the potential and the capability to solve its own problems
- Organisations are maintained in the status quo by their routines
- Organisational change involves changing routines in an organisation that maintain stability
- These routines are embedded in people's head as mindsets or mental models. These mindsets or mental models are made up of assumptions, values and beliefs. More importantly, they contain formulae or codes to guide behaviour in specific situations
- Since routines create and sustain stability in an organisation, change management is largely about changing people's mindsets
- The premise for our model of change management is the assumption of free choice. We propose that change is most effective when it is based on free choice, brought about without coercing individuals
- Change management requires engagement and connection with those whose mental models need to change
- Dialogue and conversations constitute the medium of change

Having discussed our premises, we present our model of change management in the following section.

OUR CHANGE MANAGEMENT MODEL

Organisational change involves complex processes. Managing these processes is difficult because they are dynamic i.e. such complex processes are changing. In such dynamic situations, it is difficult to predict the consequences of our actions. Managing the complex process of change involves managing a set of complex activities, each of which is crucial for the overall success of change. In particular, we contend that managing change involves managing *four* complex tasks. Each of these complex tasks needs to be completed effectively in order to achieve a successful outcome. Failure in any one of these four tasks will lead to a failure in the overall change. These four tasks are: (a) appreciating change, (b) mobilising support, (c) executing change, and (d) building change capability. Figure 1.1 shows our model.

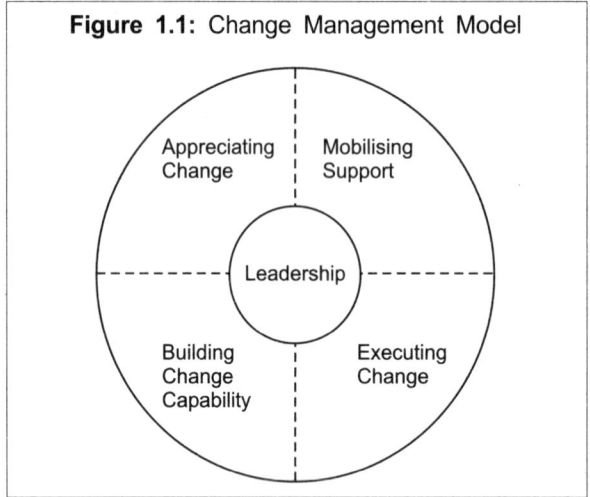

Figure 1.1: Change Management Model

The four tasks are not intended to be sequential. The dotted lines are meant to indicate that they overlap in most instances. Leadership lies at the core of change management. Most change management theories assume that managing change involves just one type of leadership. In fact, in popular change management literature, the preferred change management leader is a *transformational* leader.[7] We argue that effective change management requires four different kinds of leadership. Each of the four complex tasks requires a specific type of leadership. While most managers may have one or two of these leadership attributes, very few will have all the four attributes. In the following sections, we discuss each complex task and its associated leadership attribute.

APPRECIATING CHANGE

Appreciating change involves understanding the forces of stability and change in an organisation. This requires inquiry into routines and mental models that sustain the status quo. There are two ways in which an organisation can change. One is called *unplanned* change, which typically involves changes due to new ideas, conflict between individuals, departments or teams and political and power struggles inside the organisation. Obviously, unplanned changes are hard to predict and can lead to unanticipated consequences. In this book, we focus on the other source of change in an organisation called *planned* change. Change management is mostly about planned change. As the term implies, before you change an organisation, the change has to be planned. You can't plan change, if you are unaware of the need for change. Occasionally, you may be aware of the need for change but may be unwilling to go through with it. The appreciation phase aims to make you aware of the: (a) need for change, (b) consequences of changing and not changing, and (c) options that you have for undertaking change in the organisation. Appreciation cultivates the habit of thoughtfulness and allows you to reflect on the costs and options associated with organisational change. Let us examine these three aspects:

THE NEED FOR CHANGE

Why do organisations need change? A model first proposed by three researchers in the United States—Hebert Simon, Richard Cyert and James March, provides the key to the answer. This model, called the *experiential learning model*, explains why individuals and organisations change,[8] and has two aspects:

First, it suggests that organisations are purposive, goal-oriented systems. They set themselves targets or goals, which represent the organisation's aspirations about its performance. Performance for an organisation could be sales, profitability, market share, return on investment and so on. In other words, organisations aspire to a certain level of sales, profitability, market share, and return on investment. Periodically, organisations compare their actual performance to their targets or aspirations.

Second, if the performance exceeds their aspirations, they consider themselves to be successful. However, if performance falls below targets or aspiration levels, they see themselves as having failed. Perceptions of failure lead to change. Organisations institute a process of search to determine causes of failure and take corrective actions. However, if they see themselves as successful, they continue to do whatever they were doing more intensely. Also known as trial-and-error learning, this simple model suggests that behaviour that is linked with success is repeated while behaviour that is connected to failure is not repeated.

To put it simply, the model proposes that *organisational change is triggered by performance falling below expectations or aspiration levels.* An alternative way of expressing this idea states that change is initiated by *disconfirmation*. An individual, group or organisation must experience some kind of disconfirmation if they are required to change. Professor Edgar Schein has noted that *all* forms of learning and change start with some form of dissatisfaction or frustration generated by data that disconfirm people's expectations or hopes. Whether we talk about adapting to some new environmental circumstances or about genuinely creative learning, some disequilibrium based on disconfirming information is a pre-requisite. Whatever its source, disconfirmation functions as a primary driving force in the quasi-stationary equilibrium.

The key aspect of the experiential learning model is setting goals or expectations. Do all organisations have clear goals? Not necessarily. Most organisations have a clear idea of what they want to achieve, although this may not be stated as an organisational goal. Many organisations pursue multiple goals without a clear idea of priorities. Many organisations have goals that may be unrealistically high or low.

If the goals are low, they may be under-achieving. If the goals are too high, they may be trying too hard to achieve the impossible. As a manager, if you set yourself and your team low goals, you may not feel the need for change because your performance may meet or exceed your expectations. However, this does not mean that your team doesn't need change. The converse is also true. It would be unwise to embark on change just because you feel the need for change. Your feelings may be due to unrealistic expectations that your team hasn't met.

Therefore, the first step in appreciating change is to examine your aspirations and expectations. What are your goals? How did you set them? Are they realistic? How do you know that they are realistic? These questions require careful consideration and more importantly they need data. You can't answer these on the basis of your or others' opinions. It is not a good idea to launch organisational changes on the basis of feelings and opinions. You need to validate these feelings and opinions with concrete data. For instance, you could benchmark your organisation against your competition. What goals have your competitors set for themselves? You could study the business environment. What is the market potential? Is the market growing/declining? You could study your own organisation; what is its capacity?

Table 1.1 shows the Change Need Analysis tool[9] that can help you to analyse the need for change. A team of independent individuals who have sufficient knowledge about the organisation to answer the questions should complete it. If the average score is below 3 on the different measures, you need to seriously consider introducing change in the organisation.

To sum up the above points, organisational change must be based on metrics i.e. concrete performance measures. A number of organisations introduce change based on top management perceptions or feelings. In many instances, change is introduced without a clear idea of the underlying performance problems.

In such instances, the change effort has a high likelihood of failure. The appreciation phase is intended to focus the attention of the organisation on performance measures, comparisons and analysis.

Even if your goals are realistic and your performance meets your current goals, you may still need to consider introducing change. This is because the environment in which your organisation operates may be changing. This may threaten the future performance of the organisation. In a competitive market place, you cannot wait till the environment has changed before introducing change. You may have to anticipate the environmental shifts and introduce changes—now. This will make your job as a change manager quite difficult because others in the organisation may not share your expectations of environmental change. This is why anticipatory changes are more difficult to introduce and manage.

Table 1.1: Change Need Analysis

A. Compared to the performance of the *best performing organisation* in your sector, industry, or line of activity or business, how does your organisation rate on each of the following? (Please circle the appropriate number)

1.	Level of profitability	Very low	1 2 3 4 5	Very high
2.	Growth rate of revenue/sales/level of activity	Very low	1 2 3 4 5	Very high
3.	Morale/motivation of employees (as judged by levels of absenteeism, turnover, co-operation with management and so on)	Very low	1 2 3 4 5	Very high
4.	Financial strength (liquidity, reserves, borrowing capacity and so on)	Very low	1 2 3 4 5	Very high

(*Contd.*)

Table 1.1 (*Contd.*)

5.	Public image and goodwill (as judged by customer or client loyalty, premium on price and employment with the organisation)	Very low	1 2 3 4 5	Very high
6.	Adaptability (ability to quickly diversify, change strategies quickly, seize opportunities, etc.)	Very low	1 2 3 4 5	Very high
7.	Stability in the level of performance from one year to another	Very low	1 2 3 4 5	Very high
8.	Operating efficiency (judged by labour productivity, ratio of overheads to revenue, etc.)	Very low	1 2 3 4 5	Very high
9.	Innovativeness (ability to come up with new ideas)	Very low	1 2 3 4 5	Very high
10.	Social impact (producing socially relevant products or services)	Very low	1 2 3 4 5	Very high

B. What are the three indicators of performance where you would like to see significant improvements in this organisation?

1.
2.
3.

One way to manage anticipatory change is to keep track of what is happening in the environment. This has significant implications for planning your change, if you do decide to launch change. The analysis of operating environment will help you determine the content and timing of change: content as to *what* you want to change in the organisation, and timing as to *when* you want to introduce change. Let us first examine the content issues.

CONTENT OF CHANGE

While there are very few general rules in organisational change, some general principles hold true for all organisations. In our experience, a good place to start for most organisations in competitive, dynamic environments is to look at the four content levers of change.[10] These are *technology, quality, costs and marketing*—four areas that can be targeted for change.

Technology does not refer only to tools, equipment and machinery. It also includes information, knowledge and activities that are involved in the physical transformation of inputs into outputs. The outputs may be products or services. Any physical transformation task has a choice of technologies associated with it. In a business environment characterised by increased global competition, management of technology has become a major area of concern for organisations. We shall examine technology in detail in the next chapter.

Quality is all about meeting or exceeding customer expectations. It is a critical element in any change effort because customers are the ultimate judge of the success of the change effort. If the change does not result in products and services that meet or exceed customer expectations, it has obviously not achieved its purpose.

Costs or productivity constitutes the third content area of change. In today's business environment, customers are very cost-conscious and are unwilling to pay for products or services that do not meet their expectations. With increased competition, they have more choices. Consequently, they are no longer dependent on a single supplier or a few suppliers for products and services. Widening the choice has resulted in customers demanding more value for their money. A challenge for most organisations is to enhance quality while reducing costs. This requires carefully planned processes, systems and work habits.

Marketing refers to the mechanisms for delivering products and services to the customer. It includes: attracting new customers to your organisation's offerings; retaining existing and new customers; and examining your distribution channels, marketing structures and procedures.

Each of these content areas is supported by a set of structures, processes and procedures such as human resource practices. Any changes in the content areas will also require corresponding changes in these structures, processes and procedures. In the first phase of appreciation, it is not necessary to work out these details but you need to be aware of the linkages that need to be strengthened at the implementation stage.

ROLE OF MENTAL MODELS

The preceding discussion may give the impression that the appreciation phase is a straightforward process of collecting and analysing data for making informed decisions. However, in practice, it is not as clear-cut. There are organisational features that can prevent managers from understanding the change issues that confront the organisation. These are the mindsets and mental maps of the top management. Managers at the top of the organisation will have a certain picture of their organisation and its strengths and weaknesses. We refer to these mindsets and mental maps as mental models. When everyone shares the same mental picture, it becomes the dominant mental model of the organisation.

In an organisation, managers have mental models about their organisation, industry, customers, competition, government and so on. These mental models may be based on assumptions and beliefs that may no longer be valid. However, managers may be unaware of this and may continue to use old mental models to deal with new situations. In such instances, our decision-making can sometimes be seriously flawed. The appreciation phase is aimed at making us aware of our assumptions, beliefs and mental models, so that we can prevent or at least minimise such instances.

The task of appreciating change also involves understanding the fundamental source of the organisation's revenues, profits and growth, and the distinctive service that the organisation provides to its clientele and how these are being impacted by changes in the firm's operating environment. In business jargon, we use terms like value proposition and business model to understand what is unique about an organisation. A *business model* refers to the way in which a business organisation defines its customers and identifies what they value. A *value proposition* is the foundation of a business model. It refers to the distinctive way in which an organisation structures its activities to offer products or services that meet or exceed customer expectations. More generally, it is what makes the organisation unique or different in comparison to its competitors.

If you are a manager in an organisation, what makes your organisation unique or distinctive to your customers? How has your organisation achieved this uniqueness? What structures and processes inside the organisation contribute to its distinctiveness? To explore these important questions, we shall learn more about value propositions and business models in Chapter 3.

Thus, the critical task of appreciating change is intended to make key people in the organisation mentally ready for change in light of the analysis of operating environment. These are people who have the credibility to make things happen in the organisation. Usually they will be in top management positions but all of them need not be at the top. A common mistake most managers make is in assuming that just because they are ready for change, everyone else in the organisation should be ready too. This is of course a flawed assumption. If you are at the top of a large organisation, chances are that the rest of the people in the organisation don't see the world the way you see it. You need to convince others about the need for change. This is the next critical task of change management.

MOBILISING SUPPORT

This phase is closely related to the earlier phase of appreciating change. Even as you begin to analyse your organisation, its environment and its distinctiveness, you need to begin the process of testing the organisation's readiness for change. This phase is not only meant to gather support for the change effort but also aimed at collecting information and ideas that would give you a better appreciation of change.

WHY IS SUPPORT NECESSARY?

Broadly, there are two ways of bringing about planned change in an organisation. One way is to *impose* change on the organisation. In this approach, organisational change is a non-participative process. The other way is to convince people in the organisation about the need for change so that the whole organisation is involved in the change process. This is the participative approach to change. It does not impose change but *exposes* people to the possibility of change. In our change management model, engagement, involvement and participation are essential to bring about meaningful change. In order to understand this, we need to look at the various roles that people play in a change process.

According to Jick, there are three categories of people who play a role in any change process. First, there are *change strategists*.[11] These are the people who decide that the organisation needs change and set a direction for the change effort. They are usually in the top of the organisation. Change strategists don't implement the change; they design the change process. Second, there are *change implementers*—those who actually implement the change by creating new structures, rules, procedures and processes. Typically, they constitute the middle management of an organisation. Third, there are *change recipients*—people whose jobs change as a result of the changes launched in the organisation. They are usually at the lower levels in an organisation. But these are the people who are crucial to the success of the change effort. They can make or break the change effort. They are also the people who are at the frontline, directly dealing with clients and customers. Success of the change effort ultimately depends on what these frontline individuals do and don't do. In order to bring about successful change, all these three categories of people need to work together. The change effort can be derailed if any one of these fails to support the change process: the success of change depends on the consent of the people in the organisation.

GETTING CONSENT FOR CHANGE

In any organisational change effort, consent cannot be taken for granted. Consent has to be generated and sustained throughout the change process. Typically, in larger organisations, you can expect about 20 per cent of the people to be enthusiastic about change. Another 20 per cent will be strongly opposed to the change, and the rest will be sitting on the fence. Just because they do not oppose the change, a manager cannot assume that they will support the change. Conversely, just because they don't openly support the change, it doesn't mean that they are opposed to it. These are people who are unsure; they may be a little confused. They may not have all the information for making an appropriate choice. These are the people that need to be convinced about the change process.

Getting consent and mobilising support is not an easy process. It requires persistence and patience; a willingness to engage with people opposed to your ideas and opinions. If you are a manager in an organisation facing this challenge, what should be your strategy for mobilising support? How would you build participation, involvement and ownership that are crucial for effective change? We examine these issues and concerns in Chapter 4.

POLITICS OF CHANGE

You also need to be aware that organisational change is a political process. As a manager if you are planning to launch change, you need to have the support of key and influential individuals in the organisation. Therefore, you need to identify people who will support change and those that will oppose change. Unlike the earlier phase, where you could use diagnostic instruments to analyse the organisation and its environment, in this phase you can't rely on questionnaires and survey instruments to identify proponents and opponents of change. You will have to rely on informal means to 'feel' the pulse of the organisation. You have to use your networks of contacts to gather information. We will discuss these aspects also in greater detail in Chapter 4. We also refer to change as a political process because it involves influencing, persuading and negotiating with people in order to bring about a change in their mental models. The second phase is intended to gather a 'critical mass' of people in the organisation who will actively support the change process. This phase also gives the change manager an opportunity to test her ideas about what kind of changes are appropriate for the organisation. Once the organisation has the support of a critical mass of people, it is ready to move to the next task.

EXECUTING CHANGE

The third task is about executing change. This involves creating and putting in place new structures, processes or procedures. It entails creating co-ordinating mechanisms such as cross-functional teams and new routines for improvements and innovations. Most change management efforts fail at the implementation phase. Typically, most organisations underestimate the resource requirements, in terms of time, money and people, for implementing change. It has been found that organisations run into a host of problems while implementing change. For example, implementation takes more time than originally allocated; major problems surface during implementation; lack of coordination, competing activities and crises detract attention from implementation; and capabilities and skills of employees involved in implementation fall short of requirements.

Execution is, perhaps, the most critical aspect of change. Obviously, if an organisation hasn't managed the previous two tasks well, its change plan or programme will never take off. However, even if an organisation has carefully thought through its change issues and options and has gathered enough support for change, it can still fail at this critical stage.

Change execution almost always requires more resources than what has been allocated by an organisation. This is because organisational change is not a neat, orderly process. There may be unexpected events and surprises. Key people may leave the organisation during the change execution. There may be sudden changes in the market; competitors may introduce new products or policies that demand a quick response. Such factors can contribute to more resource requirements, such as more time, more staff and more money, for the change project. Allocating adequate resources for change requires a clear-cut strategy for change. In other words, the key managers need to decide the *type* of change that they wish to introduce in the organisation.

TYPES OF CHANGE

The type of change an organisation undergoes depends on four crucial decisions made by key managers: (1) Deciding the *goal* or purpose of change. What do we want to achieve? (2) Deciding the *scope* of change. Do we want change throughout the organisation or in a few selected units? (3) Deciding the *intensity* of change. Do we change a few things or do we change many things? (4) Deciding the *timeframe* for change. How quickly or slowly do we want to execute the change? Goal, scale and timeframe shape the nature of change that people will experience in the organisation.

Let us look at these decisions in a simplified way to facilitate understanding. Each decision, to simplify understanding, can be framed as a choice between two options. For instance, the goal for the change could be general or specific. A general goal is 'we want to enhance our competitiveness in the market place' whereas a specific goal is 'we want to increase our market share by 5 per cent.' Similarly, scope could be few units or organisation-wide. Intensity could be low (changing few aspects) or high (changing many aspects). Timeframe could be slow (indefinite or many months) or quick (few months or weeks).

Scope, intensity and timeframe decide the nature of change. Again, to simplify matters, let us look at two extreme situations. One situation could be a change programme that is slow, covering few units and changing few aspects of the organisation: we refer to this as frame-living change. The other situation could be a change programme that is fast, covers the whole organisation and changes many aspects: we call this frame-breaking change.

People in the organisation are likely to experience the frame-living change as a continuous change whereas frame-breaking change will be experienced as a discontinuous or disruptive change. The nature of change depends on the goal or purpose. If the goal is general, frame-breaking change will be experienced as a chaotic, confusing process. Frame-breaking changes have greater chances of success if the goal is specific. A number of organisations attempt to execute frame-breaking change without a clear idea of what they want to achieve. It is not surprising, therefore, that the failure rate of frame-breaking changes is high. There are other factors that make these changes risky. We will discuss these in detail later. Whether an organisation should engage in frame-living or frame-breaking change depends on the change issues facing it. If it faces a crisis and if there is not much time for responding, a frame-breaking change may be necessary. However, if it has time and does not have a specific change agenda, then frame-living change may be a good starting point. These four choices lead to the next three choices relating to *how* the change is to be executed.

STYLES OF CHANGE

The four decisions discussed in the earlier section constitute the content of change. The other two that are equally important make up the style of change. Again, to simplify matters, we present these as choice between: (a) deciding whether the change execution should be directive or participative, and (b) deciding whether the changes should focus on structures or on processes. Directive changes are, typically, top-down changes whereas participative changes may be initiated at the top but will involve extensive consultations with people in the organisation. Completely participative changes may also allow people lower down in the organisation to initiate changes.

In an ideal world, all changes would be participative, carried out with the active involvement of employees in an organisation. However, organisations do not operate in an ideal world. Whether changes should be directive or participative should not be based on the whims and fancies of top managers. The important considerations are the skills and motivations of employees and the availability of change tools. If employees lack the skill and/or the motivation for change, a directive approach may be necessary. In addition to skills and motivation, employees also need change tools to initiate and carry out change successfully. These need to be provided as part of the execution process.

The other dimension relates to the focus of change. Typically, most organisations focus on structures. Structure refers to reporting relationships, clustering of people into sections, departments and decisions and decision-making authority. Process, on the other hand, refers to norms and culture of the organisation. Some change practitioners use the terms hard vs. soft to refer to structure vs. process. Structures are seen as the 'hard' part of the organisation (perhaps as hardware) and processes are seen as the 'soft' side (the software). Sometimes, this can be a misleading terminology because changing processes in an organisation is actually quite difficult. Changing structures is relatively easier.

Most change programmes focus on structures and are usually framed as reorganisation or restructuring. However, these may not result in any significant changes in norms, habits, customs and traditions in the organisation. Not surprisingly, such restructurings do not lead to lasting change.

These six decisions discussed above shape the content and style of change in an organisation. Another crucial choice that managers face is, whether to adopt a ready-made change programme or design their own.

PROGRAMMATIC CHANGE

Over the last decades, a variety of change programmes have emerged, each promising effective and successful change. Many have not survived the passage of time. Some, however, are well established. We refer to these as change packages. Examples are Six Sigma, Lean Production, Total Quality Management and Business Process Reengineering. Change packages offer a ready-made approach that can be customised for each organisation. Many organisations choose a package because it has worked in another organisation. Managers think it is less risky to use a change approach that has proven itself in another organisational setting. This is not strictly true. Just because a change approach has worked in another organisation, there is no guarantee that it will work in your organisation. Organisational change is very context dependent. Your organisation's norm, values and culture will shape the success or failure of your change effort.

Research indicates that organisational change initiatives that succeed have little to do with the package, technique or tool employed. Critical success factors include whether there is a clearly focused strategy, quality of operational execution, performance oriented culture and a flexible structure.[12] On the other hand, packages provide a framework and model to guide the organisation and can save an organisation from having to re-invent the wheel as long as managers are aware that it is not the package but its execution that will bring results.

Executing change requires the creation of new structures and establishing new processes. Many organisations create a task force or a transition management team to spearhead the change. It is not uncommon for organisations to create cross-functional teams. These new structures also require new processes. Newly created teams have to work together to come up with ideas and decisions that will result in meaningful change. Teams require tools and skills to enable them to work together. Many organisational efforts fail to achieve their goals because organisations do not provide the necessary tools to their managers and teams. Many teams also require problem-solving skills because they begin to grapple with complex issues that had been ignored earlier. Thus, for effective execution, organisations require a methodical and systematic approach based on a clear goal.

Another challenge pertains to managing people's responses to change. It is during the execution phase that managers come face-to-face with people's reaction to change. For many managers, this can be an unnerving experience. In the face of hostility and negativity, they may conclude that the change is not going well. Employees are blamed for their lack of enthusiasm for change; they are seen to be 'resisting' change. However, hostility, negativity and lack of enthusiasm are normal, human responses to change. These factors do not indicate that the change is going badly, nor should the people be labelled as 'resistors.' People undergo a psychological transition while dealing with change because they have to let go of their old mental models. This transition takes time and may throw up negative feelings and emotions. Managers need to be prepared for these. They need to learn to deal with these emotions with sensitivity and tact. This critical task of execution calls for qualities of persistence and patience.

BUILDING CHANGE CAPABILITY

A well-known model of change management views organisations as going through long periods of stability punctuated by short bursts of discontinuous change.[13] According to this model, periods of stability are periods of convergence. During periods of convergence, organisations make only minor or incremental changes to their strategies, structures, people and processes. These may include: refining policies, procedures, and methods; creating specialised units and linking mechanisms to improve efficiency and quality; improving selection, training and appraisal procedures; promoting organisational commitment among employees; clarifying roles, status, power and procedures in the organisation, expanding a sales territory or introducing new machinery.

What is the process that is involved in introducing and implementing such changes during convergence? Generally the following activities would be required: generation and objective examination of alternatives; creating acceptance of the need for change through education and communication; participation of those affected by the changes; providing time to learn new activities; establishing role models; rewarding positive successes; evaluation and refinement. These changes can be designed and introduced by middle and senior level managers. During convergent periods, an organisation becomes more efficient and effective. As it grows and becomes successful, it also develops internal forces of stability. As the organisation becomes more stable, it also becomes more impervious to change. Therefore, it requires a frame-breaking change or an upheaval to ensure that it is in tune with environmental changes.

Frame-breaking change usually involves: (a) a new definition of company mission and core values, (b) an alteration of the distribution of power, (c) a modification in structure, systems and procedures, (d) a change in the way people work together in the organisation, and (e) new executives brought in from outside the organisation in key managerial positions. In any upheaval, all the features listed above take place simultaneously and rapidly.

While this is robust model with empirical support, it was developed in the 1980s when business environments were relatively more stable. In today's world, organisations have relatively shorter periods of stability. More importantly, frame-breaking change is inherently risky. In fast-changing environments, characteristic of high-technology firms, there may not be enough time for a planned, organisation-wide, frame-breaking change. In such situations, organisations need to have an in-built capacity for adapting to change.

How can managers create such a capability? This is an exciting new area in management research. While we do not have all the answers, there is growing realisation that knowledge creation and diffusion is one way of creating such capabilities in the organisation. This means managers need to pay attention to learning mechanisms in the organisation. More importantly, how do we retain what we have learnt? How can organisations retain learning and knowledge despite the turnover of its staff?

We usually associate learning and knowledge with people but organisations store, or more correctly embed, the knowledge that they create in their systems, structures, habits and processes. These processes can potentially become the source of competitive advantage. They are also difficult to imitate by other organisations. Organisational studies suggest that capability can be built by attending to a number of areas such as: developing inquiry skills and building mindsets of systematic problem solving; building systems for identifying improvement opportunities, rewarding knowledge sharing and searching for and testing new knowledge; strengthening linkage and integration mechanisms in structures and also building in greater discretion and flexibility; articulating stretch goals and capabilities required for achieving those goals in a manner that communicates excitement of achievement; and creating a culture of free and frank conversations, risk-taking and seeking to be the best.

Finally we propose that self-efficacy, focus and energy are the three elements contributing to capability. Self-efficacy refers to the confidence an individual has in his or her ability to achieve challenging goals. It is the belief that one has the capability to master difficult tasks. A high level of self-efficacy makes it easy for an individual to learn new things because he or she experiences less learning anxiety compared to another individual with lower level of self-efficacy. Therefore, a critical role for change managers and leaders is to devise ways of enhancing the self-efficacy of people in their organisations.

Apart from enhancing self-efficacy, a change leader should attend to focus and energy. Focus implies that individuals and groups have clear understanding of the goals to be attained, requisite capabilities and the specific steps to be taken for this purpose. Aimless pursuit of learning has little value; learning is valuable only when focused on well-defined agenda. Energy signifies that actors are determined to do what is required to achieve the goals; their actions are fuelled by intense personal commitment.

Typically, most managers and organisations do not pay attention to this crucial task of capability building. As a change leader or manager, it is important to realise that if you haven't built change capability, it can undermine an organisation's effort to change itself.

LEADERSHIP OF CHANGE

Despite the enormous attention paid to leadership in popular management literature, the importance of leadership in change management cannot be over-emphasised. Research has shown that many change programmes fail because they lack commitment and support from the top management. While effective change management requires credible and visible leadership in all the phases, it is crucial in the execution phase. Large-scale, organisation-wide change efforts require sustained efforts and the role of leadership is to ensure momentum for the change effort. Contrary to popular belief, organisational change does not necessarily require charismatic leadership.[14] It does require different leadership roles for the four different tasks. The key idea here is that change management requires four different leadership roles:

COGNITIVE TUNER

The task of appreciating change requires the leader to understand the mental models inside the organisation and forces of change impacting on the organisation. In other words, the leader must tune into both the prevailing mindsets inside the organisation and the forces of change in the environment. We refer to this process as cognitive tuning because it is largely a process of reflection, analysis and thinking. It occurs through the medium of dialogue and conversations. Leaders must be skilled in initiating dialogue in the organisation to both understand prevailing mindsets and make people aware of their mindsets. They also need to pay attention to the environment and understand how the environment of an organisation is evolving. Cognitive tuning is all about paying attention to mental models both inside and outside the organisation. However, one cannot understand the mental models of others unless one is aware of one's own mental model. Therefore, as cognitive tuners, change leaders need to be able to reflect on their own mindsets and mental models. Once again, it is important to emphasise that cognitive tuning is not merely about understanding the need for change. The very act of cognitive tuning initiates change in an organisation.

PEOPLE CATALYSER

Our change management model rules out coercive persuasion as a strategy of change. Therefore, change leaders need to influence and persuade people to reflect on and change their mental models. They need to mobilise support to the idea of change. Change leaders don't bring about change; they facilitate its emergence. Individuals relinquishing their old mental models and embracing new ways of thinking and acting ultimately bring about change. The role of a leader is to act as a catalyst to speed up the process of letting go of old mental models and adoption of newer ones. In an organisational setting this involves mobilising support and resources, building networks and relentlessly communicating the message of change. Change leaders catalyse change by helping people to cognitively redefine their mental models. In order to do this, they need to have the skills for influencing and persuading others. They need to be able to 'frame' the change in a way that permits people to let go of their old mental models. They may also need to build support through negotiations, if necessary.

SYSTEMS ARCHITECT

Executing change involves creating the right structures and processes in an organisation. It is particularly important to establish effective coordination mechanisms. One way to do this is through cross-functional teams. It is also important to sustain the momentum of change by ensuring that people are highly focused and energised during the change process. Change leaders play a crucial role in executing change because that can facilitate or derail change by the kind of architecture that they put in place for the change process. One reason why many change efforts flounder is because leaders do not think of change in systemic terms. They fail to appreciate that they have a crucial role in designing, building and sustaining a social architecture that can facilitate others to change. Leaders underestimate the importance of establishing new routines that can replace old mindsets or mental models. The role of a systems architect is vital in ensuring the success of change efforts in an organisation.

EFFICACY BUILDER

Building change capability is an important aspect of change management. The essence of capability building is making people believe in their own ability to face challenges and master new tasks. We refer to this as enhancing self-efficacy. Change leaders play a central role in creating and sustaining a positive climate that enhances people's self-efficacy in an organisation. They perform this role by enhancing the aspirations of people inside the organisation to face challenging tasks. This requires them to pay attention to creating positive role models for others to emulate. They need to design incentives that induce people to set high goals for themselves. They must ensure that there are support mechanisms to help people achieve their stretch goals. They must promote learning as a desirable goal in the organisation. In short, they need to structure opportunities for people to set challenging goals and achieve them. Popular change management literature has not paid sufficient attention to this fundamental role of a change leader. In very simple terms, effective change leaders make change happen by engendering a feeling of optimism and hope in the organisation. This fosters a positive belief in people that they can face the challenges of change and overcome them. This helps people view change as an opportunity rather than a threat. Figure 1.2 shows the four crucial roles that are required in change leadership.

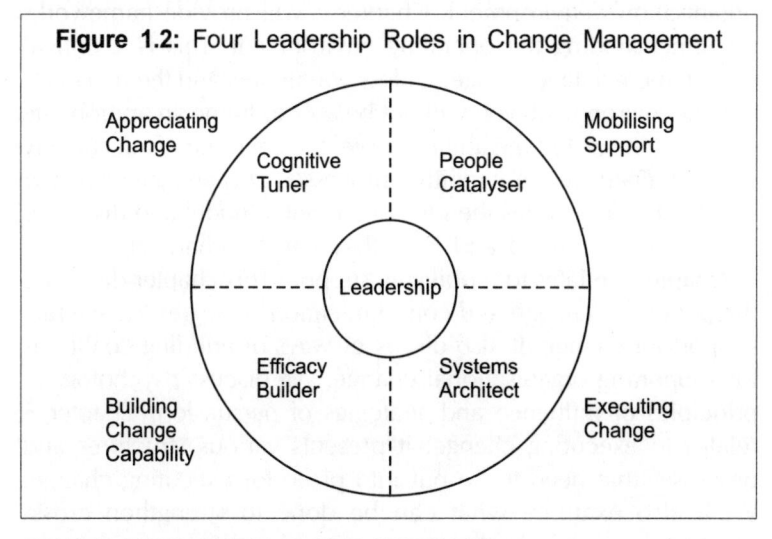

Figure 1.2: Four Leadership Roles in Change Management

Appreciating Change — Cognitive Tuner | People Catalyser — Mobilising Support

Leadership

Building Change Capability — Efficacy Builder | Systems Architect — Executing Change

CHANGE MANAGEMENT IS NOT SEQUENTIAL

So far we have outlined the four tasks involved in effective management of change. While we have discussed the different tasks of change sequentially above, organisational change is not a sequential, step-by-step process. Some of the activities discussed above will proceed simultaneously. For instance, just as managers begin to appreciate the change issues, they need to informally feel the pulse of the organisation for mobilising support. Even as they are mobilising support, they may need to start creating structures and processes for executing change. In addition to initiating activities simultaneously, managers also need to be aware that change management is a recursive process. This means that, managers may have to fall back on earlier phases as the change proceeds. For instance, while mobilising support, new information may surface that may contribute to a newer appreciation of change. Similarly, while executing change, managers may encounter roadblocks and may need to mobilise support to remove these. In view of these, change management should be more appropriately seen as a cyclical process.

In the first chapter, we develop and discuss our model in greater detail. The next two chapters deal with appreciating change. Appreciating change is all about making sense of the organisation's environment. Chapter 2 will provide frameworks for understanding the operating environment. This is a critical part of appreciating change. Unless you understand the dynamics of your environment, you will not be able to frame an appropriate change strategy. But the ability to 'see' the environment accurately is constrained by the cognitive processes of managers. Chapter 3 of the book includes the idea of a mental model and discusses how they are formed and how they can be changed.

Chapter 4 relates to mobilising support. This chapter discusses the politics of change and communication strategies to generate support for change. It also discusses ways of building coalitions for supporting organisational change. We discuss psychological principles of influence and strategies of persuasion. Chapter 5 relates to executing change; it presents various structures and processes that need to be put into place for executing change. We'll also examine what can be done to strengthen cross-functional linkages in the organisation, how new routines can be instituted for improvements, and what can be done to create hope and optimism to sustain focus and energy during execution.

Chapter 6 discusses how managers can create change capabilities in their organisations. It considers how capability can be built by setting challenging goals, creating ownership, structuring activities for reflection and action, instituting learning processes, fostering a positive behavioural context in which people learn to believe in their own abilities to achieve their aspirations. Chapter 7 begins by discussing one of the fastest-growing and popular change management strategies currently called Appreciative Inquiry. Then we examine the mindset and attitudes required for managing change. Finally, we conclude the book with a brief discussion of the key leadership roles in change management.

NOTES AND REFERENCES

1. Kotter, J. P. (1995). Leading change: Why transformation efforts fail. *Harvard Business Review*, 73(2): pp. 59–67; Kotter, J. P. (1996). *Leading Change: Why Transformation Efforts Fail*. Boston, MA: Harvard Business School Press.
2. Huber, N. (November 5, 2003). Hitting targets? The state of UK IT project management. *ComputerWeekly.com*.
3. Schein, Edgar H. (August, 1989). *Organisation Development: Science, Technology, or Philosophy?* Working Paper. WP# 3065-89-BPS. Sloan School of Management, MIT.
4. Giddens, A. (1984). *The Constitution of Society: Outline Of The Theory Of Structuration*. Berkeley: University of California Press.
5. Aldrich, H. (1999). *Organisations Evolving*. London: Sage Publications.
6. Schein, E. (August, 1989). *Organisation development: Science, technology, or philosophy?* : Sloan School of Management, MIT. WP# 3065-89-BPS; Schein, E. H. (1995a). Dialogue and learning. *Executive Excellence*, 12(4): p. 3; Schein, E. H. (1995b). Process consultation, action research and clinical inquiry: Are they the same? *Journal of Managerial Psychology*, 10(6): p. 14; Schein, E. H. (1999). Empowerment, coercive persuasion and organisational learning: Do they connect? *The Learning Organisation*, 6(4): p. 163; Schein, E. H. (Autumn 1993). On dialogue, culture, and

organisational learning. *Organisational Dynamics*, 22(2): p. 40; Schein, E. H. (Fall 1996). Three Cultures of Management: The Key to Organisational Learning. *Sloan Management Review*, 38(1): p. 9; Schein, E. H. (Spring 1990). A general philosophy of helping: Process Consultation. *Sloan Management Review*, 31(3): p. 57; Schein, E. H. (Winter 1993). How can organisations learn faster? The challenge of entering the green room. *Sloan Management Review*, 34(2): p. 85.

7. Nadler, D. A. & Tushman, M. L. (1990). Beyond the charismatic leader: Leadership and organisational change. *California Management Review*, 32(2): pp. 77–97.
8. Cyert, R. M. & March, J. G. (1992). *A Behavioral Theory Of The Firm*. Cambridge, Mass.: Blackwell; March, J. G. (1999). *The Pursuit Of Organisational Intelligence*. Malden, MA: Blackwell; March, J. G. & Simon, H. A. (1993). *Organisations*. Cambridge, Mass.: Blackwell.
9. Based on Khandwalla, Pradip N. (1995). *Managerial Styles*, New Delhi: Tata McGraw Hill.
10. Nilakant, V. & Ramnarayan, S. (1998). *Managing Organisational Change*. New Delhi: Response Books.
11. Jick, T. D. (1993). *Managing Change: Cases and Concepts*. Homewood, IL: Irwin, McGraw-Hill.
12. Nohria, N., Joyce, W., & Roberson, B. (July 2003). What really works. *Harvard Business Review*, 81(7): pp. 42–55.
13. See Romanelli, E. & Tushman, M. L. (1994). Organisational transformation as punctuated equilibrium: An empirical test. *Academy of Management Journal*, 37: pp. 1141–1166; Sastry, M. A. (1997). Problems and paradoxes in a model of punctuated organisational change. *Administrative Science Quarterly*, 42(2): pp. 237–275; Tushman, M. L., & Anderson, P. (Eds.). (1997). *Managing Strategic Innovation And Change: A Collection Of Readings*. New York: Oxford University Press; Tushman, M. L., Anderson, P. C., & O'Reilly, C. (1997). Technology cycles, innovation streams, and ambidextrous organisations: Organisation renewal through innovation streams and strategic change. In M. L. Tushman & P. Anderson (Eds.), *Managing Strategic Innovation and Change: A Collection of Readings*. New York: Oxford University Press; Tushman, M. L. & Romanelli, E. (1985). Organisational evolution: A metamorphosis model of convergence and

reorientation. In L. L. Cummings & B. M. Staw (Eds.), *Research in Organisational Behavior* (Vol. 7: pp. 171–222). Greenwich, CT: JAI Press.
14. Nadler, D. A. & Tushman, M. L. (1990). Beyond the charismatic leader: Leadership and organisational change. *California Management Review*, 32(2): pp. 77–97.

CHAPTER 2

Appreciating Change: Industry Analysis

OVERVIEW

This chapter is about the core task of appreciating change and of understanding the impact it may have on the strategy of an organisation, which involves understanding the organisation's external context. Here, we focus on the external context and discuss the dynamics of industry evolution. We explain the *population ecology theory* to discuss ideas of organisational births (entry) and deaths (exit), giving examples from various organisational populations. We also explain how business cycles impact organisations and discuss the effect of three forces—*competition, technology* and *institutional rules* on organisations. We show how *technology cycles* lead to industry evolution and how *changes in institutional rules* can lead to dramatic industry and organisational changes. These basic ideas are explained with examples drawn from a variety of industries. We suggest that any agenda for change must be based on a sound analysis of the organisation's operating environment. This chapter shows how you can analyse the industry in which your organisation is located to understand the pressures and forces on your organisation.

EXTERNAL ENVIRONMENT AS DRIVER OF CHANGE

Organisational change could be viewed as a response to pressures and forces outside an organisation or its 'environment'. Derived from *environ*—meaning 'to surround'—the word environment means 'the surroundings' i.e. everything that surrounds an organisation, everything that exists *outside* it. In fact, a variety of things surround an organisation including: customers, competitors, suppliers, and government agencies. Organisations also exist within a society and an economy. Therefore, their environments include: social habits, customs, norms, values and general economic conditions such as growth rate, rates of interest, inflation and so on.

It is important to understand that the term 'environment' does not refer to a single phenomenon or organisation, but includes a variety of both. An organisation is likely to undergo change if its environment changes, or if change is anticipated. In order to better understand this fundamental idea, it is useful to look at an organisation as something that gets resources from outside, converts them into products and services, and then returns these products and services to the surroundings.

An organisation's ability and willingness to change is expected to determine the uncertainty regarding its survival and growth. We can understand the reasons for variation in performance across organisations using population ecology. The Population Ecology framework suggests that firms survive by investing in development of distinctive competencies.

POPULATION ECOLOGY FRAMEWORK

Here, *population* refers to organisations that are similar—restaurants, cotton textile firms, automobile manufacturers, newspapers and so on. Each of these populations occupies an *ecological niche* in the environment. The niche provides resources for the organisations constituting the population. The environment, therefore, consists of a number of different niches. Organisations survive in their niches by developing distinctive capabilities such as skills, patterns of behaviours and management systems suited only for their specific niches.

An organisation competes for resources in its environment. If it does not meet the demands of different resource providers, the organisation's existence can be threatened—sooner or later—by those that *do* meet these demands/expectations. Thus, organisations that lack requisite capabilities are unable to get the required resources and, therefore, fail to survive. Consequently, some organisations die while new ones are born into the population.

Why do some organisations die while others survive? Population ecology theorists propose that there are three types of processes leading to change: *variation, selection* and *retention*.[1] Variation includes those processes that lead to differences in organisations—in terms of strategy, structure, systems, skills and culture. This could be a result of both management action and random chance. Selection refers to the process through which the environment selects those organisations that have the required features i.e. the 'right' goals, boundaries and routines. Organisations which do not conform to environmental requirements are *selected out* i.e. they under perform and may subsequently die. Retention constitutes those processes that help organisations retain the features that are required by the environment. However, when the environment changes again, these features may not be required and the organisations face the threat of extinction and new organisational forms are selected.

Change, at the population level, follows an evolutionary dynamics arising out of variation, selection and retention. What drives this process is the struggle for resources in the environment. When we portray change in this manner we are looking at not only organisational change, but also at changes in the environment. In other words, both organisations and their environments are undergoing evolutionary change. This is one of the reasons why managing change is a complex and challenging task. Not only does a manager need to pay attention to his/her organisation's goals, boundaries and routines, but he/she also has to track changes in the environment. One way to do this is by understanding the forces that lead to industry evolution. However, before we do that, let us look at an example of population-level change.

An illustration from New Zealand is helpful to understand the dynamics of change in organisational populations. In New Zealand, a small and medium enterprise (SME) is defined as an organisation employing 19 or fewer full time equivalent employees (FTEs). Figure 2.1 shows the distribution of organisations by size for 1996 in New Zealand. SMEs constitute 96 per cent of all organisations.[2]

Table 2.1 shows the percentage change in births and deaths between 1988 and 1998. Over the same decade, enterprise dynamics has increased significantly—with births rising by 136 per cent and deaths rising by 112 per cent. 95 per cent of this increase can be attributed to a rise in births and deaths among small enterprises, as illustrated in the table. SMEs also have smaller survival rates. Of all small businesses started in 1995, 71 per cent survived the first year, 56 per cent survived the second year and 47 per cent survived the third year into 1998.

Interestingly, the industries with the highest survival rate into 1998 were: electricity, gas and water supply; finance and insurance; and government administration and defence. With the exception of finance and insurance, these sectors have a proportion of SMEs significantly below the sector average. The lowest survival rates were shown by enterprises in the sectors: accommodation, cafes and restaurants; communication services; and cultural and recreational services. Each of these sectors has a proportion of SMEs higher than average. However, these figures need to be treated with some caution. Research suggests that actual failure rates may be two-thirds of those indicated by statistics. Organisational death does not necessarily mean liquidation or bankruptcy; it could also be a merger or acquisition.

Here, an interesting question would be: how many of these smaller organisations expanded and became larger? Take a guess! What percentage of enterprises with less than six people would have grown larger? According to data, of those employing 0-5 FTEs in 1995, only a small proportion graduated into larger size brackets, with 97 per cent of these firms still employing 0-5

FTES in 1996, 96 per cent in 1997 and 95 per cent in 1998. Table 2.2 shows these transition rates. The level of expansion and contraction indicates the dynamic nature of organisations. These figures are only to illustrate the dynamics of change in organisations. While the actual distributions may differ in each country, the overall trends will be similar.

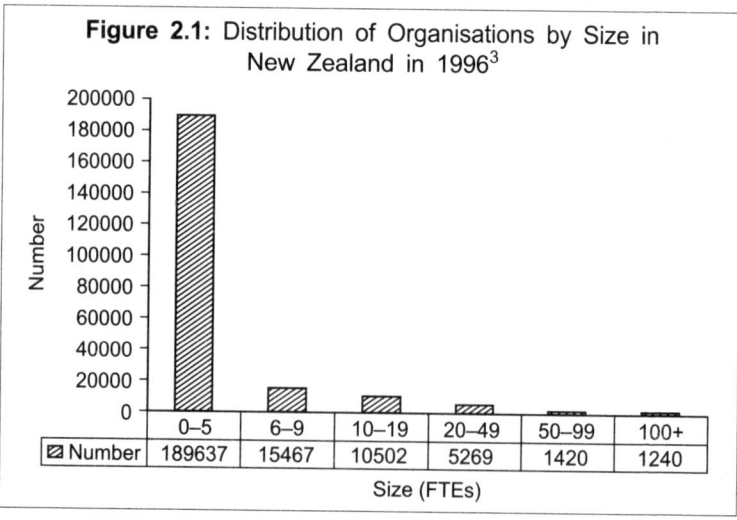

Figure 2.1: Distribution of Organisations by Size in New Zealand in 1996[3]

Size (FTEs)	0–5	6–9	10–19	20–49	50–99	100+
Number	189637	15467	10502	5269	1420	1240

Source: *SMEs in New Zealand: Structure and Dynamics*, Ministry of Commerce, New Zealand, May 1999

Table 2.1: Percentage Changes in Births and Deaths 1988–1998[4]

Enterprise Size	Percentage increase in births	Percentage increase in deaths
0-5 FTEs	142	126
6-9 FTEs	84	35
10-19 FTEs	90	27
20-49 FTEs	37	7
50-99 FTEs	14	12
100+ FTEs	–6	13
Total	136	112

Source: *SMEs in New Zealand: Structure and Dynamics*, Ministry of Commerce, New Zealand, May 1999

Table 2.2: Transition of Firms 1995–1998[5]

Enterprise Size 1995 (FTEs)	Percentage smaller in '98	Percentage same in '98	Percentage larger in '98
0-5	–	95	5
6-9	40	40	21
10-19	37	50	14
20-49	32	59	9
50-99	33	48	19
100+	33	67	–

Source: *SMEs in New Zealand: Structure and Dynamics*, Ministry of Commerce, New Zealand, May 1999

FORCES OF CHANGE

The two main factors that can trigger changes in organisations by impacting on their performance are *business and industry cycles*. Let us first look at business cycles.

BUSINESS CYCLES

An obvious factor in organisational births and deaths is the overall economic activity. When the economy as a whole is growing, organisations, too, are likely to grow. When the economy declines, organisations will either contract or die. However, economic conditions do not have a uniform impact on all organisations. Organisations are likely to be affected differently, based on the populations to which they belong. Economists use the concept of a business cycle to study the overall level of economic activity. A business cycle refers to alternating periods of contraction and expansion in the economic activity. Although economists have data ranging back to early 19th century, they still cannot agree on what causes these contractions and expansions. But the periods of booms and busts are a reality that impact on organisational performance. According to the National Bureau of Economic Research in America[6]:

A recession is a significant decline in activity spread across the economy, lasting more than a few months, normally visible in real GDP, real income, employment, industrial production,

62 Change Management

and wholesale-retail sales. A recession begins just after the economy reaches a peak of activity and ends as the economy reaches its trough. Between trough and peak, the economy is in an expansion. Expansion is the normal state of the economy; most recessions are brief and they have been rare in recent decades

NATURE OF PAST CYCLES

We observe that the world's largest economy has experienced fairly stable growth over recent decades. The recent performance, in the decade of the 90s in particular, had many politicians and economist arguing that economic cycles may be a thing of the past.

The charts below do suggest that the US economy has experienced recession more frequently during the 40s and the 50s. The economy grew at a steady rate during the 60s, and then during the 80s and 90s. 90s could be considered the golden years as the economy experienced significantly lower variability of growth rates (measured in terms of coefficient of variation of quarterly growth rates), compared to earlier periods (Figure 2.2 presents Gross Domestic Product—Seasonally Adjusted Annual Rate: Change from Previous Period). But the last five years, have seen a decline in growth rate, coupled with an increase in its variability (Figure 2.3).

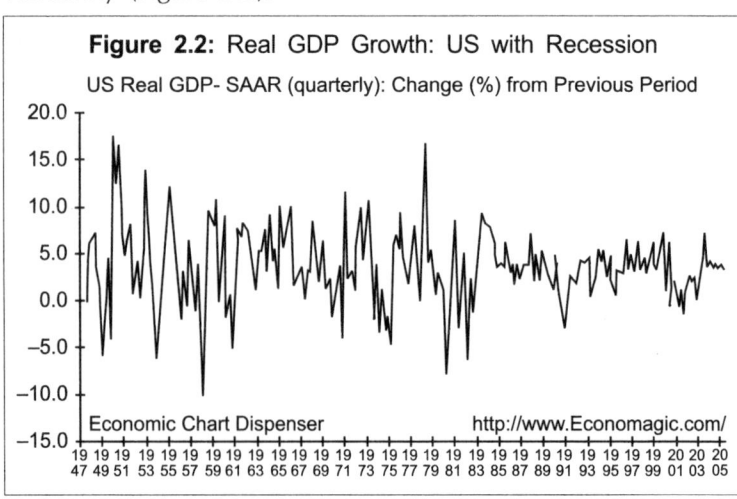

Figure 2.2: Real GDP Growth: US with Recession

Source: *www.economagic.com*

Appreciating Change: Industry Analysis 63

Figure 2.3: US Economy: Real GDP Growth Rate across Time

US Real GDP: Quarterly Growth Rate and its Variability

Period	GDP	Coefficient of Variation
1947-50	4.67	1.49
1951-60	3.09	1.71
1961-70	4.32	0.80
1971-80	3.42	1.40
1981-90	3.19	1.12
1991-2000	3.42	0.59
2001-05	2.61	0.76

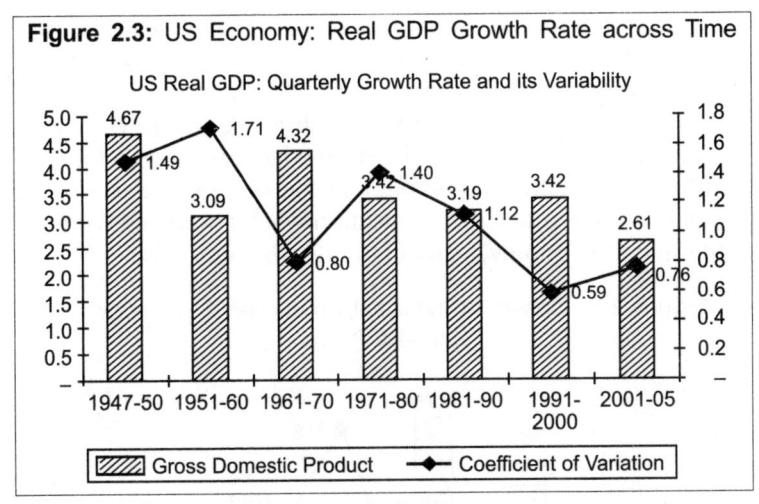

Source: based on www.economagic.com

A review of performance of the Indian economy also suggests that the economy has experienced significantly different levels of variability in performance across different plan periods. While the rate of growth has been stable over the period under study, the variability of growth rate has fluctuated significantly (Figure 2.4 below).

Figure 2.4: Indian Economy: Real GDP Growth Rate across Time

GDP at Constant Prices: Growth Rate and its Variability

Plan Period	Plan Period CAGR	Plan Period Variability
1980-85	5.62%	34.40%
1985-90	5.93%	46.27%
1990-92	3.41%	87.95%
1992-97	6.69%	16.96%
1997-02	5.46%	16.11%

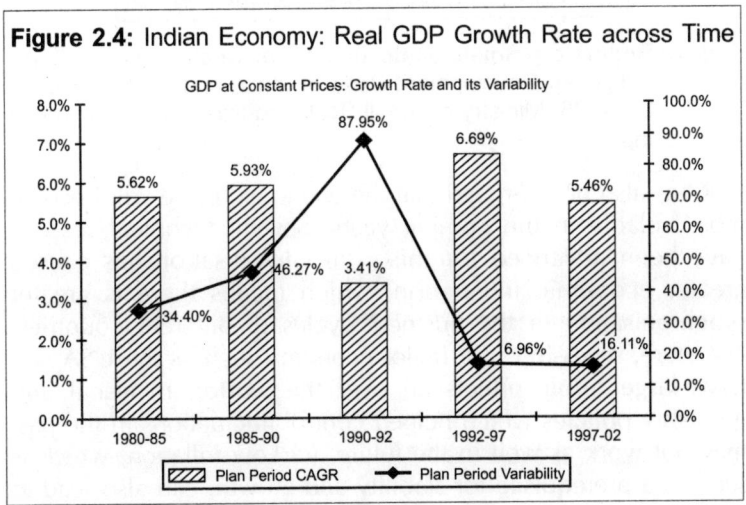

Source: Economic Survey and our Analysis

Similarly, our review of performance for the small scale industry in India suggests that the sector has experienced a significant variation in performance across years. We observe a slowdown in growth rates, in line with the growth in the Indian economy. The variability of growth rates is observed to be higher in the 90s, than in the 80s. This may imply that the small scale sector has found it difficult to sustain competition when compared with rest of the Indian economy, particularly during early 90s.

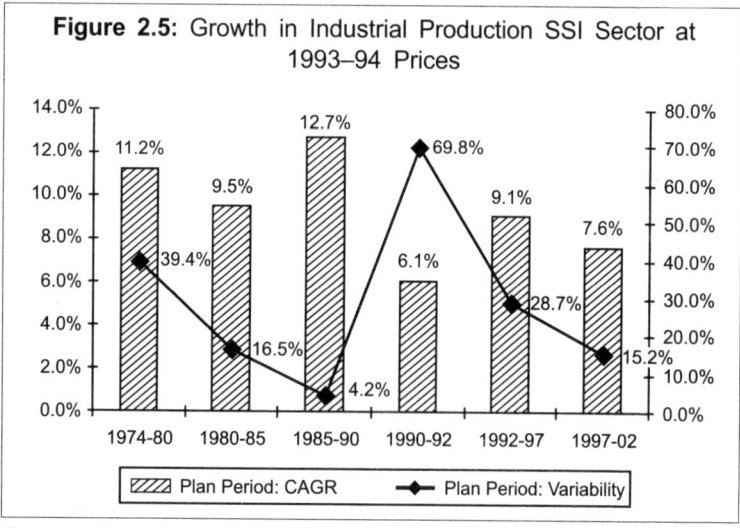

Figure 2.5: Growth in Industrial Production SSI Sector at 1993–94 Prices

Plan Period	CAGR	Variability
1974-80	11.2%	39.4%
1980-85	9.5%	16.5%
1985-90	12.7%	4.2%
1990-92	6.1%	69.8%
1992-97	9.1%	28.7%
1997-02	7.6%	15.2%

Source: Report on Small Scale Industries Sector: 2000, Small Industries Development Bank of India, and Annual Report: 2004–05, Ministry of Small Scale Industries, Government of India

It has also been argued that the economic cycle will become more volatile in the coming years. Several technical reasons have been advanced for this[7] : (a) Globalisation has caused greater economic integration, which means there is greater synchronisation in the business cycles of different countries. Therefore, recession in a major economy such as the USA will have large ripple effects all over the world; (b) Fiscal and monetary policies which helped control fluctuations in the past may not work as well in the future; (c) Low inflation, which is seen as a prerequisite for stability and growth, can also lead to fluctuations in business cycles due to volatility in equity and property prices. As over-inflated equity and property prices settle to their fair value, they may lead to a big drop in their nominal prices in low inflationary conditions. Therefore, the expectation based on past data that the world economic conditions will be less volatile and more stable seems unrealistic.

PREDICTABILITY OF BUSINESS CYCLES

Business cycles would not hurt us, if they could be predicted with some amount of reliability. However, economists—who ought to know more about these than anyone else—have been notoriously unreliable in predicting recessions. However, there are agencies in the United States, such as the Conference Board and the Economic Cycle Research Institute (a private research group), which have so far been relatively successful in predicting recessions through the use of multiple leading indices for different parts of the economy. One of the factors that can cause recession is the excessive amount of capacity build up in anticipation of demand. We saw a fairly significant increase in capacity in the 90s along side the higher growth in most quarters. But at some stage the capacity build up exceeded the historical peaks. Consequently, when the expected level of demand failed to materialise, it led to a significant decline in growth rates (Figure 2.6).

We also observe that the periods of high capacity build-up may result in pricing power going out of producer hands—implying a significant impact on business profitability (Figure 2.7). This may require an organisation to adjust its capacity as quickly as possible to lowering of demand. We did observe this to be the case during the last few years, as evident in Figure 2.6.

In a situation where the industry has built significant excess capacity, the restructuring effort itself can accentuate the decline in demand, as an increasing number of jobs are lost.

The fund-management industry illustrates the effects of business cycles on organisations. In the 80s and the 90s, pension funds, mutual funds, banks and individuals entrusted their money to fund managers for investments in the stock market and in other financial products. Till the late 90s, fund-managers had to do precious little as stock markets around the world followed the lead of American stock markets and continued to climb. The

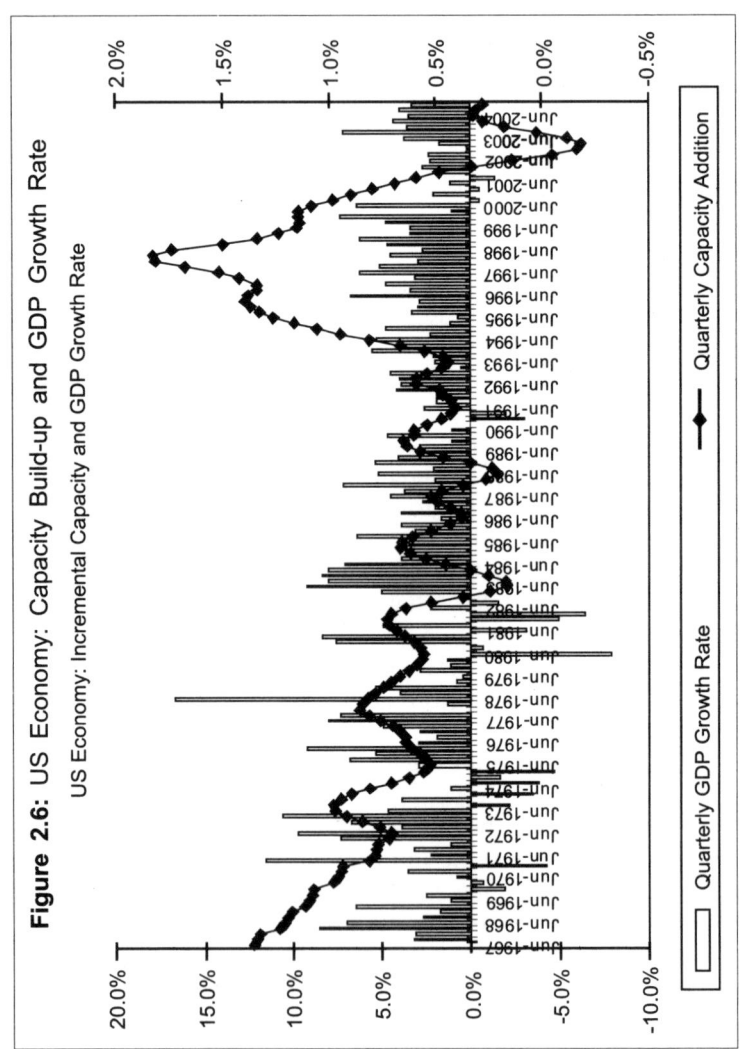

Figure 2.6: US Economy: Capacity Build-up and GDP Growth Rate

US Economy: Incremental Capacity and GDP Growth Rate

Source: based on *www.economagic.com*

Appreciating Change: Industry Analysis 67

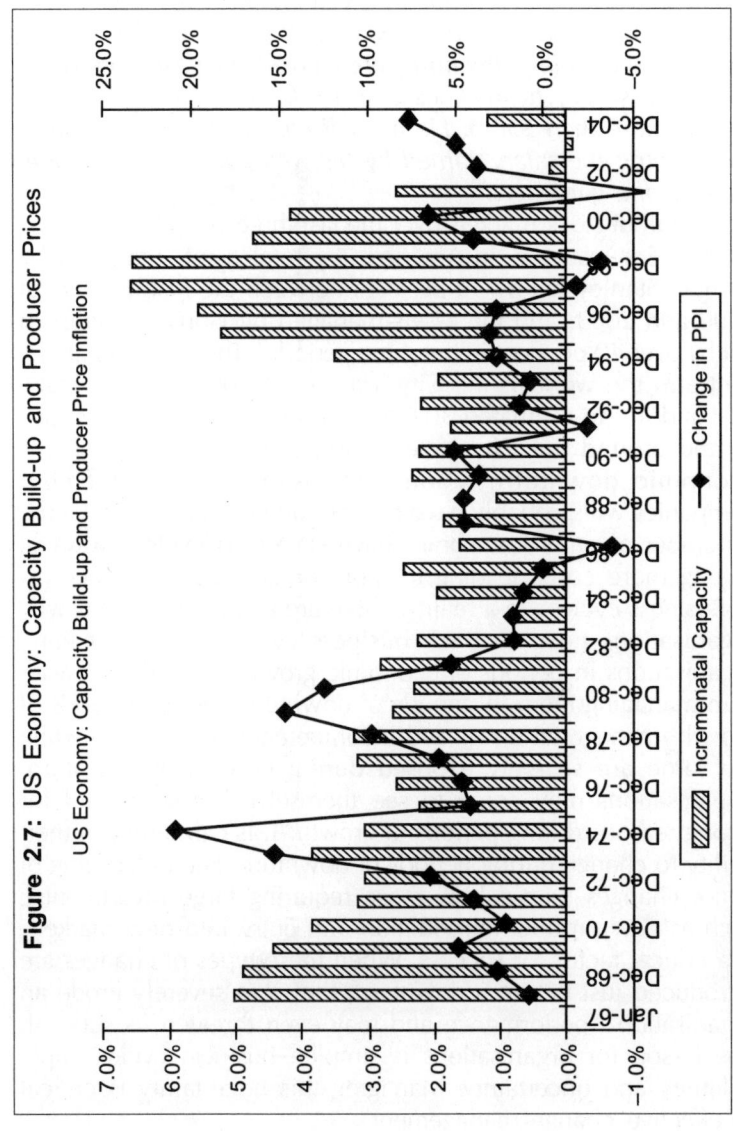

Figure 2.7: US Economy: Capacity Build-up and Producer Prices

clients of fund-managers were happy because their wealth was increasing. Fund-managers enjoyed enormous perks and rarely got fired.[8] Most were probably overpaid for their work: *'Ten years ago, says a former board member at a big investment bank, a couple of people in the firm were paid $1m a year worldwide. Three years ago, he reckons that 1,000 were, and a handful earned more than $50m. He himself has an impressive pile in the country; the salary earned by his well-paid wife just about pays for the gardeners.'*[9]

The fall of stock markets over the last three years has changed all this. For instance, in America, the total assets managed by Morgan Stanley fell by 30 per cent between the first quarters of 2000 and 2003, and the assets managed by Janus and Putnam fell by over 40 per cent in the same period.[10] The largest financial centre in the world is the City, one of 33 boroughs that make up London. An estimated 30,000-60,000 financial services jobs in and around the City have disappeared as a result of this economic downturn.[11] Some of these fund-management companies will probably have to close down. More importantly, a number of other companies have started to explore ways of cutting more costs, leading to more organisational changes.

Business cycles are a reality. There are two main reasons why organisations need to track business cycles: First, managing organisations in periods of economic growth is relatively easier than managing them in periods of downturn. During periods of growth, managerial errors and incompetence are masked while the same are severely exposed during periods of downturn. Organisations may come to see themselves as successful for wrong reasons during periods of growth. This can diminish their ability to change during periods of downturn. Second, timing of major changes (particularly those requiring large investments), such as new product introduction and entry into new markets, is a critical factor for success. When these types of changes are introduced just before a downturn, they can severely erode an organisation's performance and may even threaten its survival. The lesson for organisations is simple—business cycles imply volatility and uncertainty. Managing this uncertainty is critical to effective change management.

A firm's ability to build flexibility, responsiveness and efficiency in its operations is the key to managing across cycles. Flexibility implies a firm's ability to adjust the scale of its operations, depending on demand. Higher flexibility would help lower investment risk (as shown in the illustration presented in Box 2.1). On the other hand, responsiveness to consumer needs allows the firm to offer products and services that meet specific needs and it is also able to price them accordingly (Box 2.2 outlines a case illustration of this type). Pricing power combined with lower investment risk will really allow the firm to achieve consistent performance across cycles. To illustrate this point, presented here are two different examples (Box 2.1 and Box 2.2) from the automobile industry.

Box 2.1: Cost Advantages from Flexibility in Plant Capability[12]

- General Motors (GM) will save $120 million on each new vehicle model it builds, by using robots that can be programmed to handle a variety of cars or trucks on an assembly line
- GM's 'C-Flex' system allows multiple vehicle parts (hoods, engine compartments, and steel floor pans) from a variety of car or truck models to be welded with the same set of robots and tools
- Programmable robots allow GM to cut the size of plant body shops, where vehicles are assembled, by as much as 150,000 sq ft. Additional savings comes by decreasing the investment in tooling
- Five years ago, GM spent at least $150 million on a new body shop that was not very flexible. With the new system, GM is able to introduce a new model into a plant for as little as $30 million to $50 million. *'The less capital that is required to do a programme, the lower that break-even point'*
- By cutting the costs of a building a new car or truck, GM is able to consider building more low-volume, niche vehicles. C-Flex also gives it more flexibility to respond to changing market demand and shift production to more popular models
- All major automakers have made their main vehicle assembly lines flexible, able to build a multiple number of vehicles using a variety of components. Now, they are working to make major and minor subassembly lines, which build vehicle components, also flexible
- Earlier this year, the Chrysler arm of Daimler Chrysler said that it shaved 10 per cent from its projected costs of building new vehicles over the next five years by using factory tooling longer, and making its plants more flexible
- In the past, as automakers typically redesigned vehicles every five or six years, they would also replace all the factory tooling. Chrysler was now expecting 10 years to 25 years of life from its machinery

> **Box 2.2: Market Knowledge as Source of Responsiveness and Pricing Power**[13]
> - While rebates and 0 per cent loan deals are helping auto firms improve their sales, they are souring their bottom lines. GM's first quarter profits weakened as prices dropped 3.2 per cent, even as its market-share slipped
> - But Ford's prices increased by 0.2 per cent in the quarter, contributing $260 million out of its Q1 profit of $896 million. Ford also increased its share by 0.5 per cent at 21.2 per cent
> - Ford was able to hold its prices in 2002, while GM's net prices fell 2 per cent
> - Ford is careful to spend its marketing cash to promote moneymakers that are not selling e.g. high margin F-150 pickup truck and promote lucrative options that fatten its profits. It has managed an increased of $90 on Taurus
> - Ford raised its revenue per vehicle by $868 in Q1 at $21,716—$1400 above GM. As compared to GM, Ford spends $300 less on incentives
> - Ford collects sales data daily from dealerships and runs computer models to forecast which incentives will produce the best results in which region
> - Revenue management also concentrates Ford's spend on the most lucrative vehicles and options
> - It also encourages its customers to spend lavishly on expensive extras, like the Japanese e.g. power folding seats and power running boards add $1700 to Lincoln Navigator

INDUSTRY CYCLE

While business cycles affect all industries, each industry also undergoes specific types of changes. Although we identified three other forces—competition, technology and institutional rules, these are related to one another. Instead of examining them separately, it is more useful to study their joint impact. The key idea in understanding their joint impact is the notion of *industry evolution*. The basic idea in industry evolution is that a population of organisations evolves due to changes in competition, technology and institutional rules.

COMPETITIVE STRUCTURE

In the beginning when the industry is formed, there may be a large number of small organisations. However, over a period of time, consolidation takes place and some organisations emerge as winners. They continue to grow till the industry cannot sustain any more growth. At this stage, the industry is mature and may begin to decline later. An important *variable* for understanding industry evolution is the notion of *concentration*. *Concentration refers to the number, size and relative strength of competitors.*

In the early stages of an industry, competitive structure is *fragmented* and disorganised. There may be a large number of competitors whose positions relative to each other may be constantly changing. At this stage, a competitor may emerge with a superior technology. This technology is adopted as the industry standard and the remaining organisations need to conform to this technology. This may mean making costly investments in new capital equipment, training workers and managers in new skills and developing new routines. Organisations that are not capable of conforming to the new technology either remain in the periphery of the industry or are forced to exit the industry. This *shakeout* leaves a few organisations at the core, which start to consolidate their operations around the new technology. Inevitably, the industry is populated by fewer organisations with larger shares of the market. This results in an increase in the industry concentration.[14] As market growth slows down, the industry reaches a stage of *maturity*. If, subsequently, the market begins to shrink, the industry goes into a stage of *decline*. Figure 2.8 illustrates these ideas.

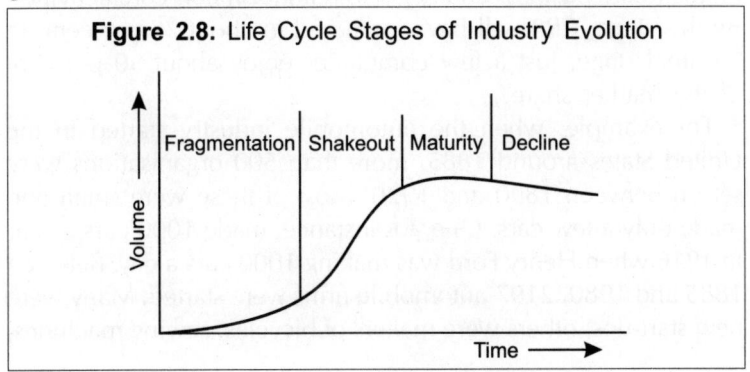

Figure 2.8: Life Cycle Stages of Industry Evolution

To frame these ideas in terms of population ecology theory, we can say that when a new population is formed, there may be a number of new start-ups together with entry of existing organisations from other populations. In the initial stages of a population's life, there is likely to be a great diversity of organisations. These organisations are likely to be small, innovative and opportunistic in exploiting resources and uncertainty in the early stages of a population's evolution. These are called *r-strategists* ('r' refers to intrinsic rate of population increase in the population ecology theory). At the initial stages, the population is still growing and there is excess carrying capacity. Resources are plentiful and therefore r-strategists thrive. During the later stages, however, the carrying capacity is full and resources are scarce. At this stage, organisations called *K-strategists* (termed in this manner to denote that the population is limited by carrying capacity 'K') dominate the population. These are larger organisations that have a selective advantage in efficiently utilising scarce resources.

In their book titled *Winning the Merger Endgame*, Graeme Deans, Fritz Kroeger and Stefan Zeisel argue that industries evolve through four distinct stages.[15] Stages differ from one another in terms of concentration, which is measured in terms of the combined market-share of the three biggest companies, or CR3 as it is called. In the first stage, with a number of r-strategists, CR3 is less than 20 per cent. In the second stage, a number of companies begin to merge to form bigger entities. CR3 increases to around 30–45 per cent. In the third stage, companies focus on their core business and begin to relinquish non-core activities. By this stage, CR3 will have increased to about 70 per cent. In the final stage, just a few companies enjoy about 90 per cent of the market share.

For example, when the automobile industry started in the United States around 1885, more than 500 organisations were set up between 1890 and 1920. Most of these were small and made only a few cars. One, for instance, made 1000 cars a year in 1916 when Henry Ford was making 1000 cars a day. Between 1885 and 1980, 2197 automobile firms were started. Many were new start-ups; others were makers of bicycles, sewing machines, carriages and precision machines. The rest were a result of acquisitions, mergers, and splitting of existing firms. By 1981, however, only 106 survived. The automobile industries in Britain, France and Germany have followed similar trends. Of the 995 firms starting between 1885 and 1980, only 57 survived in Britain in 1981. Only 33 of the 828 firms started in France during the same period were still in existence in 1981.[16] Today, about a dozen firms dominate the global automobile industry. The largest, General Motors, has about 25 per cent of the market-share.

The global beauty industry is even older than the automobile industry. Estimated to be around $160 billion a year today, it consists of make-up, skin and hair care, fragrances, cosmetic surgery, health clubs and diet pills. The skin-care, perfumes, hair-care and make-up segments constitute a market of around $100 billion a year. Even though the industry is growing at the astounding rate of seven per cent a year, six multinationals account for 80 per cent of American make-up sales, while eight brands control 70 per cent of the skin-care market.[17]

The food-services industry consists of organisations that provide breakfast, lunch, snacks and dinner to consumers too busy to cook for themselves. Fast food chains such as McDonald's and full-service restaurants account for 60 per cent of the $400 billion market. In the United States, the industry is not expected to grow at more than 2 per cent a year till 2010. Therefore, the industry is intensely competitive as different organisations vie for a bigger market share. Dinner is the most favourite meal outside the home in the United States constituting nearly 50 per cent of all meals consumed outside the home. It is also expected to grow at an annual rate of 6 per cent. The challenge for the different organisations is to offer what the consumers have started to demand: Quickly served fresh food in a casual but distinctive environment. Fast-food chains are good at offering quick service but traditionally they haven't offered fresh food and they tend not to be distinctive. Full-service restaurants are distinctive and do offer fresh food but they do not provide quick service. The challenge for both these organisational forms is to undergo change to cater to this 'fast-casual' market that is expected to be worth around $35 billion annually by 2010.[18]

The potential for economies of scale or scope and the degree of risk are the main drivers of nature and degree of consolidation. For instance, similarity in consumer preferences encourages the standardisation of products, and enables the standardisation in operations. On the other hand, if a business (pharmaceutical industry being a case in point) requires large investment in technology or market development, we would expect the industry to consolidate sooner than later. Similarly, the possibility of sharing resources across different stages of value chain would also create opportunities for consolidation e.g. if a firm could use a common channel for reaching a range of its products to different market segments, it would realise economies of scope—consumer goods being one such business. Similarly, the possibility of creating product derivatives from a platform also creates an opportunity for economies of scope—automobile industry is a case in point.

Industry evolution does not always lead to an increase in concentration. There are a number of factors that can lead to a fragmented or de-concentrated industry even at later stages of an industry's life. Technology and institutional rules are two such factors. Let us first examine different aspects of technology.

TECHNOLOGICAL CHANGES

As stated in the previous chapter, 'technology' refers to tools, equipment, machinery and information, knowledge and activities that are involved in the physical transformation of inputs into outputs. These outputs may be products or services. Any physical transformation task has a choice of technologies associated with it. In a business environment characterised by increased global competition, management of technology has become a major area of concern for organisations. Selection and utilisation of the appropriate technology is a key factor of competitive success in the new environment. More importantly, technology has to be integrated with the other aspects of the organisation.

There are two aspects to technology. First, certain technologies referred to as *general-purpose technologies* affect all organisations. Examples of general-purpose technologies include the steam engine, electricity, microprocessors (including personal computers) and the Internet. Today, electricity has become so indispensable for normal human activity that we tend to take it for granted. Similarly, computers and the Internet have become ubiquitous. General-purpose technologies have had a huge impact on our quality of life. Second, every industry has its own unique types of technology. In other words, there are *industry-specific* technologies. Interestingly, as industries evolve, industry-specific technologies may change.

The concept of a *technology cycle* is useful in understanding industry evolution through technological changes.[19] Anderson and Tushman point out that technological change is cyclical. Each technology cycle begins with a *technological discontinuity*. For instance, shift from mechanical typewriters to electric typewriters first and subsequently to word processors represents discontinuous technological change because each innovation is radically different from the previous one. Similarly, the shift from mechanical watches to quartz movements is an example of technological discontinuity.

According to Anderson and Tushman, discontinuities are breakthrough innovations that lead to a radical change in the industry's state-of-the-art technology. Technological discontinuities lead to an *era of ferment*, characterised by two over-lapping processes. First, the old technology is displaced by the new technology during an *era of substitution*. This new technology may still be crude. Second, in an overlapping process, an *era of design competition* begins. Several competing technologies may emerge, each building and refining on the fundamental breakthrough advance in a different way. The design competition ends with the emergence of a *dominant design*. This is the single basic architecture that becomes accepted as the industry or market standard.

For example, in the early stages of the automobile industry in the late 19th century United States, car engines were powered by different sources such as steam, electricity and gasoline. However, by early 20th century, gasoline engines became the industry standard for car engines edging out other competitors such as steam and electricity powered engines partly because of the success of gasoline-powered cars in car rallies in the United States.[20]

The emergence of a dominant design leads to a shakeout and the remaining organisations engage in a period of incremental change. As Anderson and Tushman (p. 48) claim, '...there is little doubt that once a design becomes a standard, it establishes a trajectory for future technical progress and changes the basis for competition in the industry.'

For example, in the United States automobile industry between 1893 and 1981, after industry shakeout following the emergence of the gasoline-powered engine as the dominant design, there were 631 product and process-related innovations. Each of these was the first significant commercial introduction or application of an innovation. These encompassed automobile features such as the drive train (engine, transmission, clutch, drive shaft, rear axle and related components), process and assembly (new machinery and equipment, new production techniques and new material uses), body and chassis (frames, suspension, brakes, springs, steering, front end parts, chassis lubrication, wheels and tires and body panels) and other parts (including exterior trim parts, instrumentation, seats and many safety-related items). Some examples: introduction of the first large scale production of the high-speed V-8 engine by Cadillac in 1915, introduction of power steering by Chrysler in 1951 and the introduction of laser robotic scanners in assembly plants by General Motors in 1981.[21]

Similarly, in the early stages of the personal computer industry in the early 80s, there were a number of organisations making personal computers with different operating systems. With the emergence of IBM PC as the dominant design, its operating system, the MS-DOS developed by Microsoft, became the dominant design for operating system software. Other competing firms could not survive leaving IBM PC and the Apple/Macintosh as the competing technologies. The bigger market-share of IBM PC gave Microsoft an opportunity to develop the software technology along its own path. Today the Windows operating system is a dominant design for software operating systems although Apple/Macintosh and Linux, a Unix-based system, are competing technologies.

Once a technology becomes dominant, it is *locked-in*. All new organisations are based on the dominant design and the evolution of the industry moves along this dominant design. In other words, industry evolution becomes *path dependent* making radical changes to the dominant design almost impossible.

There are two other aspects to technological discontinuities. First, they are relatively rare occurrences. Second, they come in two forms: *competence-enhancing* and *competence-destroying*.

Competence-destroying innovations make existing technologies obsolete. Organisations that have capabilities and competence in the existing technology have to start from scratch and acquire completely new knowledge and skills. Their existing stock of knowledge simply becomes outdated. For example, the replacement of vacuum tubes by transistors was a competence-destroying innovation. Similarly, the replacement of mechanical watches by electronic, digital watches was also a competence-destroying innovation.

Competence-enhancing innovations build on existing know-how instead of replacing it. The introduction of turbofan jets and process control in cement kilns are cited as examples of competence-enhancing innovations. They markedly improved the performance of the existing technology. Typically, most industries experience both competence-enhancing and competence-destroying innovations. Table 2.3 shows the number of competence—enhancing and destroying—innovations in three industries. Usually, competence-enhancing innovations strengthen the position of established organisations, whereas competence-destroying innovations threaten their existence.

Table 2.3: Competence-enhancing and Competence-destroying innovations in three Industries in the United States

Industry	Period	Competence-enhancing innovations	Competence-destroying innovations
Cement industry	1870-1960	Two	Three
Container glass industry	1893-1956	Two	Two
Flat glass industry	1900-1960	One	Three
Minicomputer industry	1956-1980	One	Two

Source: Adapted from Anderson, P. C., and Tushman, M. L. (1997). *Managing through cycles of technological change.* In M. L. Tushman and P. C. Anderson (Eds.), *Managing Strategic Innovation and Change* (pp. 45–52). Oxford University Press, New York

General-purpose technologies like the Internet can also have the same effect as a competence-destroying innovation. The Internet has some effects that are common across all industries. For instance, it has made each industry part of a global network enabling access to all companies. It has also made information a commodity that is more freely available. However, electronic commerce, or conducting business over the Internet has had a greater effect on some industries. In the United States, 2 million of the 15 million cars sold in 1996 were sold over the Internet. Internet sales in cars are expected to be around 25 per cent of total car sales. Music, books and gift items such as flowers make up more than half of all online consumer revenues. On the downside, the accessibility and privacy provided by the Internet has also led to a thriving pornography industry. But it is expected that other legitimate retail businesses will dominate the Internet in the coming years. Assets worth nearly $400 billion are now managed online. The Internet has also spawned new businesses such as on-line auctions.[22]

The newspaper industry illustrates the competence-destroying feature of the Internet.[23] In most western countries such as the United States, Britain, Germany and France, daily newspaper circulation figures are falling. It is a declining industry. Initially, the newspapers looked upon the Internet as a cheap distribution medium. Many newspapers started their own websites to distribute content and attract advertising. However, the Internet has the potential to unravel the basic economic model at the heart of the newspaper industry.

How do newspapers make money? We are accustomed to think of newspapers as printed content—with lot of advertisements—on paper. Alternatively, one could look at it as a package of goods coupled with income streams. Goods comprise the news, editorial section, weather forecasts, sports section and so on. The income streams are classified and display advertising, promotions and the cover price. The printing press, the paper and the distribution system are necessary to attract readers, who in turn, attract the advertising that pays for the physical inputs. The initial costs of a printing press and the distribution system make the costs of producing a newspaper very high. This raises the barriers to entry. Consequently, there are fewer competitors. The Internet eliminates the need for physical inputs and therefore allows entry of specialists into the industry. Thus, there are websites that specialise in offering each of the different sections of a newspaper. Now, areas of speciality content—such as stock market reports, sports, classifieds, weather and entertainment—can be offered by specialists over the Internet. Since they do not incur high input costs (as in a printing press or distribution system), these specialist services can be offered at lower costs as compared to newspapers.

Classified advertisements, for instance, made up nearly 30 per cent of a newspaper's revenues in the United States in 1998. This is the segment most vulnerable to the Internet where one can find specialist websites for those seeking jobs, houses, cars, and second-hand goods. Thus, Internet is hastening the demise of an already declining industry.

Another technology that is expected to revolutionise retailing is what is called 'smart labels'. Based on an old technology, Radio Frequency Identification (RFID), smart labels are tiny microchips that broadcast a signal, usually a serial number, when they are in the vicinity of a reader. The cost of these labels has fallen from $2 per label to 20 cents each, making it an attractive alternative to bar-codes that are currently in use. Prices of these tags are expected to fall to 5 cents each in the next few years, thus reducing the need for labour to scan bar-codes and count stock items in retail stores. In addition, they also act as deterrents against shoplifting.

Gillette, for instance, placed an order for half a billion of these smart labels. Yet, the impact of these smart labels will stretch beyond retailing to other areas—such as tracking luggage in airports, parts in manufacturing plants and so on. Smart labels can lead to a reduction of 5 to 25 per cent in inventories.[24] Coupling this technology with the Internet opens several new possibilities. For instance, food items stored in a refrigerator with these smart labels can 'talk' to the refrigerator's computer, which can thus keep track of what is used and what is needed. The refrigerator's computer, then, can order needed items over the Internet. A chicken with smart labels, for instance, can instruct a microwave oven how to cook it. Smart labels, therefore, have the potential to become competence-destroying innovation.

Similarly, a new breed of catalysts called metallocenes is expected to lead to radical changes in the plastics industry.[25] In 2002, more than half of the $60 billion sold in the United States was made of polyethylene and polypropylene—common ingredients of plastic bottles, plastic films such as supermarket bags and medical products such as syringes, intravenous tubes and so on. Conventional catalysts lead to a mixture of polymers with varying properties. It is very difficult to produce pure plastics with conventional catalysts such as the Ziegler-Natta catalysts because the alignment and structure of chains of molecules is difficult to control. Metallocenes, on the other hand, can let chemists control the alignment and structure of polymer chains producing plastics with definable properties. New plastic films made with this catalyst can have two to three times the tensile strength, five times the impact strength, and twice the tear strength of a traditional polymer. Therefore, thinner films can be made resulting in significant cost reductions. Union Chemical Laboratories, a division of the Industrial Technology Research Institute in Taipei, for example, is using metallocenes to develop a new class of plastic for cheap, high-quality Digital Video Discs (DVDs). According to some reports, the plastic's unique thermal resistance and electrical properties may make it suitable for flat-panel displays, printed-circuit boards and perhaps even as a silicon replacement in fibre-optic devices.[26]

The photography industry is another interesting example of discontinuous change. The basics of photography are capturing an image on a medium for processing and printing subsequently. The first step called acquisition involves a camera with its three optical components of lens, shutter and flash, if external lighting is insufficient. To get a sharp clear image, the image must be properly focused and the right amount of light must enter the camera so as to be recorded on a photographic film. Early cameras had to be manually focused and the amount of light entering the camera was controlled through aperture (how wide the shutter opened) and the shutter speed (how quickly it closed). Both aperture and shutter speed had to be manually set before taking the picture. The advent of electronics in camera technology brought electronic light meters to set the speed of the aperture and the shutter; further leading to the automation of both. Further technological innovation introduced auto-focusing. Conventional film photography uses a medium coated with light-sensitive chemicals to record the image. The photographic film is then processed using specialty equipment to produce negatives or transparencies that can be printed on special paper. The global photography industry was quite concentrated with a handful brands—like Canon, Nikon, Minolta, Olympus, Ricoh and Pentax for cameras; and Fuji, Kodak and Agfa for films and film processing—dominating the market.

The arrival of digital imaging ushered an era of technological discontinuity. Digital imaging replaces the photographic film with a sensor such as a light-sensitive charged-couple device (CCD) consisting of an array of photocells that convert light into digital signals. However, unlike film photography, these digital signals need to be processed before storage. This involves interpolation and compression to ensure image resolution and storage of more pictures in a given medium. Images are stored on magnetic or optical disks or on special flash data storage cards. This allows for the retrieval, printing and transmitting of these images using personal computers, standard or specialized printers and the Internet. A major change in digital imaging is that images can be viewed and erased before being printed and transmitted, cutting down on film and processing costs in conventional film photography.

Digital imaging has also altered the structure of the photography industry with the entry of a number of new players from the consumer electronics industry such as Casio, Sony, Philips, Samsung, Sega, Matsushita and Hitachi. In addition, personal computers and peripherals firms such as IBM, HP, Apple, Epson, Lexmark, and Xerox are also seeking to enter specific niches. By 2005, the sale of digital cameras is expected to overtake that of film cameras. However, both digital and film cameras face a new threat—the camera-equipped mobile phones, the sale of which is expected to exceed the combined sales of digital and film cameras.[27] While the future of the

82 Change Management

industry is uncertain at this stage, it is safe to assume that printed photos will decline in the future, with most images being viewed on-screen.

TECHNOLOGY AND STRATEGIC CHANGE

We illustrate how some of the firms are changing the industry structure and creating new opportunities for growth or competitive advantage in technology-led consumer focused businesses. Our case in point is Apple in the digital music industry and Nokia in the mobile phones industry (outlined in Box 2.3 and Box 2.4 respectively). While Apple achieved phenomenal success in the last two years, Nokia has had to struggle a bit to retain its dominant position. Apple represents an organisation that was under-performing, as compared to its peers in the computer industry; while Nokia was doing extremely well till recently as 2004. Nokia got its wake-up call in form of lost market-share and weak financial performance.

Box 2.3: Digital Music and iPod Phenomenon[28]

Apple's emergence from being a niche player in the computer industry to a dominant player in the digital music industry is an interesting case of a firm's ability to leverage technology for fulfilling a latent consumer need—music of choice anytime, anywhere. iPod lets consumers control how and when they would listen to their music. Apple commands 80 per cent of MP3 player market and 75 per cent of the online music sales.[29]

iPod had its share of sceptics at the time of its initial launch in October 2001, in the middle of technology slump. The main concerns being the product-price and Apple's ability to compete in the consumer electronics market. These concerns invited jokes like 'idiots price our products' or 'I prefer old-fashioned discs'. Not any more. Apple has products across a range of prices in form of iPod Mini and iPod Shuffle. The ability to choose music from iTunes makes discs look old-fashioned. The global sales of hard-format music have continuously been declining for last 5 years and are now at US$ 33.6 billion in 2004, a decline of 1.3 per cent from the previous year.[30] At the same time, the cumulative sales at iTunes increased to 500 million on July 2005, up from 250 million in January 2005.[31] As for Apple's ability to compete in consumer electronics industry, it is the players in the consumer electronics industry who now have to compete with Apple today. In this sense, Apple has a game-changing innovation on its hand.

Sony, after years of resistance to selling MP3 players, had to give in. iPod's success encouraged Sony to launch Network Walkman, with capabilities that are qualitatively similar to those of iPod. Sony, one of largest content owners in the world, is still resisting the open standards approach. While Apple does not have to protect its content, iPod users can download music only from iTunes at present. So is the case with Sony.

While, for some time to come, we may not know the winner in the race for standards, digital music success has already initiated a debate about consumer preference: would a user want to own music or simply rent it out? If the songs are to be delivered anytime and anywhere, we may need some more technology solutions to deliver music for renting through wireless networks. We are probably not far from that solution; mobile phone firms like Motorola are bundling iTunes with their handsets and car manufacturers like BMW are incorporating facility to play iPod into their new models. It may not be surprising to see music playing capability in mobile phones becoming as ubiquitous as photography capability today. Apple's success has also led to 'podcasting' being one form of broadcasting technology.

iPod's success highlights the fact that the ability to leverage technology coupled with simplicity of design could create a game-changing strategy. At this stage of evolution, a business leader may ask: What are the opportunities opening up for convergence of computing, consumer electronics, mobile telephone and entertainment industry, and how can a firm be at the forefront of this change? Interestingly, Apple is an outsider for three of the four industries in question.

Box 2.4: Strategic Change in Mobile Phone Industry[32]

Nokia, world's biggest mobile phone maker, selling over 200 million phones per year in a market that sold over 650 million handsets in 2004, saw its market-share slip from over 35 per cent to below 30 per cent in that year. The reason: it missed anticipating a product-design based change in consumer preference. We are talking about flip-open or clamshell phones. Motorola, Samsung, LG and Sony-Ericsson took a significant bite out of Nokia's share. Since then, it has regained lost share through a combination of new products and aggressive price cuts.

How did Nokia lose track of its own insight—that mobile phones were increasingly becoming a fashion product—and, consequently, required increased, consistent and continuous attention to product design?

It is quite possible that Nokia ignored its own understanding of the market to leverage scale in its manufacturing operations. This hypothesis is supported by the fact that Nokia has been reluctant to offer customised products to mobile operators. This has led many mobile operators to turn to original design manufacturers (ODMs). Nokia has now reversed this position. And its reconfigurable Nokia Series 60 software has enabled the reversal of 'we would not customise' strategy. Software reconfiguration allows it to support different operator requirements without having to reconfigure its supply chain.

While Nokia has successfully negotiated the recent challenge, it is firms like Samsung that are leading the way in technology. Samsung showcased a phone that uses voice-recognition technology to convert speech into text. It was the first firm to launch a phone that could work with CDMA as well as GSM networks. Samsung is now competing with Motorola for the number-two position in the handsets market.

In some ways, the mobile phones market is at crossroads. The market is large and growing. Consequently there are huge opportunities for realising economies of scale. At the same time, the product life cycle is getting shorter due to changes in consumer preferences. Thus a firm has to invest in market development for its new products in a fiercely competitive market. It has to invest in product as well as market development activity without being certain about whether the realised volume will allow it to recover these investments— a strategic dilemma indeed! Probably this is what Nokia faced at a time when its competitors were able to take away some share of its market.

In a large volume, high-growth market like the mobile phones, we may also see a trend toward 'horizontalisation' of supply chain, which may make the advantage of scale irrelevant. Horizontalisation refers to the process of outsourcing different components of a product to specialist producers. In such a situation, the design-brand focused firms do not have to worry about economies of scale in manufacturing, as component manufacturers through pooling of supplies across the entire industry provide the scale. In such a situation, even the smaller players, willing to invest in product development, can lead the way for changes in consumer preferences.

INDUSTRY EVOLUTION AND CONCENTRATION

Now, returning to the earlier question, does industry evolution always lead to increase in concentration? The answer: it depends! One of the things it depends on is, whether the dominant design is standardised and accessible to new entrants. If the design is standardised and embedded in machinery and equipment that can be purchased relatively easily, then smaller firms in the periphery can mount a challenge to larger firms that dominate the market. If skills and machinery that contain the dominant design can be purchased relatively easily, then smaller firms in the periphery will compete on the basis of costs and prices. An example of such competition is the emergence and growth of Asian competitors in last two decades. Overseas firms from Asia entered markets where the technology was available for purchase such as in manufacturing of hand and machine tools, textiles and consumer durables. Alternatively, when large firms dominate the centre of the market, smaller firms may focus on niche markets.

In population ecology terminology, phenomenon of the co-existence of r-strategists and K-strategists in a concentrated industry is called *resource partitioning*.[33] In industries where resource partitioning exists, the market would have been partitioned into segments—some of these are held by larger organisations called *generalists* while others are held by smaller organisations called *specialists*. Generalists focus on broader segment of the market whereas specialists concentrate on narrower segments. Population ecology researchers have shown the existence of such resource partitioning in the brewing, music recording, book publishing, and microprocessor industries.

The commercial airlines industry is an interesting example of lack of concentration and resource partitioning. The car industry came into being just a little after the first aeroplane was flown, yet the commercial airlines industry is nothing like the automobile industry.[34] There are around 265 international airlines and a little over 500 domestic ones. The biggest, American Airlines, has only 7 per cent of the global market share. One of the reasons for the low concentration in the airlines industry is that competition is still restricted in this industry. In the aftermath of the terrorist attacks in the United States on September 11, 2001, the industry was expected to lose $10 billion that year. However, even before this, the industry was declining. Passenger numbers were down. Over the last 30 years, most airlines in the industry have not generated enough profits to cover their cost of capital. Since September 11, 2001, at least three international carriers—such as Swissair and Sabena—have had to close down operations. Many are teetering on the edge of bankruptcy. Despite this, new airlines are being launched the world over.

Why are there new entrants into an industry that is in decline? The reason is that some airlines are still profitable. For instance, in the United States, there are two types of airlines—the large network carriers and the low-cost carriers (LCCs). The network carriers such as American Airlines and Delta Airlines are generalists. They operate on the basis of what is known as the 'hub-and-spoke' model. They consolidate passengers at their 'hub' airports fed by smaller 'spokes'. The low-cost carriers (LCCs) such as Southwest, AirTran, JetBlue and EasyJet, offer a no-frills, point-to-point service—often flying from secondary, smaller airports. LCCs are the profitable, growth-segment of this industry. Given the industry decline, there are plentiful aircraft available for leasing. The dominant design is standardised and available for purchase. Not surprisingly, most new entrants are LCCs leasing Airbus A320s for about $150, 000 a month and set themselves up as LCCs. The LCC segment of the airlines industry may be around 25 per cent of the market, but is expected to increase.

The major reason for fragmentation of the airlines industry has to do with rules that govern the conduct of business in this industry. For example, there are restrictions of foreign ownership of state-owned, international flag carriers. Foreign airlines are not allowed to compete in the domestic routes in the United States. Other restrictions ensure that British Airways cannot fly to the United States from Paris or Frankfurt. Similarly, Air France cannot fly to America from London's Heathrow airport. In the United States, the big network carriers face barriers to exit due to union and local community pressures to retain jobs. These are example of *institutional rules* that govern the conduct of business in any industry. Together with technology and competition, institutional rules shape the evolution of an industry.

INSTITUTIONAL RULES

Institutional rules refer to the formal or written and informal or unwritten constraints that preside over the exchange of goods and services in a society.[35] Formal constraints are Acts of legislation—such as the law pertaining to setting up companies with limited liability, health and safety, employment, fair trade, consumer protection and guarantees, monopoly restriction and so on. Informal rules are codes, conventions and norms that evolve over time. Institutional rules include both what organisations are permitted to do and what they are prohibited from doing. Organisations cannot—and do not—operate with unlimited freedom. They cannot choose to do what they like, but have to conform to both written and unwritten rules of conduct.

A useful way to understand institutional rules is to compare them to competitive sport. Institutional rules are similar to rules of the game in any competitive sport. Any competitive sport is played under strict rules that are rigorously enforced by referees and umpires. There are both written and unwritten rules that govern the conduct of players. Unwritten rules are as important as written rules. While violation of written rules leads to legal sanctions against the offender, violation of unwritten rules can lead to widespread condemnation of the action by the community. The offender suffers a loss of reputation and legitimacy.

For instance, none of 42 laws of cricket explicitly state that a player may not punch someone in the opposing team on the nose, but the preamble to the rules of cricket affirm that the spirit of the game involves showing respect to opponents. Therefore it is understood that the player should not violate the spirit of the game. However, violations do occur and they not only cause controversy but also lead to making informal rules formal.

When cricket was first played, a bowler sent the ball to the batsman in an under-arm throw.[36] According to cricketing folklore, about one hundred and fifty years ago, a young lady was trying to bowl for her brother. She wore a crinoline dress with a long, full skirt. The skirt had hoops in it to make it stand out stiffly. When she tried to bowl under-arm, her crinoline stopped her arm swinging forward. She then began to swing her arm backwards and upwards, to throw the ball from above her head. In doing so, she became the first over-arm bowler. A number of people copied her action but over-arm bowling did not become legal till much later, although under-arm bowling was not considered illegal till the early 1980s.

On a fateful day on February 1, 1981, the one-day World Series cricket match between Australia and New Zealand gave rise to one of the greatest controversies in the history of cricket.[37] Greg, his captain and brother, instructed Trevor Chappell to bowl the last ball of the match under-arm, preventing New Zealand's batsman Brian McKechnie from scoring a six, which the Kiwis needed to tie the match. Although legal, the act was considered against the spirit of cricket. The incident caused outrage around the cricketing world, especially in New Zealand where the then-Prime Minister Robert Muldoon called it 'an act of cowardice', while Melbourne newspaper *The Age* wrote: 'Australian cricket is today in disgrace and the country's reputation as a sporting nation is severely damaged.' Greg Chappell has since gone on record as saying he 'bitterly regrets' making that decision, one that resulted in the laws of cricket being rewritten. Back in 1981, underarm bowling was permitted as long as the umpire was informed of the bowler's intention—as Greg Chappell did on the day in question. Now, law 24 (1b) of cricket states: *Underarm bowling shall not be permitted except by special agreement before the match.*

This episode from cricket illustrates an important point about institutional rules. Institutional rules become formal constraints embodied in acts of legislation when the conduct of organisations violates widely held beliefs about what is appropriate. In organisation theory jargon, we refer to this as loss of *legitimacy*. When organisations squander their legitimacy by engaging in deceitful and unprincipled behaviour, they invite scrutiny and control over their actions from the community and its representatives in the government.

For instance, between 1999 and 2002, there were a number of corporate scandals in America involving cooked-up books, exorbitant salaries and loans to chief executive officers (CEOs), conflicts of interest by auditors, and hyped-up stock reports by securities analysts at some well-known business corporations and investment banks.[38] Thousands of shareholders and employees lost billions of dollars of retirement savings, as share-prices of these companies collapsed. Predictably, these scandals led to widespread outrage and demand for greater control over corporate activities. In 2002, the United States Congress drafted a piece of legislation titled the Sarbanes-Oxley Act to prevent such behaviour of business firms.

The Sarbanes-Oxley Act of 2002 contains far-reaching provisions affecting some 15,000 public-traded companies in such areas as auditor independence, corporate responsibility, improved financial disclosure, analyst conflict of interest and accountability for corporate criminal fraud. Among other things, including stiffer jail terms for errant executives, the legislation[39]:

- Requires CEOs and chief financial officers to personally attest to the accuracy of earnings reports and other financial statements
- Sharply curtails the kinds of non-auditing consulting services that outside auditors can provide to companies whose books they review
- Protects whistle-blowers i.e. employees who legitimately complain about their organisation's illicit activities
- Strengthens criminal penalties, including fines and jail terms, for certain misdeeds by executives
- Requires investment firms to take steps to improve the objectivity of reports by securities analysts
- Establishes a Public Company Accounting Oversight Board to oversee the audits of companies that are subject to securities laws
- Bars executives and directors from coercing outside auditors to issue misleading financial statements and requires them to relinquish any compensation they earned as a result of bogus statements

The Act is leading to changes in the ways in which corporate organisations govern themselves in America. The Sarbanes-Oxley Act of 2002 also illustrates another aspect of institutional rules. Just as in any game like cricket, these institutional rules also undergo change. In other words, institutional rules evolve, although their rate of evolution may be slow. However, when institutional rules change, they change the rules of the game in a competitive industry. An organisation that doesn't anticipate and prepare for this change can experience a fall in its performance. A change in institutional rules, therefore, can trigger changes in an organisation.

When the institutional rules that govern transactions of business are reduced, the industry moves towards *deregulation*. Deregulation does not, however, imply absence of rules. When the institutional rules are increased, the industry is re-regulated. Some changes in institutional rules have the same impact as a competence-destroying innovation. For example, deregulation of industries that were previously regulated can lead to radical changes in the rules of the game. For instance, in many countries, industries such as telecommunications, banking, and electricity generation and distribution were once highly regulated, restricting competition. Deregulation of these industries paved the way for increasing competition resulting in both industry-level and organisational changes.

One of the functions of institutional rules is to reduce uncertainty for organisations. They render the environment more certain and predictable, thereby reducing the need for the organisation to expend resources in trying to make sense of an uncertain environment. When industries are deregulated, such institutional rules are eliminated. Therefore, deregulation raises the level of uncertainty faced by individual organisations. Organisations that are better able to cope with the uncertainty thrive in the new environment. Usually such organisations are likely to be smaller, newer entrants into the industry.

However, more regulations do not necessarily imply less uncertainty. For most organisations, frequent and unanticipated changes to the rules and regulations governing an industry are a major source of uncertainty. Therefore, *change* in institutional rules—not whether there are less or more rules—is the trigger for organisational changes. For the organisations in the industry, any change implies a degree of uncertainty that they need to manage. Deregulation usually results in more competition and technological changes. The telecommunications industry in the United States is an illustration of this phenomenon.

Britain and India offer dramatic illustrations of the effects of deregulation.[40] A series of changes in institutional rules in the 1980s and 1990s have led to Britain becoming one of the most open economies in the world. It is the fourth largest economy now, behind the United States, Japan and Germany. Deregulation has led to dramatic changes in many industries. Traditional industries such as steel, coal and shipbuilding have almost disappeared to be replaced by a thriving services industry. London is the leading international financial centre in the world. Formerly known as the British Airports Authority, BAA manages airports in America, Europe and Asia-Pacific. Well-known British firms such as ICI and Rolls Royce have significantly declined. British Airways, Marks and Spencer and BT (British Telecom) are all struggling. On the other hand, Vodafone, having acquired an American and a German mobile-phone company, has emerged as the world's top mobile phone company. Deregulation can, therefore, lead to both creation and destruction. New industries may emerge and the old ones may die, while new entrants may transform the others.

India offers a more dramatic example of industry creation and change, as a result of deregulation. The information technology (IT) industry in India is made up of firms that provide hardware and peripherals, software and training. Firms specialising in software include firms that provide software products and those providing software services. In 2002–2003, the total turnover of this industry was roughly $18 billion. Software services accounted for 75 per cent of this turnover. Within software services, exports contributed to 60 per cent of the turnover. In other words, export-oriented software services sector dominate the industry. The software industry is comprised of firms that undertake software projects and firms that offer IT-enabled services (ITes) such as call centres, processing credit card and back-office transactions.

The Indian software services industry emerged in the late 1960s and early 1970s. It has grown rapidly at an average compounded annual growth rate of around 40 per cent since early 1990s. Today, it is a global industry catering primarily to markets in North America and Europe. The World Bank rates India as a leading outsourcing destination for software services. Exports of software services has grown from less than $2 billion in 1997–98 to over $10 billion in 2002–2003 at a compounded annual growth rate of 41 per cent. In the same period, the global market for software services grew by around 6 per cent from $359 billion to $475 billion. In 2003, the volume of Indian exports was about four times the size of the Indian domestic market for software services. The United States was the main export destination, accounting for nearly 70 per cent of the exports. Nearly 73 per cent of the export revenues were through software projects. In the same year, the ITes segment contributed to about one-third of the export revenues. For last ten years, three firms have dominated the industry: Tata Consultancy Services (TCS), Infosys and Wipro. Currently, each employs about 25,000–30,000 people. To summarise, the Indian software industry is rather distinctive in its features:

➤ It is almost exclusively oriented to export of software services, either as projects or through business process outsourcing
➤ It is concentrated with three firms providing nearly a quarter of the exports
➤ It comprises a large pool of young professionals with relatively high levels of education
➤ Its main export market continues to be the United States

Why has India been particularly successful as an exporting nation in software services? According to the international consulting firm, McKinsey and Company, there is a potential cost savings of 60–65 per cent for organisations in the United States that outsource to India. In concrete terms, whereas a chip designer with a post-graduate degree and five years experience would cost around $7,500 per month in the United States, an individual with the same education and experience can be hired for around $1,500 per month in India. Partly this is because the availability of skilled labour is in relatively large quantities. In 2003, there were more than 230 universities and 1,000 engineering colleges producing about 100,000 engineering and 2 million non-engineering graduates each year. Since the medium of instruction in these institutions is English, it provides them an advantage compared to graduates from non-English speaking countries in East Asia.

However, this explanation based on cost differences and supply of skilled labour doesn't answer some important questions. First, given that the same factors would have also bestowed them with competitive advantage, why didn't India's manufacturing industries experience similar success? Second, labour costs in India have been rising between 14–30 per cent a year during a period when the average rate per hour for offshore work dropped from $75 to $12.50. Despite this, how has the industry continued to grow? Third, as a developing country, the Indian software industry faced formidable barriers in building a successful export-oriented industry. It lacked infrastructure facilities, was saddled with institutional constraints as a result of misguided government policies, and lacked credibility in overseas markets as a supplier of software services. How did the software industry overcome these obstacles?

The success of this industry was built around a unique business model that was shaped by both the opportunities and constraints in the institutional environment. The articulation of this business model into firm level success was the result of both government policies and firm level strategies. Government policies created a favourable context that helped organisations develop capabilities to put their business models in operation. Therefore, the emergence and growth of the Indian software industry was the result of both institutional dynamics and firm-level capability development. In other words, changing the 'rules of the game' in the institutional environment and continuously upgrading firm capabilities through human resource practices were as important as the supply of low-cost intellectual labour in the success of this industry.

The three forces of change—competitive structure, technology and institutional rules—are inter-related. Together, they not only influence industry evolution but also require organisations to change in order to survive and grow. As long as they undergo only slow change, industry evolution is gradual and predictable. Managing change under these conditions is relatively easy since the level of uncertainty faced by managers is low. However, as the rate of change in these three forces begins to increase, managers begin to face a dynamic environment and higher levels of uncertainty. *The challenge of change in the present environment is coming to grips with this uncertainty and managing it.*

DEVELOPING A CHANGE AGENDA

The purpose of analysis of operating environment is to understand the forces that are impacting or likely to impact on your organisation's performance. Industry analysis gives you the big picture of what is feasible in your business environment. It facilitates the setting of realistic targets for your organisation. The targets that you set for growth, market share, profitability or customer service shapes your change agenda. These targets need to take into account the realities of your business environment. More importantly, they also need to be based on your organisation's capabilities and competencies. In other words, as Bossidy and Charan suggest, your change agenda should be based on three factors: (i) Business environment or industry dynamics, (ii) Financial and non-financial targets, and (iii) Internal capabilities and competencies. Figure 2.9 illustrates this.

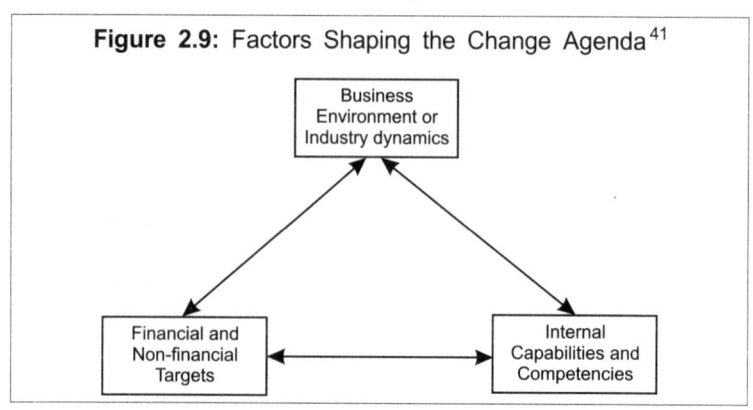

Figure 2.9: Factors Shaping the Change Agenda[41]

The change agenda must address the following questions[42]:

- What is our assessment of the external environment?
- How well do we understand our existing customers and markets?
- What is best way to grow our business profitably?
- How can we make money on a sustainable basis?
- What are the obstacles to growth?
- Who is the competition?
- What strategy do we need to grow in this environment?
- Do we have the internal capabilities and competencies to execute this strategy?
- What capabilities are we missing? What do we need to develop?
- How do we balance the short term and the long term?
- What are the important milestones in executing our change agenda?
- What are the critical issues facing our organisation?
- How do we address these issues?

This change agenda needs to be developed through a process of dialogue and conversations with key managers in the organisation. The questions listed above are a useful starting point for these dialogues and conversations. However, organisations face a formidable barrier in effectively addressing these questions. The dominant mindset or mental model prevailing in the organisations can prevent managers from seeing and confronting reality, both externally and internally. Mental models shape our thinking and mediate between the reality outside and us. They can be significant obstacles in times of change. Therefore, we need to understand the nature of mental models and how they can affect our perceptions and actions. In the next chapter, we address this important topic.

NOTES AND REFERENCES

1. Aldrich, H. (1999). *Organisations Evolving*. London: Sage Publications.
2. *SMEs in New Zealand: Structure and Dynamics*, (May 1999). Wellington: Firm Capability Team, Ministry of Commerce, New Zealand.

3. *SMEs in New Zealand: Structure and Dynamics.* (May, 1999). Ministry of Commerce, New Zealand.
4. Ibid.
5. Ibid.
6. *The NBER's Recession Dating Procedure.* (2003). from http://www.nber.org/cycles/recessions.html
7. After the bubbles. (September 26, 2002). *Economist;* Crystal balls-up. (September 26, 2002). *Economist;* Keeping a lower profile. (September 26, 2002). *Economist;* Of shocks and horrors. (September 26, 2002). *Economist;* The unfinished recession. (September 26, 2002). *Economist;* United we fall. (September 26, 2002). *Economist.*
8. Other people's money. (July 3, 2003). *Economist.*
9. Financial services: Goodbye to the City. (February 6, 2003). *Economist.*
10. Other people's money. (July 3, 2003). *Economist.*
11. Financial services: Goodbye to the City. (February 6, 2003). *Economist.*
12. Source: *Economic Times,* December 14, 2002.
13. Source: *Business Week Online,* May 2003.
14. Abernathy, W. J., Clark, K. B., & Kantrow, A. M. (1983). *Industrial Renaissance: Producing a Competitive Future for America.* New York: Basic Books.
15. Deans, G. K., Zeisel, S., & Kroeger, F. (2002). *Winning the Merger Endgame: A Playbook for Profiting from Industry Consolidation.* Europe: McGraw-Hill Education.
16. Carroll, G. R. & Hannan, M. T. (2000). *The Demography of Corporations and Industries.* Princeton, New Jersey: Princeton University Press.
17. The beauty business: Pots of promise. (May 22, 2003). *Economist.*
18. McPherson, J. R., Mitchell, A. V., & Mitten, M. R. (2003). Fast-food fight. *The McKinsey Quarterly* (2).
19. Anderson, P. C. & Tushman, M. L. (1997). Managing through cycles of technological change. In M. L. Tushman & P. C. Anderson (Eds.), *Managing Strategic Innovation and Change* (p. 45–52). New York: Oxford University Press.
20. Aldrich, H. (1999). *Organisations Evolving.* London: Sage Publications.
21. Abernathy, W. J., Clark, K. B., & Kantrow, A. M. (1983). *Industrial Renaissance: Producing a Competitive Future for America.* New York: Basic Books.
22. Tremble, everyone. (May 8, 1997). *Economist.*
23. Caught in the web. (July 15, 1999). *Economist.*

24. The IT revolution: The best thing since the bar-code. (February 6, 2003). *Economist*.
25. Designer plastics. (December 6, 2001). *Economist*.
26. Ibid.
27. Mobile snaps. (July 3, 2003). *Economist*.
28. Source: Various *Economist* articles including The meaning of iPod (June 10, 2004), Crunch time for Apple (Jan 13, 2005), The Race to catch the iPod (July 23, 2004), *A Big Week for Apple* (July 29, 2004)
29. Source: www.boston.com, *Digital Competitors ready to take bite out of Apple*
30. Source: www.ifpi.org
31. Source: http://playlistmag.com
32. Source: Various issues of *Economist* including As good as it gets? (Jan 13, 2005), The Giant in the palm of your hand (Feb 10, 2005), *The Giant's makeover* (June 16, 2005) and Battling for the palm of your hand (April 29, 2004)
33. Aldrich, H. (1999). *Organisations Evolving*. London: Sage Publications.
34. Business: Airlines. A way out of the wilderness. (May 1, 2003). *Economist;* Business: Airlines. The unpalatable truth. (November 22, 2001). *Economist;* Business: America's airlines and the war. The darkest hour. (March 20, 2003). *Economist;* Business: Low-cost airlines. Cheap and cheerful. (May 22, 2003). *Economist;* Opinion: Airlines. Flying blind. (October 11, 2001). *Economist*.
35. North, D. C. (1990). *Institutions, Institutional Change and Economic Performance*. Cambridge: Cambridge University Press.
36. http://www.cricketweb.net/resources/history.shtml (2003).
37. http://www.bangkokpost.net/chiangmai/news/140402_news07.html (2003).
38. *Has Sarbanes-Oxley Made a Dent in Corporate America's Armor?* (2003). Retrieved July 31, 2003, from http://knowledge.wharton.upenn.edu/print_version.cfm?articleid=823&catid=2
39. Ibid.
40. British business: A bruising boom. (October 19, 2000). *Economist*.
41. Based on Bossidy, Lawrence and Charan, Ram, (2004). *Confronting Reality: Doing What Matters to Get Things Right*. New York: Crown Business, p. 79.
42. Based on Bossidy, Lawrence & Charan, Ram, (2002). *Execution: The Discipline of Getting Things Done*. New York: Crown Business. pp. 188–189.

CHAPTER 3

Appreciating Change: Mental and Business Models

OVERVIEW

We begin by describing four types of change and identifying two strategic errors that can arise while appreciating change. Type 1 error is defined as engaging in too little change, while Type 2 error is launching too much change. We discuss the role of cognition in appreciating change and identify the root cause for the two strategic errors. These errors arise from inappropriate mental models. We examine how mental models are shaped and present ideas for avoiding these errors by engaging in appropriate learning processes. Finally we bring together the key ideas from the previous chapter and this one, to diagnose the change issues and decide on a change agenda. This involves becoming aware of industry dynamics and identifying the value proposition and the business model appropriate for an organisation in its present context. By the end of this chapter, you would know about reactive change, anticipatory change, Type 1 and Type 2 errors, cognition, mental models, organisational learning, defensive routines, value propositions and business models.

APPRECIATING CHANGE—A FRAMEWORK

In the previous chapter, we examined the dynamics of change in an industry. Evolutionary changes in an industry form the context for organisational changes. This is because organisational change is largely an adaptive response to pressures and forces in the environment. According to the experiential learning model, change is driven by a gap between performance and aspirations. If we assume that aspirations are likely to be stable over a period of time, any actual or anticipated reductions in current or future performance should trigger change. However, in reality it is not as simple as that.

Generally, organisations can engage in two types of changes.[1] One, called *reactive change*, is fairly straightforward. Organisations launch reactive change when they experience a drop in performance as a result of changes in the environment. For instance, an organisation might lose market-share and experience lower profits as a result of competitor action. In this instance, there is a clear felt need for change that is quite visible. Managers are likely to have a clear idea of what caused the performance reduction and can, therefore, initiate changes to correct the situation. When they do take corrective actions they are engaging in reactive change.

The other type of change, called *anticipatory change*, is a little more complex. Organisations can also initiate changes in anticipation of changes in the environment. For example, managers in an organisation may anticipate a reduction in performance as a result of the possible entry of new competitors. They may launch changes to prepare the organisation for the new competitors who have not yet entered the market. Another organisation could introduce changes in anticipation of technological shifts in the industry. In both these instances, organisations are engaging in anticipatory change. Obviously anticipatory is relatively more risky. The anticipated shifts in the environment may not take place or the environment may shift in a direction different from what the managers anticipated.

What distinguishes reactive and anticipatory change is the level of uncertainty in the environment. Reactive changes are usually low on uncertainty; the performance drop is visible and the cause is usually clear and concrete. However, in anticipatory change, there is no disruption to current performance and the causes for future disruption are likely to be uncertain and unclear. This aspect of increased uncertainty makes managing anticipatory change challenging. In the current globally competitive environment, few organisations can afford the luxury of reactive change. In fast-paced markets, resorting to reactive change will seriously compromise an organisation's competitive position. Firms that engage in reactive change tend to follow—rather than lead—their competition. Therefore, and despite its difficulties, managing anticipatory change is vital for an organisation's survival as well as growth.

Reactive and anticipatory changes represent one dimension of change management. The other dimension is about the tempo of change, it relates to the content and process of change that the organisation is planning to introduce. This is a fairly important dimension; organisational change researchers distinguish between two types of change based on this dimension. *Incremental change* refers to small, continuous changes introduced over a longer time frame. *Radical change* stands for large, discontinuous changes implemented rapidly over shorter time frame.

In simple terms, incremental changes are little changes introduced slowly, over a period of time; whereas radical changes are lot of changes introduced rapidly. Radical changes also tend to be discontinuous in that, unlike incremental changes, they do not build on existing structures and processes. They tend to replace existing structures, processes and people with newer ones. Radical changes also tend to be episodic i.e. they occur infrequently.

Change management effort can be mapped into a grid (Figure 3.1), so as to enable us to look at change as an opportunity as well as a challenge. Given the nature of change, the leadership role would be significantly different across situations. For instance, the leadership role for situations described in the lower half of the grid (Figure 3.1) has higher managerial content i.e. the decisions are likely to be made within an existing framework using existing decision rules. In situations described under the top half of the same grid, the change management effort would require dealing with the unknown. There may not be any past experience or strategy that would help meet the challenge or realise opportunities in the market place.

Figure 3.1: Managing Change: Impact and Magnitude Grid

Radical Change (Leadership Approach)	**Crisis Management** (Organisation and Business Restructuring with limited degrees of freedom)	**New Competitive Positioning** (Innovation led changes in Organisation and Business Model)
Incremental Change (Managerial Approach)	**Damage Control** (Recouping the lost position within Existing Organisation and Business Model)	**Strengthening Existing Competitive Position** (Realising Opportunities within Existing Organisation and Business Model)
	Reactive Change (Problem Situation)	**Anticipatory Change** (Potential Opportunities)

The top, right-hand quadrant (Figure 3.1) represents the situation where the firm has an opportunity to change the rules of game in industry, led usually by product or process innovation. Sony Walkman and iPod are two examples of product innovation. On the other hand, Dell and Walmart's competence in managing their respective supply chains are the classic cases of process innovation that enabled them to change the rules of game. While product innovation enabled Sony and Apple to create new businesses or redefined the market completely, Dell and Walmart used different business models to change the competitive structure of the market.

The need for incremental change may arise when different industry players are experimenting, at margin, to strengthen or protect their position or there are imperfections in learning (an issue discussed later in the chapter) that require a relatively conservative strategy. Conservatism could also stem from the fact that an organisation is culturally averse to making significant strategic changes. At the individual level, conservatism may have its roots in fear of failure.

The core task of appreciating change exposes managers to two errors that can seriously affect their organisation's performance, survival and growth. First, they may either not launch any changes or may introduce changes that are too little relative to what is required in their environment. Alternatively, they may introduce the right quantum of changes but the same may be initiated too late. We refer to these errors as Type 1 error: either there is no change or too little change is initiated too late. Second, managers may initiate too many changes relative to what is required in their context or they may introduce changes too quickly. These errors constitute Type 2 error: organisational change that is 'too much or too soon.'

Both Type 1 and Type 2 errors have the potential to jeopardize the performance and growth of an organisation. Type 1 errors render the organisation uncompetitive over a period of time; it may end up trying to catch up with its competitors. Type 2 errors lead to disruptive changes that eventually degrade the organisation's performance. While Type 1 errors will lead to organisational stagnation and loss of vitality, Type 2 errors will lead to what is known as 'initiative overload' and cause change fatigue in the organisation. Over a period of time, high levels of change fatigue among employees will lead to cynicism, mistrust and lack of enthusiasm for any future changes.

The key to effective change management is striking the right balance of change, initiated at the right time. Therefore, while appreciating change, managers need to guard against Type 1 and Type 2 errors. These errors can be minimized and eliminated if managers are aware of the root causes for these miscalculations. As we stated earlier, organisational change is an adaptive response to the environment. In other words, organisational changes are initiated based on what managers 'see' in the environment. Thus, both Type 1 and Type 2 errors flow from managers' faulty perceptions of their environment.

When managers underestimate or fail to see shifts in the environment, they are more likely to commit a Type 1 error. When they overestimate or miscalculate the extent of these shifts, they are more likely to commit a Type 2 error. Accurate perceptions of the environment, therefore, are crucial in effectively managing change. Let us examine the process of perception or what is referred to as cognition.

COGNITION AND ORGANISATIONAL CHANGE

The word 'cognition' means the 'act or faculty of knowing.' Cognition also signifies awareness, comprehension, discernment, insight, intelligence, perception, reasoning and understanding. In change management, cognition implies knowing when to launch change in an organisation. This act of knowing is based on the collection and interpretation of data from outside. In other words, the way in which a manager collects and interprets information about the world outside the organisation shapes her knowledge about change.

Specifically, managerial cognition in the context of change is the recognition and interpretation of signals from an organisation's environment that denote impending shifts in the environment. If a manager recognises and interprets the signals accurately, she is unlikely to commit Type 1 or Type 2 errors. On the other hand, both type of errors are more likely when recognition and interpretation are flawed. Then the key question is: what leads to flawed recognition and interpretation of environmental signals? If cognition is the recognition and interpretation of the world outside, what leads to faulty cognition on the part of managers?

Although this seems like a simple question, the answer is quite complicated. There are a number of factors that can cause flawed cognition, which can be broadly classified in two categories: (i) organisational factors that can lead to defective cognition, and (ii) personal or human factors that can cause errors in cognition.

Let us look at the organisational factors first. Knowing when to launch change depends on recognising and interpreting signals from the environment. Managers are unlikely to recognise signals if they don't notice them. Thus, even if there are strong signals from the environment, managers may not recognise them because these signals do not capture their attention.

In fact, managerial attention in an organisation is a scarce resource. Managers can only pay attention to a limited number of things and are most likely to miss crucial signals from the environment if their attention span does not encompass the signals. Therefore, factors that shape, influence or constrain managerial attention can lead to either absence of cognition or flawed cognition. Therefore, we need to look at organisational factors that influence managerial attention and cognition.

As discussed in the previous chapter, a large proportion of activities in any organisation are routine activities driven by the formulae, which people hold in their heads. More importantly, these explicit and implicit rules structure people's attention and thinking by helping focus their minds on specific activities. Organisations with strong routines will have a powerful influence over managerial attention and thinking. Unless these routines require managers to pay attention to the environment, they are not likely to notice signals from the environment. Obviously, if they don't notice signals, they are more likely to commit a Type 1 error, i.e. not recognise the need for change when there is a real need for change.

Apart from organisational factors, a set of human factors can also affect the cognitive processes in managers. A major factor is the cognitive limitation of the human brain. Regardless of their intelligence, human beings have limited computational capacity for absorbing and interpreting complex data. The human brain can get easily overloaded when presented with a lot of information.

As human beings, we rely on mental short cuts called *heuristics* to solve problems and to make decisions in complex situations. Heuristics can be thought of as formulae that have helped us navigate similar complex situations in the past. However, most of us are largely unaware of these mental short cuts that we take. Although they make our decision-making efficient, these heuristics can be inappropriate for dealing with new, unfamiliar situations.

Cognitive psychologists have made important contributions to understanding the thinking and decision-making processes in individuals. One of their important contributions is the notion of a *mental model*—the key to noticing, recognising and interpreting signals from the environment. In change situations, erroneous mental models can lead to both Type 1 and Type 2 errors. Therefore, it is important to understand the mental models that we use for dealing with change situations.

MENTAL MODELS AND CHANGE

Kenneth Craik first proposed the notion of a mental model in 1943. According to Craik,[2] the mind constructs 'small-scale models' of reality that it uses to anticipate events. Mental models can be concrete (as a visual image) or abstract. Psychologists have used this concept to study how children develop mental models, the relationship between mental models and emotions and, more importantly, deductive reasoning.[3] Management theorists also use words like beliefs, assumptions, rules, regulations, habits, mindsets, paradigms and managerial frames to refer to mental models.

For our purposes, we will use the term mental model to signify the 'picture' managers have of the world outside. This picture will be made up of assumptions and beliefs about their own organisation, their competitors, customers and suppliers. It will be a simplified representation of the reality that they face. Mental models will also include perceived causal linkages between various aspects of their organisation. Finally, mental models will also have a 'formula' for dealing with the outside world. *Mental models can be thought of as 'codes' that we download whenever we encounter a problem or a situation.*[4]

Mental models are not only mental pictures but they also have emotional and behavioural consequences. We are attached to our mental models because they facilitate our task of navigating through a complex environment. They give us a sense of stability and identity in an otherwise precarious world and also guide our actions. We tend to act in accordance with our mental models. If we succeed, we tend to reinforce our mental models and become confident of our ability to deal with similar situations. We stop looking for alternatives to our current mental model. This confidence can also prevent us from noticing signals from the environment that disconfirm our mental model.

The American automobile companies provide illustrations of these ideas. In the 50s and the 60s, automobile firms in the United States were extraordinarily successful and began to dominate the global auto industry. Their success led to complacency bordering on arrogance; resulting in their ignoring market shifts that favoured Japanese carmakers in the 70s. An American journalist, David Halberstam, presents certain interesting insights based on an in-depth study of Ford and Nissan.[5] In the words of David Halberstam:

There were clear signs in the early seventies that the domestic market was changing. Some of the more iconoclastic people at Ford and GM had been bothered by Volkswagen's success with Beetle in America, not so much by the sales numbers as by the fact that comparatively affluent and sophisticated people were buying it. There were other signs of alienation. In California by 1970 the Japanese cars were beginning to sell vigorously in the lower echelons of the market. The cars were relatively inexpensive and were winning an enviable reputation for quality and economical gas mileage. Franklin Murphy, who was on the Ford board and who was head of the Los Angeles Times, *would mention the Japanese invasion to his fellow board members when he came to Detroit for meetings, but they would always put him down. It was serious, he insisted; the Japanese were doing very well in California, a state that tended to signal trends to the rest of the country, and doing well with an educated, young, expanding part of the market. But his colleagues seemed to feel if the people of California were buying Japanese cars, then it was because California was an unreliable place, filled with health faddists that did not eat meat, worshipped strange gods, and preferred to play in the sun rather than work all day at a real job. It was simply very hard for the Americans to take the Japanese seriously.*[6]

Why do intelligent and competent managers occasionally make serious strategic errors? The reason is that they are unaware of their mental models. A Harvard university psychologist, Ellen Langer, has written a fascinating book about how mental models influence people's thinking, emotions and behaviour.[7] Langer argues that we are mostly unaware of the assumptions that underlie our thinking and behaviour. As a result, our behaviour, for most part, is largely automatic. We tend to react to situations unthinkingly; it is as if our behaviour is 'mindless.' Langer devised numerous interesting experiments to test this argument. She describes one such experiment in her book:

> *In a similar experiment, we sent an interdepartmental memo around some university offices. The message either requested or demanded the return of the memo to a designated room— and that was all it said. ('Please return this immediately to Room 247,' or 'This memo is to be returned to Room 247.') Anyone who read such a memo mindfully would ask,'If whoever sent the memo wanted it, why did he or she send it?' and therefore would not return the memo. Half of the memos were designed to look exactly like those sent between departments. The other half was made to look in some way different. When the memo looked like those they were used to, 90 per cent of the recipients actually returned it. When the memo looked different, 60 per cent returned it.*[8]

Langer's other experiments also strongly support the notion of automatic, mindless behaviour. She suggests three manifestations of mindlessness:

1. We tend to get trapped by the categories we create. When we construct a mental model of the world around us, we create categories and make distinctions between them. These categories could be like: 'We are a customer driven organisation', 'Our competitors can't match us in product quality' or 'Customers are not interested in any product attribute other than price.' According to Langer, mindlessness sets in when we rely too rigidly on the categories and distinctions created in the past.
2. As the experiment above indicates, automatic behaviour is another reflection of mindlessness. Habit or any repetitive behaviour is more likely to lead to mindlessness.

3. Acting from a single perspective is a reflection of mindlessness. According to Langer, 'So often in our lives, we act as though there were only one set of rules. For instance, in cooking we tend to follow recipes with dutiful precision. We add ingredients as though by official decree. If the recipe calls for a pinch of salt and four pinches fall in, panic strikes as though the bowl might explode.'[9]

What are the roots of mindlessness? Langer lists six causes for mindlessness:

1. Whenever we perform any task repeatedly, we become 'experts' at it. In psychological terms, we 'overlearn' the task. Subsequent task performance becomes an automatic, mindless behaviour.
2. We tend to form a mindset when we first encounter something. Subsequently, we have a tendency to cling to it when we reencounter the same thing. Langer calls this *premature cognitive commitment.* This implies that our mindsets—that are formed on the basis of first impressions without much reflection—are quite difficult to change, even though those first impressions may be incorrect.
3. When we believe that the resources we require are limited, we are more likely to be trapped by the categories that we create. In organisational change situations, this may manifest as a call for immediate change on the premise that the organisation does not have much time to reflect on the need for change. Here time is seen as a limited resource.
4. We may think of time as a linear entity when in fact under some conditions it may make more sense to think of it as a cyclical entity. The linear view of time translates into a step-by-step sequential approach to change management, which may be inappropriate in a complex dynamic environment.
5. Both in education and at work, we tend to be outcome-oriented. We are focused on results rather than the process for achieving the results. Outcome orientation restricts our categories and we may operate from a single perspective. This does not permit reflection and critical thinking that are essential prerequisites for mindfulness.

6. Our context can powerfully influence our mindsets and behaviour. In an organisation, the routines of a firm are a powerful context that can shape people's thinking, mindsets and behaviour.

Langer's research has significant implications for change management. In appreciating change, inappropriate mental models of managers can lead to both Type 1 and Type 2 errors. Therefore, managers need to be aware of their mental models. Langer suggests that we can become aware of our mindsets and mental models through mindfulness. Mindfulness, she suggests, can be cultivated by:

a) Continually creating new categories to enrich our mental models,
b) Opening ourselves to new information,
c) Considering different points of view before acting on change,
d) Consciously limiting the power of context on our thinking and behaviour, and
e) Paying attention to process before outcome.

Langer suggests that we adopt an orientation of inquiry and learning in order to act mindfully in change situations. Within the field of management, there is a growing literature on organisational learning that echoes this sentiment. We briefly examine some of the ideas from this literature.

ORGANISATIONAL LEARNING AND CHANGE

In previous sections, we discussed the relationships between Type 1 and Type 2 errors and mental models. Flawed mental models are more likely to lead to Type 1 and Type 2 errors. How can managers know if their mental models are flawed? More importantly, how can they constantly update their mental models? Changing and refining one's mental models requires paying attention to how one learns because learning leads to mental model change in an individual. However, we also need to understand mental model changes within the context of an organisation. Learning in an organisation tends to be lot more complicated than learning in an individual. In this section, we will discuss three perspectives on organisational learning: (i) We discuss organisational learning from a systems perspective (ii) We discuss the ideas of Chris Argyris, who views organisational learning in terms of barriers, such as defensive routines (iii) we discuss the behavioural perspective of James March and his associates.

SYSTEMS APPROACH: CONTRIBUTION OF PETER SENGE

One of the influential thinkers in the area of organisational learning is Peter Senge of the Massachusetts Institute of Technology in the United States. In 1990, Senge published, *The Fifth Discipline: The Art and Practice of the Learning Organisation.*[10] In this book, he uses the notion of mental models to discuss organisational learning and puts forward—what Senge calls—five new 'component technologies' that can create a learning organisation. These five disciplines (elaborated in Box 3.1) are components of a whole and—when present together—can promote learning in an organisation. Senge uses the term *ensemble* to refer to five disciplines as a whole: (i) *systems thinking*, (ii) *personal mastery*, (iii) *mental models*, (iv) *building shared vision*, and (v) *team learning*.

The idea of systems thinking is based on the notion of *dynamic complexity*. Senge distinguishes detail complexity—which is a situation involving many variables—from dynamic complexity—a situation where linkages between different variables are not clear. How does dynamic complexity arise?

A major cause of dynamic complexity is *feedback loops*. Feedback loops arise whenever an action leads to a reaction that requires a modification of the original action or a new action. For example, a firm may attempt to improve its performance relative to its competitors through a change management programme. However, its competitors who may notice this, in turn, will launch their own performance improvement programme. This will nullify the initial advantage gained by the first firm.

A common instance of feedback loops in large organisations is when a department or a division launches change on its own. However, since it has linkages with other departments or divisions within the firm, these changes will impact on those departments and divisions. In turn, they will take corrective measures that will affect the original department that launched the initial change. It will react to these corrective measures and soon the organisation—as a whole—will experience a cascade of changes that were not anticipated earlier.

Feedback loops can make it difficult to predict and control change. However, when combined with other effects, prediction and control can become almost impossible. These are lag effects and non-linearities. Lag effects arise when there is time lag between a cause and its effect. For instance, when a firm spends money on advertising, it is unlikely to have an immediate effect on its sales. Potential customers would first have to become aware of the advertisements and then decide to purchase the firm's product or service. Thus, there will be a time lag between the initial advertisement and increased sales. Long time lags can confuse managers and lead to inappropriate decisions.

Non-linearities arise when small causes have disproportionately large effects. Specifically, the cause-effect relationship will not show features of linear relationship. Thus, incremental changes in the cause will lead to varying effects. For example, in competitive industries, the relationship between price of a product and its market-share will usually be non-linear. Small increases in the price of one firm may cause disproportionately large reductions in its market-share.

Most of us are used to linear thinking. Therefore, when we encounter non-linear situations, we take inappropriate decisions. Thus, non-linearities and time lags, coupled with feedback loops, can render a situation dynamically complex—making it very hard for managers to comprehend the situation and take appropriate decisions. This is mainly because their mental models are not geared for dynamic complexity. In such instances, awareness of their mental models and dynamic complexity can help prevent Type 1 and Type 2 errors.

Senge suggests that awareness of mental models requires two kinds of skills, reflection and inquiry. Skills of reflection involve slowing down our thinking processes so that we can become aware of the formation of our mental models. Skills of inquiry relate to working with others on a face-to-face basis for solving complex problems. One way to develop skills of reflection is to identify the assumptions we have made about our organisation and the business. Once identified, these assumptions need to be questioned. They need to be tested against real, concrete data. If the data does not support the assumptions, these assumptions need to be discarded.

Senge argues that managers need to develop two kinds of skills in inquiry. They need to be good advocates and they also need to be good learners. However, these skills are mutually incompatible. When you are advocating a point of view, you are not open to learning. Similarly, when you are on a learning mode, you haven't reached a point of view that can be advocated. Senge believes that balancing inquiry and advocacy is the key to understanding and changing mental models. Senge acknowledges that there may be routines and codes that we have adopted, which can act as barriers to learning. He has borrowed the ideas of Chris Argyris, who has a different perspective on organisational learning. Let us discuss this.

Box 3.1: Senge's Five Disciplines[11]

Systems Thinking

Senge calls systems thinking the fifth discipline because it integrates the other four disciplines. 'Systems' is the discipline of treating organisations, issues and problems as a whole. It is a framework for seeing patterns of relationships instead of static snapshots. 'Systems thinking' is not so much a technique as it is a state of mind. Systems thinking is a vital tool for managing in a world characterised by complexity and interdependence. Senge distinguishes between two types of complexity, detail complexity and dynamic complexity. While detail complexity refers to a situation where there are many variables, dynamic complexity refers to situations where the relationship between cause and effect is not always clear. It is dynamic complexity that is more important than detail complexity. Senge insists that the essence of systems thinking lies in seeing interrelationships rather than linear cause-effect chains and seeing processes of change rather than snapshots.

Personal Mastery

It is more than competence and skills and involves taking a creative rather than a reactive stance to issues, problems and life itself.

Personal Mastery includes two aspects: (a) ceaselessly making clear what is important to us, and (b) continually learning to see current reality more clearly. Therefore, managers with a high level of personal mastery share these basic traits. They have a sense of purpose that lies behind their vision and goals. In specific terms, personal mastery involves expressing one's vision and listening to others' visions, developing a systemic worldview, learning to uncover tacit and hidden assumptions and jointly inquiring into different people's views of current reality.

Mental Models

These are the deeply held images of how the world works; we all carry mental models. They guide our thinking and action in familiar ways. In order to change, we need to change our mental models. We can't change these models unless we understand what they are. Surfacing, testing and improving our internal pictures of how the world works is an important aspect of learning and change.

Shared Vision

People have a shared vision when they all have the same mental picture. When people truly share a vision they are connected together by a common aspiration. Shared visions are potent forces for change. It is a shared vision of freedom from colonial domination that led the Indian people to rally behind Mahatma Gandhi. A shared vision provides focus and energy for learning. Learning how to build a shared vision is an important tool of change management.

Team Learning

It is the process of focusing and developing the capacity of a team towards achieving its shared vision. Team learning has three critical dimensions: (i) developing the ability of the team to think insightfully about complex issues, (ii) learning to act innovatively in a co-ordinated way, and (iii) fostering learning in other teams in the organisation. Senge makes an important distinction between dialogue and discussion. According to him, 'In dialogue, there is the free and creative exploration of complex and subtle issues, a deep 'listening' to one another and suspending of one's own views. By contrast, in discussion different views are presented and defended and there is a search for the best view to support decisions that must be made at this time. Dialogue and discussion are complementary, but most teams lack the ability to distinguish between the two and to move consciously between them'.

ORGANISATIONAL LEARNING: CONTRIBUTION OF CHRIS ARGYRIS

Over the last two decades, Chris Argyris has been a prolific writer on the topic of organisational learning.[12] Argyris's starting point is his observation that both individuals and organisations seem to avoid change by not confronting real issues that hinder their effectiveness. He has built an elaborate theory to explain this marked reluctance to confront the real issues that inhibit individual and organisational effectiveness.

The foundation of his theory is the idea of a mental model. Argyris refers to a mental model as a 'theory of action.' According to him, individuals have mental models on how to act effectively in any interaction. However, they are unaware of this mental model. If asked about their mental model, they are likely to espouse a theory of action, which is quite different from the one that they actually use. The mental model that actually drives their behaviour is called 'theory-in-use.' The one that they advocate is called 'espoused theory.' Based on empirical research, Argyris claims that human beings in different parts of the world may have different espoused theories but they all seem to have the same theory-in-use. He calls this Model I theory-in-use.

Model I theory-in-use has four governing values: (i) achieve your intended purpose, (ii) maximise winning and minimise losing, (iii) suppress negative feelings, and (iv) behave according to what you consider fair. These governing values lead to individuals advocating their positions, evaluating their own and others' thoughts and actions, and attributing causes for whatever they are trying to understand. This mental model also guides managerial behaviour.

Specifically, managers carry a mental model about what leads to effective performance. The implicit or tacit mental model that managers carry assumes that organisational goals can be achieved if individuals know the specifications of their jobs (job requirements), have the skills to achieve these specifications (skills and abilities), wish to achieve these specifications (motivation) and are enabled to achieve them (enablers).

Therefore, managers see their job as providing job specifications, training for skills and abilities, motivation for job performance and right policies and procedures to enable performance. Their job is to define the roles, create the enablers and train employees. Once employees begin to perform the activities, their actions will become routine and the knowledge to perform these becomes tacit. What happens when performance fails to meet specifications? Can a manager identify the real causes behind performance failure?

Argyris claims that the governing values of Model I also suppress inquiry and exploration into the real issues that might be inhibiting performance. Model I theory-in-use leads to what Argyris refers to as 'defensive routines.' Defensive routines are actions or policies that are aimed at protecting an organisational member from experiencing embarrassment or threat. These are activated whenever organisational members face situations that are potentially embarrassing or threatening.

Defensive routines are, in fact, anti-learning and over-protective. The logic of defensive routine is something like this: (a) send a message that is inconsistent ('I want you to be creative but be careful'), (b) act as if it is not inconsistent, (c) make both sending an inconsistent message and acting as if it is consistent un-discussable, and (d) make the un-discussability un-discussable.

Defensive routines are most obvious in employee performance assessment situations. Model I theory-in-use would lead to managers not confronting a poorly performing employee directly about his or her performance. They are likely to be very circumspect and beat around the bush. If questioned about their behaviour, they will justify it by insisting that they are trying to be supportive and caring. They would also claim that direct confrontation would make a subordinate defensive and hostile. The employee who is being evaluated also supports this behaviour and does not insist on authentic feedback. Therefore, most individuals in organisations rarely get authentic feedback on their performance.

The result is that individuals in the organisation collude with each other in maintaining a façade about the organisation's performance issues. In other words, authentic communication about real issues is conspicuously absent. Obviously, if there is no authentic communication between individuals, there is not likely to be any significant organisational learning.

Argyris argues that Model I theory-in-use, which is a mental model, inhibits organisational learning and change. The key to change, therefore, lies in making individuals aware of this mental model and help them change it to a different one. Argyris advocates a Model II theory-in-use that can overcome the dysfunctional features of Model I. The governing values of this alternative mental model are *valid information, informed choice,* and *vigilant monitoring of the choice implementation*. Although Model II shares the same features of advocacy, evaluation and attribution with Model I, its use leads to 'productive reasoning' rather than defensive reasoning. In productive reasoning, nothing is un-discussable. All assumptions are made explicit, the deductions and conclusions from the assumptions are also made explicit and the conclusions are constructed in such a way that they can be tested by data and logic.

Changing an individual's mental model from Model I to Model II is not an easy task. Since most of us are unaware of the inconsistency between our espoused theory and our theory-in-use, we are not likely to be pleased when some one points out our inconsistencies. We are more likely to deny the feedback, become hostile or sulk silently. When we act defensively, we also make the feedback-giver feel uncomfortable and guilty. This is the reason why such inconsistencies are rarely pointed out.

Argyris acknowledges these problems but, as a scientist wedded to truth, feels that it is the obligation of a manager or consultant to confront these inconsistencies if we genuinely wish to bring about change. He offers an elegant case study instrument to uncover people's theories-in-use and defensive routines. This technique (Box 3.2) involves asking people to write a case that states a problem that they face and their intended strategy to approach the problem. They are asked to imagine and write a conversation that would occur when they communicate their strategy to a person of their choice in the organisation. They are also asked to write the information that they would not communicate for whatever reason. This is a simple but effective technique to uncover the real thoughts, assumptions and feelings of individuals as they attempt to solve organisational problems in collaboration with others. Does the technique work? Argyris claims it does. Why not try it on yourself? What you learn about yourself may surprise you!

Box 3.2: The Two Column Approach to Uncover Defensive Routines

1. In one paragraph, describe a key organisational problem as you see it.
2. Assume you could talk to whomever you wish to begin to solve the problem. Describe, in a paragraph or so, the strategy that you would use in this meeting.
3. Next, split your page into two columns. On the right-hand side write how you would begin the meeting; what would you actually say. Then write what you believe the other(s) would say. Then write your response to their response. Continue to write this scenario for two or so double-spaced typewritten pages.
4. On the left-hand column write any idea or feeling that you would have that you would not communicate for whatever reason.

ORGANISATIONAL LEARNING: CONTRIBUTION OF JAMES MARCH AND ASSOCIATES

James March has been yet another productive contributor to our understanding of organisational learning.[13] Unlike Senge and Argyris, whose works have explicit action components in that they aim at changing organisations, March is more interested in describing the reality of organisations. Nevertheless, March's ideas are equally important for a manger or consultant in the area of change management because he alerts us to the limitations of organisational learning.

March has built his theory of organisational learning on three basic properties of organisations: (a) In any organisation, behaviour is driven by routines; (b) Actions in an organisation are history-dependent i.e. our actions are more strongly influenced by our past than our perceptions of the future; and (c) Organisations are goal-driven i.e. they are oriented to targets. If we view mental models to be made up of routines and beliefs, then learning is said to occur when there is a shift in mental models i.e. there is a change in routines and beliefs.

According to March, there are two ways in which organisations change their mental models:

i) Organisations engage in trial and error experimentation i.e. they learn by doing. Typically, they modify their behaviour based on the gap between their performance and their targets.
ii) Organisations engage in search behaviour i.e. they look for new routines that will enhance their performance. According to March, although learning generally increases average performance and reliability, both these mechanisms have built-in limitations.

Let us consider trial and error experimentation or learning by doing, first. The basis for learning here is the generation of experience. We experiment in order to generate experience. Learning occurs when we reflect on the experience, interpret it and draw conclusions. If our experience is positive i.e. performance and targets are matched, then we tend to stay with the routines and become more proficient in executing the routines. However, our increasing competency in current routines is also a trap because it inhibits learning about other routines that may be useful for future performance.

As March argues, in an organisational setting, in which learning has to occur under dynamic conditions, experience is often a poor teacher. First, there are cognitive limits to learning from experience. Learning involves making inferences from information. It involves memory. It involves pooling personal experience with the experience of others. In organisational settings, what has happened is not always clear and it is difficult to untangle the factors that caused the experience. Different individuals may interpret the same event in different ways. People also make systematic errors in interpreting events. Individuals tend to: overestimate the probability of events that actually occur, are insensitive to sample size and use simple linear rules to understand dynamic complex settings.

These cognitive limitations are heightened by organisational limitations. Political dynamics interfere with the interpretation of experience. The interpretations of people in power may dominate organisational learning. Organisations tend to record their learning in routines, stories, and myths. Stories and myths tend to be sustained even in the face disconfirming experience. Evaluation of performance, which is crucial to learning, is likely to be more mixed in organisations. Targets can change, performance indicators may be modified, and the level of aspiration may change. Occasionally, organisations can learn the wrong things i.e. learning may be superstitious. As March observes:

> *Learning does not always lead to intelligent behaviour. The same processes that yield experiential wisdom produce superstitions, competency traps and erroneous inferences. Problems in learning from experience, stem partly from inadequacies of human cognitive habits, partly from features of organisation, and partly from characteristics of the structure of experience.*[14]

The other problem with learning is related to search. In terms of search behaviour, organisations face a dilemma—should they develop completely new knowledge or should they incrementally improve current knowledge? These are competing goals and organisations have to balance the conflicting goals of developing new knowledge, referred to as *exploration*, with improving current competencies, referred to as *exploitation*.

Whereas exploitation ensures current organisational performance, exploration is necessary for future organisational performance. An organisation that exclusively emphasises exploitation may suffer obsolescence as the industry evolves; the organisation that over-stresses it may threaten current viability. Survival requires a balance between the two. However, the attempts to balance the two competing goals create imbalances in the organisation. According to March, the imbalances create three forms of learning myopia: Organisations tend to overlook distant times, distant places and failures. Despite these limitations, March exhorts managers not to give up on learning:

> *Imperfections of learning are not so great as to require abandoning attempts to improve the learning capabilities of*

organisations but those imperfections suggest a certain conservatism in expectations. Conservative expectations, of course, will not always enhance the selling of learning procedures to strategic managers, but they may provide a constructive basis for a realistic evaluation and elaboration of the role of learning in organisational intelligence. Magic would be nice, but it is not easy to find.[15]

To summarise, while learning benefits an organisation's chances of survival and growth, it suffers from limitations due to individual and organisational factors. It is important for change managers to be aware of these limitations and not blindly follow the populist exhortations to convert their organisations into learning organisations. Now that we have discussed cognition, mental models and organisational learning, how do we use this knowledge for effective change management?

BUSINESS MODELS AND VALUE PROPOSITIONS

Ideally, while appreciating change, a manager will reflect on the forces of change impacting on the organisation and become aware of the mental models that are driving the organisation. A key mental model that the manager needs to be aware of is the soul or essence of the organisation. In simple terms, what does the organisation stand for? What does it mean to its customers? What does it represent for its employees? For business organisations, the term *value proposition* captures this idea. In business organisations, the task of appreciating change also involves becoming aware of the organisation's value proposition and a related concept called *business model*. First, let us discuss the concept of a business model.

BUSINESS MODEL

The term *business model* rose to prominence in the United States in the late 90s, with the emergence of so-called 'dot-com' companies and fell into notoriety with the fall of these companies in subsequent years. Dot-com companies were those firms that were set up to transact business on the Internet. The term *business model* became the leading management buzzword of the dot-com era signifying everything and nothing. This is unfortunate because, although many people use the term loosely to signify strategy, the concept of a business model offers a powerful way of analysing the fundamentals of an organisation's performance.

Any organisation, new or established, does need a business model to survive and grow. As Joan Magretta[16] points out, a good business model answers two fundamental questions relating to any business: Who are our customers? What do they value? Or, to put it differently, a business models tells the manager how the business can make money. If we accept the premise that businesses can only generate profits by providing customers with value at an acceptable cost, then a business model signifies the underlying economic logic of an organisation. In other words, a business model reveals the profit engine that drives a business.[17]

Business models are important because, in times of change, the underlying economic logic of an organisation may need to be re-evaluated. As industries evolve and dominant designs emerge, the business models of surviving organisations become entrenched. In fact the industry may be characterised by just a few business models. For instance, as we discussed in the previous chapter, the global airlines industry is characterised by two different business models. There are the large network carriers and the low-cost carriers (LCCs). The network carriers such as American Airlines and Delta Airlines operate on the basis of the 'hub-and-spoke' model. LCCs like Southwest, AirTran, JetBlue and EasyJet, often flying from secondary and smaller airports, offer a no-frills, point-to-point service. LCCs are the profitable, growth-segment of this industry. As industries evolve, new business models may emerge to challenge existing business models. While the survival rate of new business models is not high, occasionally they may come to dominate the industry by a creative re-organisation of the underlying economic logic. The case of Dell Computer in the computer industry illustrates this.

DELL COMPUTER[18]

Dell Computer exemplifies the concept of a business model better than any other organisation. Michael Dell, the founder and chief executive of Dell Computer is widely regarded as the business guru who introduced the direct marketing model in the personal computer industry. A number of organisations have sent their key executives to Dell Computer to study its business model and operations. There are books and business school case studies on what makes Dell Computer so successful in a highly competitive industry. However, no organisation has been able to replicate the business model and success of Dell Computer. Before we examine the Dell business model, we need to understand the evolution of the personal computer industry.

Evolution of the Personal Computer Industry in the United States

Like most industries in the early stages of evolution, in 1976, the personal computer industry was highly fragmented with low entry barriers and the absence of a dominant design. Early personal computers were sold by popular electronics magazines such as Radio-Electronics and Popular Electronics, in the form of a kit. Four technological developments in 1977 paved the way for significant changes in the industry. First, 8-bit microprocessors were launched which were a significant improvement over the previous Intel 8080 microprocessors. Second, CP/M-80 became a standard operating system leading to the development of a wide variety of application software. Third, a 5-and-¼ -inch disk drive was introduced that replaced the earlier cumbersome external cassette tape drives. Fourth, technological improvements led to a rapid drop in the costs of random access (RAM) and read-only memories (ROM).

By 1977, personal computers were mainly distributed through electronic stores, computer retail stores and smaller independent specialty stores. Personal computer users were mainly hobbyists and 'hackers' who were willing to travel long distances to buy these computers. These developments also led to a wave of new entrants into the personal computer industry.

In 1977, three entrepreneurial firms, Apple, Tandy Radio Shack and Commodore entered the industry with their own model of personal computers. They were followed by established companies such as Zenith and Texas Instruments. By 1980, due to its superior technology, Apple had established itself as the industry leader. Although the market still comprised of mainly first-time users, hobbyists and educational users, the American personal computer market began to grow at an annual rate of 30 per cent and started to pose a threat to the mainframe and minicomputer manufacturers such as IBM, Hewlett-Packard (HP) and Digital Equipment Corporation (DEC). A number of larger established firms such as IBM, HP, Xerox, Wang, ICL, Philips, Olivetti, NEC, Toshiba and Fujitsu also entered the market to cater to the business segment of the market.

By 1983, IBM had captured 43 per cent of the personal computer market. Its strategy for its personal computer business was radically different from its mainframe business. For its personal computer business, it outsourced both hardware and software components. It adopted an 'open architecture' and encouraged third-party software firms to develop software applications at their cost. It used the more powerful Intel 8086 chip facilitating development of higher performance software. More importantly, with the help of Microsoft, IBM introduced a new operating system standard—the PC-DOS. In sharp contrast to Apple, this new industry standard was made available to all personal computer manufacturers building IBM-compatible machines. IBM also recruited retail dealers to stock, service and sell its personal computers.

However, IBM was so successful that it created a demand for personal computers that it could not satisfy. This led to the entry of IBM PC-compatibles or 'clones' into the market to satisfy this excess demand. Compaq was one such clone manufacturer. Established in 1982, it had no previous experience in the computer industry. By 1987, it had emerged as a serious contender to IBM. IBM addressed the threat posed by Compaq by introducing a new internal proprietary hardware configuration for personal computers called MCA that did not allow third-party add-ons. However, Compaq, in collaboration with eight other manufacturers, successfully countered this by introducing a new industry standard called EISA that was compatible with existing industry standards.

On the software front, there was an explosion of third-party software firms that developed specific application software for IBM personal computers and clones. There was a strong growth in the retail sector of the industry with retail chains such as *BusinessLand* and *ComputerLand* becoming dominant. There were more than 5000 retail outlets in the United States stocking the three most favoured brands—Apple, Compaq and IBM.

By 1990, the $40 billion personal computer segment accounted for 40 per cent of the computer industry by volume. There were dramatic breakthroughs in processing and storage technologies leading to substantial improvements in the price-to-performance ratio. Microsoft's Windows operating system started to emerge as the industry standard and power was shifting away from hardware vendors to software firms. There were a large number of entrants into the industry but most were unsuccessful. Personal computers started to become commodity-like items. This led to the entry of newer types of hardware vendors and distributors focusing on cost efficiency.

Michael Dell's Entry into the Industry

As an 18-years-old student at the University of Texas, Austin in 1983, Michel Dell spent his spare time upgrading IBM-compatible personal computers for local area businesses. What started off as an innocent hobby to make 'decent pocket money' started to consume more of his time. Dell soon realised that his upgrades were seen as good value for money by business firms in Austin, Texas. He started to buy surplus personal computers from retail at a discount, upgraded them and sold them to businesses for a nice margin. By 1984, his revenues were $80,000 a month and he wisely decided to drop out of college to found the Dell Computer Corporation.

Michael Dell was soon getting calls from the likes of Exxon and Mobil who were demanding 50–100 machines at a time. These businesses wanted a good performance machine at a reasonable price. Dell offered them upgraded machines at almost 40 per cent below the price of comparable IBM machines. Dell offered a 24-hour hotline for complaints and a 24- to 48-hour guaranteed shipment of parts. By 1985, the company was making $6 million a year by just upgrading IBM compatibles. In 1985, the company assembled and marketed its own brand of PCs and the turnover dramatically increased to $70 million a year. Most of Dell's customers were business organisations and only a small proportion comprised individual customers.

The Dell Direct Model

By 1997, in just 13 years, Dell Computer Corporation was a $13 billion company. The success of Dell is attributed to the business model that Michael Dell perfected. Called the Dell Direct Model, it was a significant departure from the prevailing industry practices. The dominant model in the personal computer industry was that manufacturers received parts from suppliers and shipped their finished products to distributors, who resold the computers to final customers. Figure 3.2 shows the value chain for the dominant model.

Figure 3.2: Dominant Model in the PC Industry

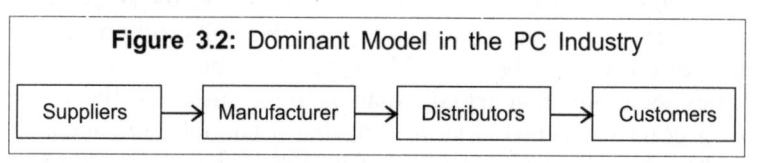

Suppliers → Manufacturer → Distributors → Customers

This business model required manufacturers to produce their machines even before they had firm orders. In other words, manufacturers estimated demand on the basis of feedback from distributors, ordered the parts from the suppliers and produced their machines. They carried an inventory of computer parts and finished goods, which added to the overall cost of manufacturing the computer. In this model, manufacturers had a bargaining, transactional relationship with their suppliers and distributors. Dell's direct model eliminates the distributors in this value chain and sells directly to the customers. Figure 3.3 shows the Dell Direct Model.

Figure 3.3: Dell Direct Model

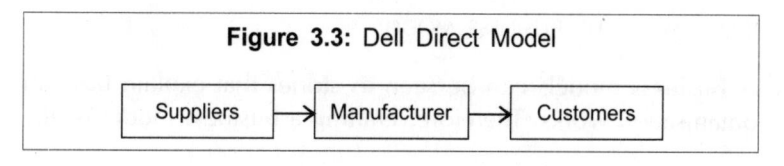

Suppliers → Manufacturer → Customers

Its business model is built on 'virtual integration.' This means that it first captures in-depth information about customers' requirements. Then, it regularly transmits that information to suppliers and by treating suppliers as in-house partners, Dell achieves the tightness of internal coordination— *without* excess personnel or costly inventory. The business model of Dell thus emphasises customer focus, supplier partnerships, mass customisation, and just-in-time, built-to-order manufacturing.[19] The Dell Direct Model is based on a sound *value proposition*. Next, let us examine this notion.

VALUE PROPOSITION

A value proposition is generally a clear and succinct statement (e.g. 2–4 sentences) that outlines a company's unique value-creating features.[20] Dell provides value to its customers by supplying high quality, low cost customised computers. Wal-Mart offers everyday low prices, McDonald's gives consistency, Domino's Pizzas makes available fast delivery, BMW presents the ultimate driving machine and *Google*'s value proposition is fast, extensive searches. In each of these instances, the company offers something that actually matters to the customer. The secret of a good value proposition is having a tangible difference in a characteristic of an organisation's product or service—one that actually matters to the customers.

Three aspects constitute a firm's good value proposition: (a) customer objectives, (b) the firm's offer, and (c) differentiators.[21] Customer objectives refer to the specific needs that customers are aiming to realise. This part of the value proposition addresses these objectives in the customers' language. The firm's offer refers to what the firm is presenting to fulfil these objectives. Differentiators refer to how the firm's offer stands out in comparison with the competitors' offers. A value proposition is the foundation of a business model.

IDENTIFYING THE BUSINESS MODEL

Business models can be seen as stories that explain how an organisation works. Therefore, crafting a business model is like writing a new story. As has been pointed out, all new stories are merely variations on old ones reflecting same universal themes that underlie all human experience.[22] Similarly all new business models are variations on the generic value chain that underlie all businesses: (a) All activities associated with making something, and (b) All activities associated with selling something.

A business model is not the same as strategy. A business model explains how the different pieces of a business fit together. It doesn't consider competition. A competitive strategy, on the other hand, explains how you will do better than your rivals. However, if your business model is based on a sound value proposition, it will have a differentiator that tells your customers how your offerings are different from other options. In this sense, a good business model can also be a winning strategy.

When business models don't work, it's because the story doesn't make sense or the numbers don't add up.[23] This is because it is not enough that your business model tells a good story. It should also be profitable. A number of new businesses fail because they have interesting business models that are just not profitable. In order to pass the numbers test, business model must address the following factors: (a) revenue sources, (b) key expenses, (c) investment size, and (d) critical success factors.[24] Table 3.1 shows the questions that need to be addressed in analysing each of these four factors. Table 3.1 can be used as a framework to analyse the need for change in an organisation.

Now that we have discussed mental models, value propositions and business models, how do we tie all these together? Specifically, what outcomes do we expect from appreciating change?

OUTCOMES OF APPRECIATING CHANGE

In the first phase of appreciating change, the management of an organisation contemplating change needs to identify its business model and the underlying value proposition. This business model needs to be compared with the dominant business model in the industry. Specifically, the organisation needs to address the following questions: (a) What are the

Table 3.1: Evaluating a Business Model[25]

Factors	Explanation	Questions
Revenue sources	Revenue sources are made up of revenue streams. Organisations can have single or multiple revenue streams based on different revenue models.	➤ How many different revenue streams will the business model generate? ➤ What is the source of each revenue stream? ➤ What is the relative size and importance of each revenue stream? ➤ How quickly is each revenue stream likely to grow?
Key expenses	Key expenses are based on cost drivers that are aspects that affect total costs	➤ What are the primary cost drivers? ➤ Are these expected to change over time?
Investment size	This is the amount of cash required before a firm achieves a positive cash flow.	➤ What are the cash requirements in the present or new business model?
Critical success factors	This refers to an operational function or competence that a company must possess in order for it to be sustainable and profitable.	➤ What are the critical success factors in the present or new business model?

industry dynamics? What stage of evolution has the industry reached? (b) Is the industry likely to experience new technology cycles or changes in institutional rules? Will these affect the dominant design? (c) Is our business model appropriate for the industry in its present stage of evolution? (d) Do we need a radical change in our business model? (e) If the answer to (d) is no, do we need refinement of our business model?

Managers need to be aware of their mental models when they address questions (a), (b) and (c) above. Mindless application of old mental models to changing situations can lead to a flawed understanding and enhance the likelihood of Type 1 and Type 2 errors. In order to increase their awareness of the present mental models, managers can address the following questions: (a) What are the organisational routines that are shaping our understanding and driving our behaviour? (b) What are the defensive routines that we seem to be using in day-to-day situations?

While appreciating change, key managers in an organisation would have come to an in-depth understanding of their industry dynamics and their organisation's business model. The critical questions that they have to address are: (a) whether this business model needs to change, and (b) if the business model needs changing, does it require *radical change* (a completely new business model) or *incremental change* (refinement of the existing business model)?

We advise extreme caution before opting for radical change. This type of organisational change is inherently risky and should not be attempted unless the managers are aware of the risks. Therefore, the top management team needs to re-evaluate its mental models before it opts for radical change. If the key managers in an organisation achieve a clear understanding of their industry dynamics and their business model, they are ready for the second phase, which involves mobilising support for their understanding and agenda for change.

REFINING THE CHANGE AGENDA

In the previous chapter, we discussed the development of a change agenda based on the analysis of the external environment. This change agenda needs to be refined, based on the analysis of the internal context. In his book *Good to Great*, Jim Collins argues that to go from good to great requires a deep understanding of three intersecting circles.[26] These three circles are an integral part of the core task of appreciating change.

Each circle represents a question that needs to be addressed in appreciating change:

1. What is our organisation *passionate about*?
2. What *can our organisation be best at, in the world*?
3. What drives our *economic engine*?

The first two questions relate to the organisation's soul, while the third question addresses the business model. Answering these questions is not easy. It requires a lot of soul searching that can only come from intense dialogue and meaningful conversations. The organisation needs to confront its external realities and internal capabilities. The following set of questions can be used to facilitate dialogue and analysis[27]:

1. What are the underlying causes of the trends and issues we identified while developing our change agenda?
2. How is money made or not made in our industry? Why some organisations do better than others?
3. What is our business model? Is it delivering results?
4. If our industry is delivering financially attractive results and we aren't, what are the reasons? How do these factors bear on our business model?
5. What do we need to change about our business model?
6. What capabilities and competencies do we need to execute a new business model?
7. Do we have the right people to pull off the new business model? Are they properly deployed?
8. What obstacles in our organisation and current thinking stand in the way of reaching our goals?
9. Are we focusing on the right initiatives for growth? What edge do we have over our competitors?
10. What is the *one* assumption we are making that can cause our change initiative to fail if it turns out to be wrong?

These questions are only guidelines to spark dialogue and debate in the organisation among key managers. The objective of the dialogue is to uncover the assumptions, values and beliefs that underlie the mental models in the organisations. These assumptions, values and beliefs need to be subjected to relentless scrutiny in light of changes in an organisation's external environment. Key managers need to be aware of the organisation's dominant mental model or mindset. They need to identify the codes that they are downloading as they confront a changing environment. Above all, they need to be sincere and honest. If the organisation's key members are willing to confront the realities inside and outside the organisation, the above questions will facilitate the refinement of the change agenda developed in the previous chapter. This change agenda needs to be taken to the rest of the organisation before it can be executed. In the next chapter, we discuss how to mobilise support for a change agenda.

NOTES AND REFERENCES

1. Nadler, D. A. & Tushman, M. L. (1990). Beyond the charismatic leader: Leadership and organisational change. *California Management Review,* 32(2): pp. 77–97.
2. Craik, K. (1943). *The Nature of Explanation.* Cambridge: Cambridge University Press.
3. See http://www.tcd.ie/Psychology/Ruth_Byrne/mental_models/index.html for an introduction to mental models and additional references on this topic.
4. Senge, Peter M., Scharmer, C. Otto, Jaworski, Joseph, & Flowers, Betty Sue, (2004). *Presence: Human Purpose and the Field of the Future.* Boston: Society for Organisational Learning.
5. Halberstam, D. (1987). *The Reckoning.* London: Bantam Books.
6. Ibid., p. 518.
7. Langer, E. J. (1989). *Mindfulness.* Reading, Mass.: Addison-Wesley.
8. Ibid., p. 15.
9. Ibid., p. 16.
10. Senge, P. M. (1990). *The Fifth Discipline: The Art and Practice of the Learning Organisation.* New York: Doubleday Currency.
11. Ibid.
12. Argyris, C. (1976). Single- and double-loop models in research on decision making. *Administrative Science Quarterly,* 21 (September), pp. 363–377; Argyris, C. (1982). *Reasoning, Learning and Action.* San Francisco: Jossey-Bass; Argyris, C. (1990). *Overcoming*

Organisational Defenses. Needham, MA: Allyn-Bacon; Argyris, C. (1993). *Knowledge for Action: A Guide to Overcoming Barriers to Organisational Change*. San Francisco: Jossey-Bass; Argyris, C. (1999). *On organisational learning* (Second ed.). Malden, MA: Blackwell; Argyris, C. & Schon, D. (1978). *Organisational Learning*. Reading, MA: Addison-Wesley; Argyris, C. & Schon, D. (1996). *Organisational Learning II*. Reading, MA: Addison-Wesley.

13. March, J. G. (1981). Footnotes to organisational change. *Administrative Science Quarterly,* 26: pp. 563–577; March, J. G. (1988). *Decisions and Organisations*. Oxford: Blackwell; March, J. G. (1991). Exploration and exploitation in organisational learning. *Organisation Science,* 2: pp. 71–87; March, J. G. (1999b). Understanding how decisions happen in organisations. In J. G. March (Ed.), *The Pursuit of Organisational Intelligence* (pp. 13–38). Malden, Mass.: Blackwell; March, J. G. & Olsen, J. P. (1986). *Ambiguity and choice in organisations*. Bergen, Norway: Universitetsforlaget; March, J. G. & Shapira, Z. (1987). Managerial perspectives on risk and risk taking. *Management Science,* 33: pp. 1404–1418; March, J. G. & Simon, H. A. (1993). *Organisations* (2nd. ed.). Oxford: Blackwell.
14. March, J. G. (1999a). *The Pursuit of Organisational Intelligence*. Malden, MA: Blackwell, p. 92
15. Ibid., p. 218.
16. Magretta, J. (May 2002). Why business models matter. *Harvard Business Review,* 80(5): pp. 86–93.
17. Ibid.
18. This section is based on *Dell Computer Corporation*. (No. 9-596-058)(September 25, 1996). Harvard Business School; *Dell Online*. (No. 9-598-116)(March 26, 1999). Harvard Business School; Didn't Delliver. (February 18, 1999). *Economist; Matching Dell*. (No. 9-799-158) (June 6, 1999). Harvard Business School; A revolution of one. (April 12, 2001). *Economist*.
19. Magretta, J. (March–April, 1998). The power of virtual integration: An interview with Dell Computer's Michael Dell. *Harvard Business Review,* 76: pp. 72–85.
20. Perla, M. L. (July 1, 2003). *What's your value proposition?*, from http://www.marketingprofs.com
21. Ibid.
22. Magretta, J. (May 2002). Why business models matter. *Harvard Business Review,* 80(5): pp. 86–93.
23. Ibid.

24. Hamermesh, R. G., Marshall, P. W. & Pirmohamed, T. (2002). *Note on business model analysis for the entrepreneur* (No. 9-802-048). Boston, MA: Harvard Business School.
25. Based on Ibid.
26. Collins, Jim (2001). *Good to Great: Why Some Companies Make the Leap... . And Others Don't.* New York: HarperBusiness.
27. Based on Bossidy, Lawrence & Charan, Ram, (2004). *Confronting Reality: Doing What Matters to Get Things Right.* New York: Crown Business; Charan, Ram, (2004). *Profitable Growth is Everyone's Business.* New York: Crown Business.

CHAPTER 4

Mobilising Support

OVERVIEW

While the previous chapters on appreciating change discussed operating environment and mental models, this chapter deals with the next core task of change management in our model called mobilising support. Here, the basic idea is that people in an organisation have to be assembled and rallied together to bring about meaningful change. We discuss principles and approaches to influence people to actively participate in a change process. There are three main ideas in this chapter. First, we argue that organisational change is most successful when people in the organisation take charge of the change. In other words, participation, involvement and ownership are crucial for effective change. Second, we contend that organisational change is both cultural and political. It involves changing mindsets. This involves influencing, inducing, negotiating, persuading and winning over people to the idea of change. Third, influencing and persuading people mainly involve communication. Therefore, effective communication strategies are crucial to change. The chapter concludes with some guidelines to mobilise support.

WHY MOBILISE SUPPORT?

Many change management efforts in organisations fail because they do not sufficiently mobilise the support of people for change. This is because most managers assume that if they appreciate a compelling need for change, then the rest of the organisation should also be able to notice it. Therefore, they tend to jump directly from appreciation to execution. However, the assumption they make is inherently flawed. The rest of the organisation may not share the manager's enthusiasm for change for a variety of reasons. Generally, others in the organisation may perceive the same reality differently because their mental models or mindsets may be different. This leads to a lack of support for change, which may manifest itself as lack of motivation, resistance or lack of cooperation. Before we discuss ways of mobilising support, it is useful to identify the different approaches to managing change that are adopted by organisations.

FOUR APPROACHES TO CHANGE

In his book *Terms of Engagement,* Axelrod[1] discusses four historical approaches to change: (a) Leader-driven approach, (b) Process-driven approach, (c) Team-driven approach, and (d) Change Management approach. Table 4.1 shows the features of each of these four approaches.

Leader-driven change is more suitable for small and medium enterprises with owner-managers. This approach works well when the manager or leader has all the necessary information and knowledge. Leader-driven changes tend to be directive and non-participative. Therefore this approach is less suitable when: (a) the workforce is young and/or highly skilled, (b) the business environment is complex and dynamic, and (c) successful change requires active involvement of a number of people in the organisation.

Process-driven changes are led by experts or outside consultants and supported by the leader (Table 4.1); these changes are more common in large, bureaucratic organisations. This approach works well when the change requires technical or specialised expertise. Also being directive and non-participative, as in the case of leader-driven approach, this approach is therefore less suitable when: (a) the workforce is young and/or highly skilled, (b) the business environment is complex and dynamic, and (c) successful change requires active involvement of a number of people in the organisation.

Team-driven approaches are most common in large, manufacturing enterprises that have skilled and educated employees. Change management strategies—such as Total Quality Management (TQM), Quality Circles (QC) and Six Sigma—exemplify this approach. These are highly participative change efforts that empower employees and provide them with involvement, participation and ownership of change. Team-based approaches that are properly executed can unleash enormous levels of employee energy and motivation. This can, in turn, lead to innovation and productivity gains. However, using this approach can also cause some discomfort for managers in an organisation because they may not be used to sharing their power and authority with workers. Moreover, this approach requires managers to shift from a directive, authoritarian style based on power and expertise to a participative style based on persuasion, coaching and helping. More importantly, the team-based approach to execute change requires the establishment of a 'parallel organisation'—a notion that has been elaborated in the following section.

The fourth approach to change is called the Change Management approach. According to Axelrod, this is a combination of expert-driven and team-driven approaches. Whereas the former provides a business and technical focus to change, the latter generates ownership, involvement and commitment. So as to gain this commitment, most specialists, experts and change management consultants have incorporated the parallel organisation concept in their process-driven approach. The Change Management paradigm[2] is the approach to change that most organisations use today. Although it seemingly seeks to integrate ownership of change with practical business focus, the Change Management approach, according to Axelrod, has shortcomings. He argues that—instead of involvement and commitment—this approach breeds cynicism, bureaucracy and resistance. He believes that it actually disempowers employees, by reinforcing hierarchical top-down management. Axelrod's book *Terms of Engagement* offers an alternative approach to generate employee ownership, involvement and commitment.

PARALLEL ORGANISATION

A parallel organisation is a series of groups or teams created in the organisation with interlocking memberships i.e. some employees are members of more than one team or group. These teams are also cross-functional i.e. each team is made of people from different departments or divisions. According to Axelrod, a parallel organisation typically consists of a sponsor team, a steering team and multiple design teams. The sponsor team is cross-functional, with senior managers from different divisions/departments. This is the team that initiates change, motivates others and provides resources for the change. While the sponsor team members are not involved in the day-to-day, nitty-gritty of change, their approval is required for major changes in policy or strategy. The steering team is also cross-functional and has people from all levels of the organisation, including employee unions. The steering team drives the day-to-day change. Design teams are also cross-functional and multi-level i.e. they include both managers and workers. These teams execute the nitty-gritty of change. In other words, they redesign processes, establish new procedures and get rid of procedures and processes that are no longer useful. These three types of teams operate in parallel with the regular organisation. This is the reason why they are referred to as the parallel organisation.

The parallel organisation is a major organisational innovation in recent years. Its purpose is to expedite decision-making—by cutting down inter-departmental barriers and improving the quality of decisions by involving employees in decision-making. Typically, decisions in these three teams are made by consensus after discussion and debate. Selection of team members is also important; usually people who command credibility and respect based on their competence get selected for these three types of teams. The parallel organisation is most effective when employees

Table 4.1: Four Approaches to Change

	Leader-driven Approach	Process-driven Approach	Team-driven Approach	Change Management Approach
Who leads the change effort?	Leader or chief executive	Experts or outside consultants	Teams within the organisation	Experts (consultants) and teams
How is change communicated and executed?	▶ Leader (CEO) announces change after consulting advisers ▶ Leader uses his/her authority and power to drive change	▶ Experts or consultants identify and recommend changes ▶ Leader supports the change ▶ Experts or consultants execute the changes	▶ Employee teams identify and recommend changes ▶ Leader (CEO) approves the suggestions ▶ Parallel organisation created to execute change	▶ Experts or consultants initiate and recommend changes with employee inputs ▶ Leader (CEO) approves the ideas and suggestions ▶ Parallel organisation created to execute change
What are the underlying assumptions?	Leader or CEO knows what is best for the organisation	Experts or consultants know what is best for the organisation	Employees know what is best for the organisation	Experts or consultants with employee inputs know what is best for the organisation

| When is this approach suitable? | ▲ Uneducated workforce
▲ Leaders have the knowledge and power | ▲ Uneducated workforce
▲ Experts or consultants have specialised knowledge
▲ Leader is supportive | ▲ Workforce educated and skilled
▲ Organisation is large and complex
▲ No single person has all the knowledge | ▲ Workforce educated and skilled
▲ Business focus needed in the change
▲ No single person has all the knowledge |

Source: Based on Axelrod, Richard H. (2000). *Terms of engagement: Changing the way we change organisations.* San Francisco: Berrett-Koehler Publishers

in different teams feel empowered so that they begin to 'own' the change. This is what is typically referred to as a 'buy-in' in conventional change management jargon. Ownership of change means that employees are not only fully involved in the change process but are also committed to the changes. Generally, with higher levels of employee involvement and commitment, there is greater probability of successful change in the organisation. By the same token, change efforts in which employees have low levels of involvement and commitment are more likely to fail. Ideally, most managers would like to have employees who are involved and committed to change. In reality, generating employee involvement and commitment is quite hard. The parallel organisation is an organisational mechanism of generating employee involvement and commitment by encouraging ownership of change.

OWNERSHIP AND INVOLVEMENT IN CHANGE

Employee ownership, involvement and commitment to change are crucial to the success of organisational change. There are two main reasons for this.

The first reason is pragmatic or practical: Today, large organisations are so complex that no single person has all the information and knowledge to take appropriate decisions. Front-line employees who are in touch with customers and the actual operations of the organisation are more likely to have information that is critical to make effective decisions. These employees also have the potential to provide creative suggestions that can significantly enhance the organisation's competitiveness and effectiveness. Therefore, from a pragmatic point of view, it makes a lot of sense to involve employees in any change process. In addition, involving employees in the change process will reduce the likelihood of opposition to change.

The second reason for the emphasis on employee ownership, involvement and participation is ethical or philosophical. The ethical aspects of participation and involvement are emphasized, not because they will make the change process more effective or easier but because they are worthy goals in themselves. In other words, we insist on employee involvement and participation because they are good for employees. Involvement and participation in change develops them as both employees and as human beings. They will become more capable and competent because involvement and participation will lead to learning and personal growth. The philosophical arguments tie into our notions of individual freedom and democracy. In very simple terms, the ultimate goal of any effort towards organisational change is to enhance the quality of life of its stakeholders. Employees constitute an important segment of the stakeholders of an organisation. Any change effort that does not give them a 'voice' or participation denies them choices and opportunities, which are most likely to diminish their quality of life.[3]

Given the practical and ethical reasons to create ownership of change by involving people, it makes perfect sense for managers to devote time and attention towards generating commitment and mobilising support for their change efforts. However, this is not such an easy or straightforward task. Mobilising support for change is, in fact, quite difficult because most individuals are oriented to stability rather than change. Change involves giving up the status quo and, for most people, that is fraught with uncertainty, which in turn can generate anxiety and stress. As a consequence of this, they will be less willing to trust a manager who tries to involve them in a change effort. Therefore, people need to be persuaded to give up the status quo. They need to be influenced to induce them into embracing change. Most importantly, they need to feel sufficiently enthusiastic to alter their mindsets and mental maps. To summarise, before change can be executed effectively, employee commitment needs to be created, consent for change needs to be generated and support for change mobilised. Change involves persuading a large number of people to stop what they have been doing and start doing something that they probably don't want to. That is why getting the buy-in for change is a very important part of the change manager's work.

MOBILISING SUPPORT FOR CHANGE

In the previous section, we argued that there are both practical and ethical reasons for creating ownership of change in an organisation. In order to be an effective change manager, you need to be *both* practical *and* ethical. If you ignore the ethical aspects, you may be seen as manipulative and cynical and are likely to lose credibility and respect quickly. On other hand, if you ignore the practical aspects and insist only on ethical reasons, you may be seen as a soft, touchy-feely manager not oriented to task or performance. Employees might like you as a person but will not respect you as a professional manager. Therefore, effective management of change requires managers to be practically ethical or ethically practical.

Most managers plan to introduce change by presenting a strong case for the need for change and the potential benefits of the change programme. They go armed with facts and figures. They anticipate objections, and prepare themselves thoroughly to puncture those with the help of powerful counter arguments. Yet great presentations and arguments run into familiar hurdles of indifference, suspicion, and resistance. Managers may get distracted dealing with these hurdles, and in the process their attention may shift from core issues and concerns. This can lead to failure. The predicament of these managers is captured by a delightful story that John Glidewell narrates[4] (Box 4.1).

Box 4.1: Getting Oscar to Eat Lunch

John was a young man studying psychology at the university. One Saturday his wife and another woman in the neighbourhood planned a daylong shopping tour, and he agreed to take care of the neighbour's two-year old son Oscar. As the neighbour was leaving, she said, 'He didn't eat any breakfast at all. Can you try to get him to eat some lunch?' Though Oscar had already built a formidable reputation in the neighbourhood for having a brain as fast as light and as sharp as a needle, John felt that the task of getting Oscar to eat some lunch was well within his area of core competence. After all he was a doctoral student of psychology, and had completed a course in child development with an excellent grade.

When lunchtime came, John called out cheerfully, 'Who would like some lunch?' Oscar's response was as quick as a flash. He snapped back, 'Not me!' John knew that Oscar liked bean soup and peanut butter sandwiches. He thought of cleverly offering a positive choice to Oscar rather than an option of answering yes or no. He got the soup and sandwiches ready, and asked, 'Who wants soup and who wants sandwiches?' Oscar said firmly, 'Didn't you hear me? I don't want any lunch!'

With phony indifference, John began to eat as Oscar played with a toy truck. But John knew that he was in a spot, because he had not been successful in getting the two-year old to eat. As Oscar continued to ignore him, John asked, 'Don't you like bean soup?' 'I like it, but not for lunch,' said Oscar. When asked what he would like for lunch, Oscar said, 'I'd like a worm!' When he saw the shock on John's face, he shouted again: '*A worm!*'

John was so annoyed that he felt a great need to rip open the little fellow's bluff. He took him outside, dug into the ground with a spade, and extracted a nice long earthworm. He gave it to Oscar. The two-year old was surprised, but he was unruffled as he said, 'You didn't cook it.'

The psychologist was feeling quite exasperated that he had still not won the battle. Quickly, he fried the worm with a little butter and put it in front of Oscar in a plate. In unbelievable innocence, Oscar said, 'Cut it up.' Now the grown-up was running out of patience. He cut the worm into two pieces, and growled, 'Eat.' Oscar replied, 'You eat with me.'

The older man who had considered himself an expert on child development couldn't bear the thought of being defeated by the two-year old. With mounting anger and tension, he decided to cheat to gain victory. He picked up half the worm, pretended to eat it, and palmed it into his pocket. The trick was performed to such perfection that Oscar was fooled. He kept gaping at John's mouth, and never looked at his pocket. Then he stared down at the other half of the worm on the plate. Then his face clouded over and he began to cry. But Oscar wasn't finished yet. In between his sobs he stuck his last blow: 'This is not my piece. You ate *my* half. *You ate my half.*' Thus the two-year old had comprehensively and almost effortlessly demolished John's strong case.

THREE COMMON MISTAKES

There are three common mistakes that managers tend to make in getting the buy-in for change[5]:

1. *Assuming that great arguments would win hearts and minds.* Most of us tend to place excessive faith in the logic and rationality of individuals and organisations. Although convincing logic is a necessary prerequisite for any change idea, great arguments in themselves do not get the buy-in for change. Unless the manager relates to the audience at the right emotional level and his/her credibility is well accepted, arguments would fail to convince people.
2. *Assuming that persistence without compromising would sell the idea.* Many mangers wrongly believe that they should present a strong case at the outset. Unfortunately, a strong decision at the very start gives opponents a clear target to attack. If the change agent persists with the idea and resists any form of compromise, he/she may be perceived as rigid and authoritarian. Needless to say, this would only yield resentment and frustration, not commitment to the idea.
3. *Assuming that persuading is a one-time effort.* Many managers give excessive importance to the formal acceptance of their ideas in a meeting. While this is certainly important, it is not the only success factor of any persuasion effort. A manager needs to listen to diverse views, keep making changes in a variety of settings, and keep up the momentum of the change campaign. Change involves a long and difficult journey and by assuming it to be a one-time effort, we run the risk of creating a 'flash in the pan', but no lasting change.

These common mistakes are illustrated (Box 4.2) in an experience of a senior manager of a medium-sized software firm, who shared the intense emotions that he had experienced during the merger of his company with another firm.

LESSONS FROM *TIPPING POINT*

How do people get influenced? What persuades them to change their mindsets and behaviour? A groundbreaking book by Malcolm Gladwell, *The Tipping Point*, provides the answer to these questions.[6] This engaging book looks at why major changes happen suddenly and unexpectedly in society, and

> **Box 4.2: When 'Push' Strategy Pushed the Issues Underground**
>
> A decision had been made to merge two software firms of equivalent size. The senior and middle level personnel of both firms had come together to sort out merger related concerns and issues. The meeting was organised in a large hall. At one point during the discussion, someone expressed a concern: 'As a multinational, we have had a certain culture in our firm. But you are an Indian firm largely owned by a single family. What would be our new culture after the merger? Are we expected to forget about our old multinational culture?'
>
> Immediately, a top manager of the 'Indian firm' (as it was referred to by the person raising the issue) arose, walked up to the podium and said, 'How can you say that our firm is not a multinational? We operate in more than a dozen countries and have offices in all those locations; at any given point of time, a third of our employees work abroad; and we earn 100 per cent of our revenues from overseas work. So we are as much a multinational as you are'. He went on with more facts and figures to bolster his argument. It seemed as if he wanted to use his finely honed debating skills to bury the cultural comparison issue once and for all, in that meeting.
>
> But the top manager's intervention only pushed the issue underground. Many people simply withdrew from the discussion. The change managers lost a great opportunity to explore what the concerns were. Perhaps people were anxious about possible loss of autonomy in the merged entity. People may have wondered and worried whether key personnel decisions would be made on personal likes and dislikes. The merging entities should have had a dialogue on issues regarding cultural integration, which people considered important. As they did not do this, several individuals seemed to have concluded that the merger would be bad for them. The organisation lost a large number of highly skilled people to competing firms. And several months after the merger, the firm had still not achieved the strategic advantages that the merger was anticipated to provide.

argues that ideas and messages leading to change mimic the spread of an infectious disease. Gladwell calls them *social epidemics* that take off after they reach their critical mass. This is what is referred to as the Tipping Point. Based on a variety of examples from fashion trends, children's television, direct mail, early days of the American Revolution, and successful high-tech companies, the book identifies particular personality types who are initiators and creators of change. Gladwell calls them *connectors, maven* and *salesmen.*

Connectors, as the term implies, are people who have a large number of social connections. They are individuals in the organisation who seem to know everyone. In management jargon, they are well-networked individuals who have contacts with people from a variety of backgrounds.

Why does Gladwell refer to this attribute of networking as a personality type? This is because connectors are pretty unique individuals. Not everyone is a connector. In his book, Gladwell illustrates this with the example of a person called Roger Horchow who kept a roster of 1,600 names and addresses on his computer. He kept a little red pocket diary in which he had the birthdays of people he knew. He sent each of them a card on their birthday.

Connectors have a large number of acquaintances, not necessarily their close friends. These are what are known as 'weak ties'—friendly yet casual social connections. In an organisation, connectors wield enormous influence and clout because of their contacts—both within and outside it. This is what makes connectors crucial in change management. If connectors become convinced about the change effort and are enthusiastic about it, they will pass on their enthusiasm to all their contacts, thus spreading the message of change very effectively. Therefore, an organisation needs to identify its connectors first, and enlist their support for change.

Mavens form the second personality type that Gladwell discusses in his book. The word maven, in Yiddish, means one who accumulates knowledge. Mavens are human equivalents of databases or databanks; they are astounding sources of information. As Gladwell puts it, 'Obviously they know things that the rest of us don't.'[7]

Mavens have the knowledge and the social skills to start social epidemics. The social skill that Mavens possess is they want to help others because they like helping others. This makes them an effective source of influence and power. Therefore, identifying and enlisting the support of mavens is crucial in organisational change management.

Salesmen comprise the third personality type discussed in Gladwell's book. They are good at persuading others to do things that they would not do on their own. A salesman can convince a skeptical employee about the need for change and convert the employee into an enthusiastic supporter of change. How do salesmen do this?

According to Gladwell, salesmen have some striking traits that set them apart from the rest of us. They radiate positive emotions and optimism. Salesmen are able to bond with other people so effectively that others are willing to be influenced by them. Salesmen build in minutes the level of trust and rapport that would take other people hours. The implications for change management are clear. The change message needs to be communicated through salesmen. Therefore, managers in charge of change need to identify people who have the attributes of salesmen—warmth, empathy, optimism, energy and positive emotions.

In a recent merger between two financial organisations, the leaders organised a series of leadership renewal workshops for a carefully chosen group of middle and senior managers. The participant groups included the three types—connectors, maven and salesmen. The workshops discussed the challenges of change, and identified the different areas that would need attention. As per their distinctive strengths, participants volunteered to make contributions that had a significant effect in ensuring successful change implementation.

Gladwell's book *The Tipping Point* prompts us to rethink the manner in which change needs to be managed in organisations. Conventional recipes for managing change provide a step-by-step sequential approach to managing change, in which the mobilising support is largely seen as a process of communication. Gladwell's book, on the other hand, suggests that change need not be a sequential, step-by-step process.

Using principles of influence and social epidemics, managers can bring about change by targeting their efforts at the right people. If an organisation can identify the connectors, mavens and salesmen among its employees and can successfully enlist their support, chances are that the message of change will spread much more effectively in the organisation and generate commitment and support that are the hallmarks of successful change. Gladewell also points to an important factor in mobilising support for change, the *critical mass.*

THE CONCEPT OF 'CRITICAL MASS'

An important idea in change management is that you don't need every single individual in an organisation to support and be committed to a change programme. What you need is the support of a proportion of employees that is referred to as the 'critical mass.' The important concept of critical mass in the change management literature is drawn from nuclear science. It is defined[8] as the 'minimum amount of fuel needed in the core of a nuclear reactor in order to start a self-sustaining chain reaction.'

In change management, critical mass refers to the minimum number of people in an organisation whose support is required to launch change. Unlike science, it is not possible to provide a precise figure as to how many people would constitute a critical mass in an organisation. Based on our own experience and the experience of other change management practitioners, we suggest that an organisation needs the support of at least 30–40 per cent of employees before launching a major transformational change.

The reality is that, in any major change effort, there are likely to be about 20 per cent of employees actively supporting the change and about 20 per cent actively opposed to it. The rest of the organisation appears to be sitting on the fence. As a manager, you need to make a choice about which group you want to target to mobilise support. Baum[9] suggests that managers need to target those 60 per cent employees who are 'fence-sitters.' He argues that there is no point in approaching the 20 per cent active supporters because they support the change anyway. Trying to convince the 20 per cent who oppose change is risky because if they fail to be convinced, the rest of the organisation may also be skeptical about change. As a manager, you only need another 20 per cent's support to reach the critical mass. Therefore, it makes a lot of practical sense to target the

60 per cent people who have not made up their mind about change.

'POLITICAL' ASPECTS OF ORGANISATIONAL CHANGE

In order to create a critical mass, a manager needs to convert at least 20 per cent of the fence-sitters into active supporters of change. How is this possible? What does the manager need to do? The crux of the issue here is that there is a large number of individuals (about 60 per cent of employees) who are undecided about change—they need to be influenced or persuaded to support the change. How can a manager motivate employees to change? Most of the change management literature overlooks the fact that people are largely motivated by self-interest. In the 90s, popular writing in Change Management exhorted managers to develop 'vision' statements to appeal to people's hearts. While there is some merit in this proposal, change managers who ignore people's minds (and by that we mean their self-interests) will find it quite difficult to garner support for their change efforts. Individuals are not solely driven by self-interests but these interests are important. In some instances, change may involve relinquishing one's self-interest. The first thing people are likely to ask when informed about change is: what is in it for me?

When Delhi Metro undertook the massive metro project, the leadership realised that it would have a number of dependencies to manage. There had to be a number of decisions to be made at every stage of the project involving large financial outlays—quickly and without political or bureaucratic interference. The decision-making process ensured this. Public support was critical for land acquisition and later for smooth execution. A number of contractors would be involved, and their effectiveness had to be ensured for the corporation to be effective. The community would be concerned about possible environmental degradation. Though the project would ultimately benefit the community, no cost could be unilaterally imposed on any stakeholder. The project owes its success to effectively managing such political aspects too. The interests of residents whose land was being acquired (e.g. fair and transparent procedures, quick compensation and remedial actions), contractors (e.g. prompt decisions, payments and clear technical specifications and support wherever required), and the community (green cover and aesthetics) were anticipated and addressed.

If the organisation's change agenda matches self-interests of employees and other stakeholders, it has little problem in gathering support. On the other hand, if the change agenda requires employees to give up at least some of their interests, then mobilising support is a more difficult task. More importantly, even if the change agenda is aligned with employees' self-interests, they have to be convinced that participating in change will advance their self-interests. Therefore, mobilising support is largely about influencing people to change despite—or because of—their self-interests. This aspect of influencing people's self-interest is what makes change management 'political'; it requires close attention to the science and art of persuasion. In other words, we need to understand the psychology of persuasion before we can devise effective ways of influencing people.

THE PSYCHOLOGY OF PERSUASION

How can we influence and persuade individuals to do something that they would not do on their own? Robert Cialdini,[10] an internationally well-known social psychologist, has done extensive research on the science of persuasion over the last 30 years. His books, *Influence: The Psychology of Persuasion* and *Influence: Science and Practice* are perhaps the most cited in the field of influence and persuasion. Both these books have sold over quarter-of-a-million copies in nine languages. What distinguishes Cialdini's book is that it is not based only on academic research; he was very interested in professions that require other people to say yes to their requests. These are professional sales people, car dealers, insurance salespersons, advertising agencies, army recruiters and so on. Cialdini wanted to study the techniques of people who were successful in these professions. Therefore, he got into training programmes for these professions. He sold cars, peddled insurance, sold portrait photography over the phone, talked to army recruiters, advertising agency copywriters, and charity organisations. His remarkable insights are distilled into six universal principles of persuasion that are discussed in his engaging book on persuasion.

Before we present the six principles of persuasion, we want you to read the previous paragraph once again and reflect on it. Even before presenting Cialdini's principles, we have attempted to influence you into accepting his ideas. How did we do this? We have used at least two of the principles of persuasion from his book—the principles of *authority* and *social proof*. We have implied that Cialdini is widely accepted as an international authority on persuasion by a large number of people (over 30 years research, books that have been translated into nine languages and sold more than a quarter-of-a-million copies, most cited, practical research by doing things like selling cars, insurance, etc). Without your being consciously aware of it, you are being primed to accept his research findings. In other words, we are attempting to enlist your support towards accepting his ideas on persuasion. In this instance, whatever we told you about Cialdini is true; none of the details are made up. More importantly, we have nothing to gain by your acceptance of Cialdini's principles. This is an important aspect Cialdini emphasizes: the use of these principles of persuasion has to be ethically acceptable and morally valid. In other words, one should not attempt to use these to manipulate, deceive or cheat. Cialdini has been particularly emphatic in stressing this point[11]:

> *The other point I wish to emphasize is that the rules of ethics apply to the science of social influence just as they do to any other technology. Not only is it ethically wrong to trick or trap others into assent, it's ill-advised in practical terms. Dishonest or high-pressure tactics work only in the short run, if at all. Their long-term effects are malignant, especially within an organisation, which can't function properly without a bedrock level of trust and cooperation.* (p. 79)

Cialdini lists six principles of persuasion: (a) Liking, (b) Reciprocity, (c) Social proof, (d) Consistency, (e) Authority, and (f) Scarcity. Let us examine these in the context of change management.

The first principle of *liking* asserts that we tend to like people who are similar to us. We also tend to like people who like us; particularly we tend to like people who praise us. Therefore, we are more likely to be influenced by people who are similar to us, familiar to us, like us and praise us. What are the implications for this in managing change? Consider an organisation, the top management of which has decided to launch change. How should the change be communicated to employees? In many organisations that have launched major transformational changes, the chief executives have sought to demonstrate leadership by personally communicating the change agenda to the rest of the organisation. The change is introduced with multimedia presentations and a great deal of fanfare in large forums. Now, imagine that you are a front-line worker in one such organisation. How similar would you consider yourself to the chief executive, who probably earns about 300 times what you earn (if you live in the United States)?[12] Not surprisingly, such communication attempts invariably lead to cynicism and mistrust, rather than enthusiasm for change.

Communication consultants, Larkin and Larkin, offer three pieces of useful advice[13] to organisations planning to introduce change: (a) communicate only facts, not values. They argue that values are best communicated through actions, not through words; (b) communicate face-to-face and not through videos, publications, or large meetings, and (c) target front-line supervisors. Front-line employees are more likely to feel a closer affinity with their supervisors than with top-level managers or the chief executive. Therefore, first-level supervisors have greater influence over their staff than the chief executive of the organisation.

In a composite textile mill, some workers were carefully identified on the basis of their credibility with fellow workers and their communication skills. After being provided special training on the challenges of change, they were entrusted the responsibility of training the other workers on what needs to be done for the success of the change and the organisation. In training sessions, they were able to quickly establish rapport with the participants and gain greater acceptability. This method worked much better than conventional training programmes in influencing workforce to actively support the change effort.

Cialdini's second principle is *reciprocity*; it leads people to repay in kind what they receive. Cialdini calls this the universal human tendency to treat people the way one gets treated—the golden rule that is common to all world religions or wisdom traditions. In simple terms it means: what you wish done to yourself, do to others. Therefore, if you expect people to help you, help them first. The implication of the reciprocity principle for change management is that the best way to mobilise support is through generosity and benevolence towards employees in normal times. Employees are more willing to trust managers who are perceived as being benevolent. On the other hand, organisations that are perceived to be miserly or mean-spirited will get very little support for initiating change.

Mahendar Reddy took charge as the Commissioner of the Cyberabad Police in early 2003 with a total of 48 police stations and about 3000 employees. The population covered was about 3 million. He realised that a major transformation was required to make the force responsive and people-friendly; but he also realised that 85 per cent of his staff were constables who did not have a place to sit in the police station. In the traditional space allocation at a police station, constables are ignored. They are not considered significant enough to be given a table and chair. They stand outside, under the trees or in shops nearby. Not surprisingly, their sense of self-worth and their work effectiveness was very low. The sub-inspectors, who were at the first level of supervision, regularly worked 12 to 16 hours a day. Rather than start with the change agenda to enhance the service quality, Reddy focused his efforts on tackling such unacceptable work conditions. By drawing on support from the local industry and others, he was able to implement innovative solutions to the problem. Later when change efforts were initiated, the employees were far more amenable to influence.

The principle of *social proof* asserts that individuals rely on people around them for cues on how to think, feel and act.[14] In simple terms, our friends, neighbours, colleagues and people around us have the most influence on us. This can, of course, also lead to mindless actions. Here is an interesting illustration of the principle of social proof leading to thoughtless behaviour.

What is a common reason for accidents to occur during rush hour when cars in all lanes are moving steadily but slowly? Events leading to the accident would start when two cars, one behind the other, simultaneously begin signalling an intention to get out of the lane they are in, to get into the adjoining lane. Within seconds, a long line of drivers—at the rear of the first two cars—would follow suit; being persuaded by social proof that a stalled car or a construction barrier is blocking the lane ahead—although nothing of that kind has actually happened. It would be in this rush to cram into available spaces in the next lane that a collision is found to frequently happen.

The way to build a critical mass of supporters is to use the social proof principle by communicating to individuals in an organisation that 'everyone is doing it.' This principle is called the *bandwagon effect*; it implies that the best way to mobilise support is through the use of teams. Individuals who are part of a team will respond more positively to the suggestions and ideas of their team members. The message for managers is to rely on peer pressure rather than direct communication to mobilise support from employees. In practical terms, this means identifying employees who are active supporters of change and asking them to enlist the support of their peers. This principle also suggests that employees are more likely to be persuaded if they are shown other organisations that have implemented similar changes. That's why Tata Chemicals arranges employee visits to progressive firms to pick up the best practices. Technical personnel from other companies who have carried out interesting innovations are invited to make presentations about their experiences to relevant groups of employees. When they see others doing it, employees are convinced that such changes are necessary.

The principle of *consistency* refers to the need for consistency in human beings between their commitments and actions. In other words, when people take a position publicly, they tend to stick to it. People also have a strong expectation that others would stick to their public utterances.[15] Not only do we have a great need to appear to be consistent, we expect others to be consistent too. The implication of this principle for change management is that if you can get active, voluntary and public commitment for change from your employees, they will tend to support the change when it is executed. A public utility organised customer meets and involved its senior operations personnel in eliciting feedback and responding to them. When they heard certain customer complaints, there was a genuine sense of surprise. They had not expected such problems to occur, but now it was clear to them that these had actually happened. When they were asked to respond, they shared their views and ideas on how the problem could be resolved. Having committed in a public forum, they felt a stronger sense of ownership in quickly implementing those ideas to overcome the difficulties.

Cialdini emphasises that commitment to change should not be forced upon employees. Given the principle of consistency, coercion and threat will have an outcome that is opposite of what a manager wants. This is because employees can now justify their action of not supporting change as a consequence of the manager's intimidation. Another implication of the principle of consistency is that people like to have reasons for what they do. This means that a manager is more likely to enlist support for change if she/he *explains* the reasons for change.

The principle of *authority* claims that we are more likely to be influenced by individuals who are perceived as 'experts.' This is the reason why the news media often get acknowledged experts to present their opinions on a topic. Research has shown that this has a significant impact on public opinion. In the context of change management, this means that employees are more likely to be influenced by a manager who is perceived to be competent in his/her job. One way you can influence people is to earn their trust and respect. The best way to do that is by developing your technical and professional competence. If people around you perceive you to be competent, they are more likely to trust you and will be willing to be influenced by you.

E. Sreedharan was invited to join the Delhi Metro as Managing Director because of his great track record over a long and illustrious career. The results that he had achieved with Konkan

Railway project were outstanding. When he met the Chief Minister, Transport Minister and the Chief Secretary before assuming leadership charge at Delhi Metro, he discussed the challenges and mentioned that the project could be completed on time and within budget only if he was given full power to handle the project, he had complete freedom to select his own team and there was no political and bureaucratic interference at any stage. The government agreed to these conditions. Later, he was able to influence different stakeholders even on highly controversial issues because of his expertise and leadership attributes.

The principle of *scarcity* makes us want more of what we can have less of. In other words, when things are available less readily, they become more valuable. The other implication of this is that we are more influenced by our expected losses than by our expected gains. In other words, when we are told that we are likely to lose money or opportunity if we did *not* take some action, we are likely to respond relatively more quickly than when we are told that we are likely to gain money or opportunity if we took some action. This has interesting implications for change management. Most popular change management books urge managers to frame their change agendas in a positive way. In other words, managers are encouraged to communicate how the change would make things *better* for the employees and the organisation. We are told that change that is framed as improvement, progress, development and growth has better chances of being supported. While this is generally true, the scarcity principle suggests that this support can be enhanced when the positive language is complemented by 'loss language.' In other words, if the employees are also told that they and the organisation stands to lose money and opportunities, then their support is likely to be stronger.

A medium-sized engineering company was experiencing considerable performance difficulties. The dominant view among the employees was that additional investments were necessary in technology and equipments to improve performance. The change leader worked out the investment costs and showed how additional investments would not solve the problem and could actually even result in hastening the firm's demise. The analysis also showed why status quo was equally unacceptable. In the final part of the analysis, he demonstrated with facts and figures what changes could lead to a turnaround. As this analysis was presented and discussed in different forums, people were convinced of the diagnosis and the need for change. They were also energised to invest efforts in making the changes happen.

As the above case illustration demonstrates, the loss language should not be framed as a threat. If, for instance, a manager indicates that there could be job losses if the change is not implemented, then employees are likely to comply with rather than support the change. On the other hand, if the manager can produce convincing evidence why there will be job losses, the employees are more likely to be actively committed to change. The principle of scarcity also implies that providing employees with strategic information that is usually not shared with them can influence employees. Sharing financial information about company performance is a potent way to induce change.

Cialdini's principles of influence and persuasion are based on research and empirical data. They are all based on the commonly observed mental models that most individuals employ in day-today situations. The psychology of persuasion is an important part of the toolkit of a change manager. Table 4.2 summarises the principles and the associated change management tactics.

COMMUNICATING TO INFLUENCE PEOPLE

The most basic way to mobilise support in an organisation is to communicate the need for change to employees. However, the purpose of this type of communication is not merely to inform employees and other relevant stakeholders about expected changes but to win them over to the idea of change. In order to do this, we need to be familiar with the psychology of communication.

For example, having to carry out a Metro project in the nation's capital required careful attention to communication to different

Table 4.2: Six Principles of Persuasion and Related Change Management Tactics

Principle	What is it based on?	Change Management Tactic
Liking	Individuals like people who are similar to them, who like them and who praise them	Use first-level supervisors and employees to communicate change to other employees; Be appreciative of employees and their past efforts
Reciprocity	Individuals feel obligated to repay in kind, when they receive help, gifts or praise without asking	Practice generosity and benevolence; Offer help to peers and staff who need help
Social Proof	People are influenced by others who are similar to them	Arrange visits to other organisations that have implemented similar change efforts; Build a 'critical mass' of change supporters and influence others through the critical mass
Consistency	People feel compelled to fulfil voluntary, public and written commitments	Enlist employee support in a public forum by asking people to indicate their commitment openly (Do not coerce or pressurize them to commit)
Authority	Individuals are influenced by others who are perceived as experts	Develop technical and professional competence in your job so that others around you see you as being competent
Scarcity	People tend to value things that are relatively in short supply	Share strategic information with employees; Identify the opportunities they are likely to miss if the organisation does not undergo change

Source: Based on Cialdini, R.B. (1993). *Influence: The Psychology of Persuasion.*, New York: William Morrow and Company; Cialdini, R.B. (2000). *Influence: Science and Practice.* Fourth ed., Boston: Allyn and Bacon

stakeholders. Not only did the project involve a huge financial outlay, it was also highly visible. After all, a large number of decisions—which affected people and their cooperation and support—had to be made, and were critical for the success of the project. Recognising the importance of public support, the senior team at Delhi Metro Rail Corporation Limited (DMRC) saw the need not merely in terms of communication, but also in terms of winning people over in so far as shaping their impression of DMRC's philosophy and approaches. Their approach has been outlined in Box 4.3.

An effective communication strategy is one which takes into account four critical elements of communication: (a) the audience, (b) purpose of communication, (c) credibility of the communicator, and (d) the context of communication. Over the years, a great deal of research in this area provides us systematic ways of structuring our communication for influencing people.[16]

In structuring effective communication, the nature of audience involvement is an important factor. Audience involvement refers to the level of interest in and concern about the specific issue being communicated. Highly involved audiences are those who are directly affected by the issue being communicated. If we are communicating the need for change to those that are likely to be directly affected by change, then we need to ensure that we emphasise logic by building a good argument for change. On the other hand, we may emphasise our credibility and context while trying to convince less involved audiences. While less involved audiences are easy to persuade, the changes in their mindsets are likely to be short-term. On the other hand, highly involved audiences are more difficult to persuade but the changes in their mindsets last longer. Highly involved audiences are also likely to move less far from their initial mindsets compared to less involved audiences. Therefore, highly involved audiences need repeated communication in order to reinforce the original message. We present an illustration (Box 4.4) of how a unit head communicated to different stakeholders in a difficult situation to influence them to support the change process.

Box 4.3: Communicating to Delhi Residents and Gaining their Support

There was clear recognition among members of the DMRC that a number of things were important to mobilise public support. First, there should be as little inconvenience to public as possible. Second, the construction activities should be carried out in a manner that was safe and aesthetically pleasing. Third, there should be no environmental degradation, such as the reduction in the number of trees in the city. Fourth, the inevitable disruptions in certain public utilities (water supply, power, sewer lines, telecom cables, etc.) resulting from construction should be anticipated and preventive actions should be taken in coordination with the relevant agencies. Fifth, public concerns and complaints should be quickly picked up and redressed. Most important, DMRC should enjoy high credibility. This would be best achieved through consistent actions that demonstrate excellence, responsiveness, efficiency, transparency and fairness.

A number of initiatives were launched consistent with the above priorities. Before taking up worksites, the same were segregated by hoardings/barricades. A number of procedures were instituted to minimise disturbances; some even specified that vehicles would not be allowed to leave worksites without their tyres being cleaned first. Since other public utilities were notorious for their inefficiency, the interface with those agencies was handled by taking on additional responsibilities to ensure that there was no public discontent. When traffic diversions had to be made, DMRC appointed additional personnel at important signals to help the traffic police maintain a smooth flow of traffic. Though it was clearly not DMRC's responsibility, it also undertook the widening and repairs of roads where necessary; thus ensuring that no road was closed at any time and no inconvenience was caused in any way. Issues such as power, water supply, sewerage, etc. were also addressed in a similarly proactive way.

Right through the process, there were regular community interaction programmes. People were provided advance intimation and regular updates through different media. Help-lines were available to report difficulties. As a result, the project consistently enjoyed a great image in the eyes of the Delhi residents and received their support whenever required.

Box 4.4: Malaysian Carpet Company

The new general manager (GM) of a Malaysian Carpet Company[17] was faced with the challenge of turning around the firm that was rapidly going downhill. He had to influence his own head office, senior executives, workers, bankers, dealers and others to support the change till the firm turned the corner. But the workers were in no mood to wait and decided to go on strike demanding higher wages and bonus. A senior executive, who wanted to cut the new GM to size, was provoking them surreptitiously. As the workers were planning to leave for the day, the GM decided—at the spur of the moment—to talk to them. He said, 'I understand that you are planning to go on strike and hold demonstrations. When you squat outside the factory gate tomorrow, there will be people from the press who will come and photograph you. Your pictures will appear in the newspapers. They will ask you questions and blow up the issue. But our bankers will also read about our problems. They already think that ours is a dying company and when you go on strike, they will reject our proposal for funds. If that happens, the company will close down. Of course, you will continue to hold demonstrations, but now no press people will come to take your photographs and write what you say. I have another job at the head office and so I will lose very little but I am not so sure if all of you can find another job when the company closes down.'

The response of the workers to the GM's impromptu address was electric; the communication had established contact with the group. He looked directly into the eyes of a worker who was listening intently, and asked him, 'Tell me, do you want to go on strike tomorrow?' The worker avoided his eyes, but the GM persisted, 'You cannot avoid my question. It is far too important for the company's future and yours. Do you want to go on strike?' For a while, there was silence. Then, slowly, the worker said, 'No.' The GM moved to another person and repeated his question. Again the answer was 'No'. The third person, fourth person, and soon ripples of a new sentiment were being generated. Towards the end of the address, the crisis had been averted. The GM quickly followed up with initiatives to strengthen employee communication and involvement to build on the positive sentiment that had come about.

The GM followed a different approach with the bankers. He met them regularly and frequently, each time with some good news about the company. He used his contacts to get certain purchase orders released, even if the deliveries were required later. Every time there was a big order, he told the bankers that it was only the tip of the iceberg, and there was more to follow. In the GM's words, 'No accounts

> were presented to the bankers unless we put lipstick and mascara and made them look as pretty and healthy as possible. Finally, the banks relented and accepted the financial restructuring package we had proposed. That helped the company turn around in a remarkably short time'.

An audience can be biased to the content of the communication in that they may hold strong opinions about change. If they are favourable towards change, they are said to be positively biased. If they hold no opinions about change, they are neutral and if they are strongly opposed to change, they are negatively biased. We have greater chances of persuading a negatively biased audience, if we use a two-sided argument. A two-sided argument considers both the pros and cons of change. In presenting a two-sided argument, we need to consider the likely opposition to change and build strong, credible arguments against such opposition. On the other hand, we may only present the positive aspects of change if our audience is neutral or positively biased. However, if we anticipate that the neutral or positively biased members of our audience are likely to be exposed to negative arguments against change later on, we need to inoculate them against negative arguments. This can be done by presenting both the pros and cons of change and systematically refuting the negative arguments against change.

The credibility of the communicator can affect the success or failure of the communication effort. There are five possible sources of credibility[18]: (1) status of the communicator inside the organisation, (2) goodwill enjoyed by the communicator, (3) perceived expertise of the communicator, (4) perceived image of the communicator, and (5) morality or fairness of the communicator. Thus, as a manager, you can erode your credibility if you demonstrate lack of expertise or fairness in your communication. However, credibility of the communicator may not be an important factor in communicating to highly involved audiences. If the issue of change is less important to your audience, your credibility will matter most in influencing their mindsets.

Bashein and Markus[19] describe a communication episode involving the task of mobilising a community to deal with a possible outbreak of a life-threatening disease. Yet, in absence of any clear evidence, the nature of actions to be taken was far from clear. This situation has been outlined in Box 4.5.

The context is another important element to be taken into account for deciding on the choice of communication approach. For example, when the mood is hostile there is a need to quickly

---

Box 4.5: Crisis and Credibility[20]

The state disease surveillance unit had picked up a signal of 'two possible cases of bacterial meningitis—two sick teenagers, down in Mankato'. This required extraordinary public health intervention as the disease could kill a healthy person within six hours. Intensive and selective vaccination campaigns were required, but Mike Osterholm, an epidemiologist realised that there was little clarity on whom to vaccinate because there was no apparent reason linking the two teenagers who had fallen sick.

As an agent of the state, Osterholm called a meeting of Mankato officials for Sunday at 6 p.m. He drew a standing-room-only crowd of forty at the Immanuel-St. Joseph's Hospital education room, including hospital staff, private-practice doctors from the Mankato Clinic, local politicians, county health officers, and Mankato school district officials. He was aware that he was talking to medical doctors not inclined to take instruction from a Ph.D. So rather than direct the audience, he guided them toward consensus. He outlined the situation, the options, and what was known and not known. 'We're here to help,' he said. 'What do you want to do?'

His communication worked. Those listening were impressed by his matter-of-fact knowledge and appreciated that he wasn't imposing his will on them. Even as the meeting ended at 9.30 Sunday night, the hospital staff was scrambling to set up a hot line to handle calls from the community. School administrators were laying plans to distribute parent permission slips. Community relations specialists were herding reporters into a news conference. And Osterholm was on the phone to order 4,000 doses of Group C vaccine to be airlifted for Monday delivery.

Mankato officials and Osterholm's staff mapped a plan based on what they did know and decided to vaccinate all junior and senior high school students in the district on Tuesday morning. As Bashein and Markus point out, Osterholm had inspired confidence in himself rather than try to inspire confidence in science. The evidence, after all, was not nearly as strong as Osterholm's poised performance.

assess what would bring the 'heat' down in the given situation and then communicate appropriately. A senior police officer said, *I have often seen that the police have resorted to the use of force to deal with a tense situation in a community because the concerned police officials did not possess the necessary communication skills. They did not know how to convey a certain message clearly and defuse the situation. As a result, the tension is allowed to escalate, and then use of force becomes inevitable to bring it under control. In most contexts, this is a poor choice because it worsens the situation at least in the medium and long run. We have, therefore sought to improve the communication skills of our people.*

FOOT-IN-THE-DOOR APPROACH

Using the principle of consistency from the previous section, we know that the level of involvement of an audience can be increased if they are induced to publicly support change. Even if someone is not convinced about change, if they express support for change publicly, they are more likely to change their attitude towards change in order to remain consistent with their behaviour. This principle can be used to create a favourable attitude to change by inducing the audience to commit to a small step in the change programme. For instance, instead of trying to sell an organisation-wide radical change to employees, we may try to get acceptance for a small pilot programme. If they commit to the pilot programme, they are more likely to support the whole programme later.

This approach of eliciting small commitments to build support for a larger programme is called the foot-in-the-door approach, or the principle of entanglement. It involves obtaining small commitments to change that can be leveraged into larger ones. If we entangle our audience in small changes, they are likely to be more favourably inclined towards larger changes. For example, when the police commissioner, Mahendar Reddy, suggested to his sub-inspectors and assistant commissioners of police that they entrust greater responsibilities to the constabulary staff, there was resistance to the idea. Seniors felt that the constables just did not have the requisite skills. Subsequently, at monthly meetings, Reddy formed small groups to generate ideas on specific problem areas. These groups comprised people from all levels. Several constables in small groups, with their in-depth understanding of ground-level realities, were able to think up excellent ideas that surprised many sub-inspectors and assistant commissioners of police. Slowly, the seniors began to perceive the constables in new light. In a few months, greater delegation had happened to constables without Reddy's prodding.

TARGETING INFLUENCE EFFORTS

Now that we understand the psychological principles of persuasion and communication, how should we go about influencing people in an organisation? Do we meet them individually or collectively? What channels of communication should we rely on? These are practical issues that are faced by any manager. Remember that, typically, a manager has limited resources in terms of time and money. Therefore, the concept of critical mass (as discussed earlier) is important. Initially, we need about 40 per cent of people to support a change initiative. How do we identify these people? What attributes should they have? Effectively persuading people to change is a core leadership skill. In order to develop this capability, managers need a systematic framework to organise their activities, which has been elaborated in some detail (Table 4.3).[21]

Table 4.3: Core Tasks for Mobilising Support

Core Tasks	Specific Activities to be Attended to Effectively Perform Core Tasks
1. Analyse the context	➤ Identify target audience; Build supportive coalitions ➤ Map the influence networks ➤ Identify the interests of people whose support is needed ➤ Evaluate how key people perceive the alternatives to change

(Contd.)

Table 4.3 (*Contd.*)

Core Tasks	Specific Activities to be Attended to Effectively Perform Core Tasks
2. Change mindsets	➤ Alter people's incentives for change ➤ Frame the change agenda in a way that evokes support ➤ Influence people's perceptions of their alternatives to change ➤ Engage in one-on-one negotiation to buy support
3. Make difficult choices	➤ Institute a process that is open, transparent and inclusive ➤ Ensure that people are included in the diagnostic phase ➤ Consult as widely as possible before making a decision ➤ Make sure that people have adequate resources for implementing tough decisions
4. Persuade indirectly	➤ Neutralise the power of informal networks ➤ Repeat the message ➤ Match the medium to the message ➤ Simplify the message ➤ Create a new story about change ➤ Build personal credibility

There are four core tasks that change managers need to undertake in mobilising support (Table 4.3). First, they need to *analyse the context*. Second, they need to *change mindsets*. Third, they need to know how to *make difficult choices* and, finally, they need to be able to *persuade indirectly*.

ANALYSING THE CONTEXT

Before initiating any communication aimed at mobilising support, a change manager needs to identify target audience. Who needs to be influenced? How should they be persuaded? The first step in answering these questions is to identify the key groups and subgroups in the organisation. The manager needs to build *supportive coalitions* that will facilitate change and also neutralise opposition to change by preventing the formation of *blocking coalitions*. In a large organisation, subgroups may include: (a) *organisational units* that consist of employees sharing common training, expertise, tasks and supervision, (b) *identity groups* that are bound together by shared ethnicity, race, age, gender or social status, and (c) *power coalitions* consisting of people who have opportunistically joined together to promote their common interests.

The second step in analysing the context is to map the *influence networks*. These are established patterns of interaction, showing who listens to whom on critical issues. This step should identify the *opinion leaders* in the organisation. These are key individuals who act as connectors and salesmen in Gladwell's terminology. When people are faced with a difficult choice such as change, they look to people that they trust and respect for clues about the 'right choice.' Opinion leaders may be trusted and respected because of their expertise or experience or because they have access to key information. They may also elicit respect and admiration because of their personality. Persuading opinion leaders is crucial to building a critical mass. A critical part of this step is also to identify the supporters, opponents and people who are undecided about the change agenda. While the supporters and opponents should not be ignored, influence efforts should be specifically targeted at people who are undecided about change.

At this juncture, it would be interesting to examine an approach that Professor Todd Jick[22] suggests to map the commitment of key players to change. Building on the ideas of Beckhard and Harris,[23] he outlines an approach to map the minimum level of support required for a change programme to succeed. Figure 4.1 presents a sample commitment chart.

To prepare a commitment chart, the change leader first lists the key players whose commitment is essential for the success of the change effort. For each individual or group, O indicates the minimum commitment required for the change to occur. For example, A has to 'make the change happen', while it would

Figure 4.1: Sample Commitment Chart

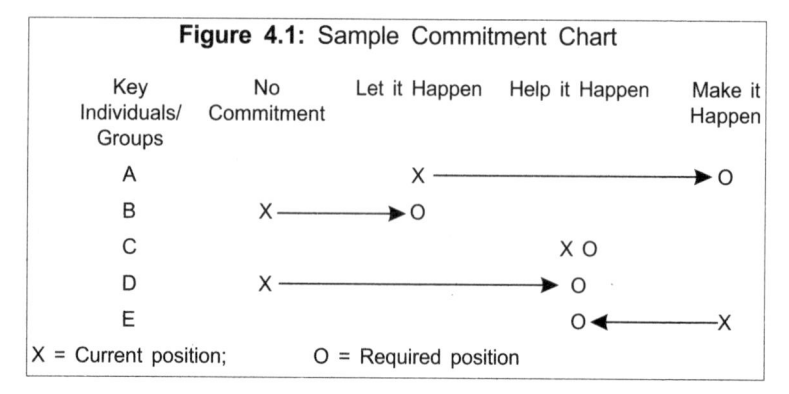

Key Individuals/ Groups	No Commitment	Let it Happen	Help it Happen	Make it Happen
A		X	→→→→→	O
B	X →→ O			
C			X O	
D	X →→→→→		O	
E			O ←———	X

X = Current position;   O = Required position

be sufficient for B to 'let it happen'. X denotes the change leaders' assessment of the present degree of commitment of key players. When X and O are in the same box (e.g. in the case of C) or when X exceeds O (as in the case of E), no additional efforts are needed to get the required commitment. For the others, change leaders need to evolve strategies to gain the minimum commitment required.

The third step in this task is to identify the interests of people whose support is needed. What do they care about? What are their concerns? Usually, in a change effort, opposition to change will arise due to a variety of reasons: (a) *loss of status quo*. The status quo may be very comfortable in terms of earning and relationships. People may experience change as giving up comforts and, therefore, may be opposed to it, (b) *loss of sense of competence*. People may feel insecure about performing effectively in a changed environment, (c) *threat to identity*. People may perceive the intended change as a threat to their values and self-image, (d) *uncertainty about the future*. The intended changes may be seen as leading to an uncertain future. This uncertainty can cause fear and anxiety, and (e) *negative consequences for others*. The intended changes may be seen as harming individuals that people care about or feel loyal to. Therefore, the changes may be opposed.

In analysing the context, an important last step is to evaluate how key people perceive the *alternatives* to change. If they do not embrace change, what are they likely to do instead? Once the key people are identified and their interests are understood,

Mobilising Support **169**

the manager can begin designing strategies for changing their mindsets.

CHANGING MINDSETS

There are four ways in which managers can alter people's mindsets about change:

1. They can alter people's incentives for change.
2. They can frame the change agenda in a way that evokes support.
3. They can influence people's perceptions of their alternatives to change.
4. They can engage in one-on-one negotiation to buy support.

We will examine the first three strategies in this section and discuss the fourth, separately, later in this chapter.

People's mindsets about change can be altered by introducing incentives to change and disincentives not to. Changing incentives will almost certainly lead to change in behaviour, but may not necessarily lead to change in attitudes. However, the foot-in-the door approach suggests that changes in attitudes can follow changes in behaviour. An organisation has a number of levers to alter incentives for change. These include the performance appraisal system, the compensation system, strategic plans, mission statements and annual budgets. These levers create expectations of reward based on desirable behaviours. Therefore, a manager may need to review and re-align some of these levers to produce incentives for change. Our experience suggests that positive incentives tend to work better than disincentives or punishments for not changing. Any changes to the organisational levers mentioned above must be communicated explicitly. Again, we recommend using an approach that is *open, transparent* and *inclusive* in redesigning incentive systems to promote change.

FRAMING CHANGE

Framing the change can also influence people's mindsets. The term *framing* refers to the use of arguments, examples and stories to create a favourable impression of the change issues facing the organisation. Framing helps people to identify their interests, which may be latent and diffused. It also helps people perceive their interest differently depending on how the change agenda is presented. There are some well-known framing techniques that managers can use in presenting their change agenda (presented in Table 4.4). Framing is a key leadership skill that managers need to develop for mobilising support in change initiatives. The purpose of framing is to present change as a choice that is easy to embrace for people in the organisation. While framing the change, managers need to be aware of research in social psychology that gives an insight into how people make choices. In general, people prefer choices that enable them to remain consistent with values and beliefs that they hold strongly. They also prefer choices that help them remain consistent with their prior commitments and obligations to others. In addition, people favour choices that preserve their sense of control, reputations and gain the approval of significant others such as opinion leaders, mentors, and experts.

Table 4.4: Techniques for Framing

Technique	What it Involves
Invoking the common good	This involves emphasising the collective benefits for the organisation and downplaying the costs to individuals. The manager may emphasise how the change will benefit the organisation as a whole in terms of increased market share, sales, profitability and growth
Linking to core values	This involves linking the change agenda to people's values about who they are or the values that define their self-identity. The change may be presented as being consistent with a company's tradition of producing high-quality products and services or as affirming the organisation's credibility and legitimacy in the community
Heightening concerns about loss or risk	This involves exploiting people's fears about potential losses to themselves and the organisation if the change is not implemented. This strategy is based on the psychological principle that people tend to be *loss-averse* (more sensitive to potential losses than to potential gains) and *risk-averse*

(*Contd.*)

Table 4.4: (*Contd.*)

Technique	What it Involves
	(prefer guaranteed gains to risky choices that may yield larger gains). Therefore, using this approach, the change can be presented as less risky and the status quo as more risky. The negative consequences of not changing can be highlighted.
Rejection and retreat	This strategy involves asking for a lot of changes initially and then settling for fewer changes. This tends to work because people's mindsets are 'anchored' on the initial request and they tend to view the subsequent move as concessions. However, the approach is potentially risky because people may become highly resistant to change when presented with the initial proposal for lot of changes.
Narrowing or broadening the focus	This involves presenting the choice of change either broadly or narrowly. When presented broadly, the change would be seen as part of a larger strategic change aimed at increasing the organisation's potential for growth. When presented narrowly, the change would be seen as an isolated initiative aimed at addressing some immediate problem.
Enlarging the pie	This involves presenting the change as a win-win choice—one that will benefit everyone in the organisation.
Neutralizing toxic issues	This involves addressing toxic issues such as potential job losses either by setting them aside for consideration later or by making up-front commitments to make people less anxious and more secure.
Inoculating against expected challenges	This involves presenting strong counter-arguments to refute potential arguments against change that may arise later in the organisation.
Providing a script for convincing others	This involves presenting the change in a way that helps the listeners to convince others in the organisation about change. This means that the arguments for change must be kept simple, compelling and lucid.

Source: Based on Watkins, M.D., *The Power to Persuade*, in Harvard Business School. #9-800-323. 2000: Boston, MA

172 Change Management

INFLUENCING PERCEPTIONS OF ALTERNATIVES

Influencing people's perceptions of their alternatives to change is another way to bring about change in their mindsets. This can be done in five ways:

➤ People can be exposed to *new options*. In a change management situation, it may be in the form of benchmarking the organisation against the best organisations in the industry—so that employees are exposed to alternative approaches to familiar tasks. This may induce them to view change in a different light

➤ The *change agenda can be controlled* to direct people's attention to specific change issues. One way of doing this is to use information selectively to define the problem and the organisation's options. Defining the need for change and the organisational choices for changing is a crucial strategic issue and can influence the outcome of change

As Managing Director of Delhi Metro, Sreedharan constantly emphasised that each day's delay on the project would cost Rs. 23 million. This figure was reinforced in communication so as not to let people's attention waver from any factor that could potentially lead to a delay in the completion of the project. This information kept all the organisational members on their toes. If there was a delay arising from a person not vacating his shop because of a disagreement on certain issue, or a contractor not progressing at the required pace because of cash flow problems, people were expected to quickly take charge of the issue and do the best possible under the circumstances. They had to remind themselves that by allowing the issue to drift through indecision, they would run the risk of losing a large amount

➤ The *'do nothing' option may be eliminated*. In an organisation, this can be eliminated through firm deadlines and time schedules for change

➤ The *'status quo' option may be eliminated* to favour change. In change management jargon, this is referred to the 'burning platform' approach to change. The origin of this term is from the allegedly true story of a worker on an offshore oil platform that caught fire. The worker, intent on saving his life, ran to the edge of the platform to jump into the sea. However, he hesitated when he saw the cold waters of the stormy sea surging 150 feet below him. Then he turned and saw the ball of fire advancing towards him and, preferring the uncertainty of the cold sea—to the certainty of burning to death—he jumped. The most celebrated example of this in history is the action of the Spanish conqueror Hernando Cortes, who ordered his men to burn the ships that carried them to shore in modern day Mexico. By eliminating the very option of retreat, Cortes effectively committed his men to war and—possibly—victory. This is also referred to as 'crossing the Rubicon,' where decision makers confront and overcome the mental barrier of making the final irrevocable commitment to a set of decisions, and then assume responsibility for the success or failure of the chosen course of action. This may be in the form of adopting new technology or a new strategy. Occasionally, a leader in an organisation may be tempted to 'manufacture' a crisis to turn their organisation into a 'burning platform' although this is not a good idea because it may adversely influence people's sense of personal efficacy. Having been pushed into a decision, people need to feel confident that they would be able to make the choices work

➤ *Alternatives to change may be explored and pruned to favour change.* This is a good way to elicit support for change in situations where change presents a difficult choice and has some unpleasant consequences such as plant closures and job losses. In such situations, it may be a good idea to let people try out alternative, less unpleasant options as long as the integrity of the larger change framework is not compromised, as demonstrated in a case illustration (Box 4.6). Change management is most contentious when it involves difficult choices. This is another crucial capability that managers need to have in effectively managing change

> **Box 4.6: Balancing Consideration and Closure in Decision-Making**
>
> When land acquisition for the Delhi Metro project ran into problems and controversies, raised by shopkeepers, affected by change and local politicians, a meeting with all the affected parties was convened with a view to sort issues and make appropriate decisions. Mrs. Sheila Dikshit, chief minister of Delhi, chaired the meeting. She was both, considerate and highly goal-oriented in her decision-making and communication.
>
> 'This project is very important for all of us in the city and we all have a responsibility to ensure its speedy completion,' she said. 'Mr. Sreedharan and his colleagues at DMRC have carefully worked out alternative locations for all the shops in such a way that minimum inconvenience would be caused. I have full confidence in their decisions. They have studied the pros and cons of each decision and have given us the best possible alternative. Their decision is final. But if there is any aspect of the decision that bothers you, and you have an alternative that is better for you and is acceptable to others, please tell me. As long as it fits within the framework of the Delhi Metro plan, I'll pass it on to Mr. Sreedharan. I am sure he would give it a fair consideration.' Mrs. Dikshit's fair and firm approach sent a powerful signal to local politicians that they should not interfere with the change; it bolstered the credibility of decision makers at Delhi Metro, and helped reach a timely closure on the issue.

MAKING DIFFICULT CHOICES

Often, change managers find themselves in a situation involving tough and unpopular decision-making. For instance, some one may be let go or transferred; some one's responsibility and authority may be curtailed; a department or plant may be shut down and so on. If the decision to be made is the right decision, then there is little choice for the manager. The decision needs to be made regardless of how unpopular the manager might become. However, tough decisions can be made acceptable by following some basic principles. In other words, it is possible to mobilise support even for tough decisions by following four guiding principles:

1. A basic human tendency is that people are very sensitive to equity and fairness. A decision-making process perceived

as being equitable and fair, can ensure that even the affected people accept the consequences of tough decision. Therefore, while making tough decisions, managers must ensure that the process is *open, transparent* and *inclusive*. Affected people must be given a chance to share their views and opinions and the manager must ensure that these people feel that they have been heard. The manager must also demonstrate that the decision was made after considerable thought, debate and deliberation. There is nothing like thoughtless, arbitrary decision making to fuel and unite opposition to change.
2. When people are involved in the diagnosis of organisational problems, they are more likely to support tough decisions for change. Managers must therefore ensure that people are included in the diagnosis phase of appreciating change, if the organisational change is likely to be painful. Sometimes, actual involvement does not occur even when sincere attempts are made to get people involved. Box 4.7 presents such a situation and what leaders did to overcome the initial hurdle.
3. When faced with tough choices, it is always a good idea to consult as widely as possible before making a decision. Good consultation is essentially about listening to people. In change management jargon, the term 'active listening' involves demonstrating interest and curiosity in what people are saying, asking questions to clarify, summarising what people have said to signal understanding, and taking notes. Before unravelling his Nissan revival plan in 1999, Carlos Ghosn spent about three months talking to various people to identify change issues facing Nissan. In his own words[24]

I met people, inspected factories, and visited suppliers in Japan and in Mexico, the United States, and Europe, as well as Thailand and other countries of Southeast Asia. I asked people what they thought was going right, what they thought was going wrong, and what they would suggest to make things better. I was trying to arrive at an analysis of the situation that wouldn't be static but would identify what we could do to improve the company's performance. It was a period of intensive, active listening. I took notes, I accumulated documents that contained very precise assessments of the different situations we had to deal with, and I drew up my own personal summaries of what I learned. In the course of those three months, I must have met more than a thousand people.

Box 4.7: Unclogging the Communication and Involvement Channels

The leadership of AVT Natural Products Company was keen to strengthen dialogue with workers. The unit was a part of the AVT group, which had been in operation for 75 years and operated plantations. The plantation culture was highly traditional with a huge divide between senior officers and workers. This traditional culture also cast its shadow on AVT Natural Products. But for strategic reasons, the new unit was faced with the necessity of getting into nutraceuticals market that was highly demanding. The leadership was keen to create a very different culture where there could be free and frank exchange of views and ideas between management and workers.

To initiate a dialogue process, 'Open House' sessions involving all the workers were planned. The first meeting began with senior executives making a few opening remarks and inviting people to share any concerns or views they may have: but there was a deafening silence. Even after repeated requests, no one came forward with any question or comment. Before the second meeting, the president talked to a few carefully identified individuals about the importance of opening the channels of communication. He urged them to set an example. In the second meeting, after the initial remarks by senior executives, one of these individuals raised an issue about why the president was given an expensive car when workers were being given the message of cost control. The president was taken aback, but he gave a response as best as he could in the spirit of dialogue. During the initial period, comments continued to be hostile and critical. But as the leaders persisted with the meetings without getting defensive, the attitudes of people started to change; they began to come up with valuable feedback and ideas. The open house sessions became extremely important in the process of cultural transformation and helped the unit realise its challenging strategic goals.

4. Giving people what they ask for in implementing a tough decision is another way of ensuring that the decision will be accepted and supported. There is nothing more disconcerting than to have the responsibility to implement a tough decision with inadequate resources.

PERSUADING INDIRECTLY

In large organisations, it is not feasible to persuade people through one-on-one communication. Particularly, if the organisation is multi-locational, persuasion has to be through indirect means such as memos, speeches and newsletters. Change leaders also need to build capabilities in persuading others indirectly. The following guidelines can help managers be effective in indirect persuasion:

1. *Neutralise the power of informal networks:* Change leaders need to develop reliable communication channels to communicate their change agenda directly to employees in the organisation. Otherwise, people will rely on informal grapevine that can distort the change message either unintentionally or deliberately. In either case, employees may develop unfavourable perceptions of the change agenda leading to opposition and resistance. Communication channels such as employee forums, town meetings and special newsletters can counter the grapevine and informal networks. Change leaders must be particularly careful in not withholding bad news because such news gets out very quickly into the grapevine.
2. *Repeat the message:* Focus and repetition are crucial for effective communication. This means that the change agenda should consist of only a limited number (two or three, at best) of themes. These themes need to be repeated and reinforced through different communication channels.
3. *Match the medium to the message:* Speeches and videoconferences are ideal to communicate vision and values; these media are also appropriate to inspire people to embrace change. On the other hand, data, graphs and charts are best conveyed in the written form—such as

memos, newsletters and web pages. Change leaders must think very carefully about appropriate media before communicating their change agenda.
4. *Simplify the message:* The change agenda needs to be conveyed through a framework that is conceptually simple and easy to grasp. Yet, change leaders must avoid the trap of oversimplification. Oversimplified messages sound trite and faddish and can significantly reduce the credibility of the communicator. Simple frameworks are easy to remember, and are also powerful in framing the change agenda to mobilise support.
5. *Create a new story about change:* Stories constitute a powerful medium to mobilise support. People are more likely to remember stories rather than facts and figures. Stories are also more effective in persuading people to alter their perceptions of change. Therefore, change leaders need to be able to craft their change agenda in the form of a story.
6. *Build personal credibility:* Change leaders who are respected, considered trustworthy and competent are more likely to be effective in persuading their employees to embrace change. Personal credibility is built on the foundation of consistency. Change leaders must demonstrate consistency between their thoughts, words and behaviour. Inconsistent, self-serving behaviour can severely erode the credibility of a leader.

NEGOTIATING FOR CHANGE

Occasionally, in any change effort, despite following the suggestions discussed above, a manager may run into another kind of roadblock: he/she may require the cooperation and support of managers in other departments and divisions, but may have no formal authority over them. Attempts to influence or persuade them to support change may fail because the change may involve a perceived loss for the other managers; this could be loss in status, power, authority, prestige or perquisites. Under these circumstances, it is not in the self-interest of those managers to support the change. Situations like these make the management of change explicitly political because, in order to gain their support, the manager may have to do some bargaining. In other words, when influence and persuasion fail, a manager may need to mobilise support through negotiation. Many managers, particularly those with technical backgrounds, find this process distasteful because it seems irrational. However, there is little that is irrational in these situations and they arise out of calculated self-interest. Just as there are sound scientific principles to influence and persuade people, negotiation and bargaining can also be based on logic and science. While part of negotiation—like management—is art, most of it is amenable to scientific analysis. In this section, we present some of the principles and tactics of negotiation based on the Programme on Negotiation (PON) at the Harvard Law School[25]—considered to be one of the premier interdisciplinary research centres on negotiation.

Preparation is the essence of being a good negotiator. Once you realise that you would not get someone's support without offering something in return, you need to prepare yourself for the negotiation. The Harvard Project on negotiation is based on a coherent framework of principled negotiation. The framework suggests that managers prepare themselves for negotiation by answering seven questions. As a manager, if you find yourself in a negotiating situation, you need to ask yourself the following questions[26]:

1. *What will you do if you can't reach an agreement?* Negotiation researchers call this your BATNA[27] (**B**est **A**lternative **T**o a **N**egotiated **A**greement). Can the organisational change still be implemented? What is your preferred course if you are unable to secure commitment to change from the manager with whom you propose to negotiate? More importantly, what is the maximum that you can offer this manager (resources, promise of future support, staff, equipment and so on) in return for his or her commitment to change? It may be a good idea to think this through and list all your alternatives.
2. *Who are the real parties in the negotiation?* Does the person you intend to negotiate with have the authority and power

to commit resources to change? Is this person the 'real' party in negotiation? Does he or she require the approval of a manager above? Will negotiating with this person increase or decrease the chances of getting a deal from another manager? This is a crucial question because you may discover opportunities and problems that were not evident before.
3. *What are the interest and priorities of the parties involved?* It may be a good idea to ask yourself why you are proposing to negotiate with this person. What are your goals? What are you willing to trade-off? Similarly, what are the interests and goals of the other party? Here, again, you may be surprised to discover new opportunities and potential problems for the change effort. We can gain further insights in this, by considering the situation presented in Box 4.8.

Analysing the situation (Box 4.8) in an interesting article, Professor Sebenius writes that—in describing the dilemma and the decision—his purpose is to highlight the significant differences between the perspectives of Perkins and his team members. The campaign team members were paralysed by the anxious obsession with their own side of the problem, and their pathetic BATNA. But Perkins recognised the essence of the negotiator's central task: understand the interests and priorities of the other party and shape how the other side sees its problem such that it chooses what you want. He looked beyond price, positions, and common ground and used Moffett's different interests to frame the photographer's choice as 'the value of publicity and recognition'.
4. *How can negotiation create value for both parties?* You need to devise a negotiation strategy that ensures that the change is supported and results in some gain for the other party to the negotiation. This is a difficult process because both parties usually want to capture the maximum value from a negotiation. Quite unlike in the incident described above, it may require you to yield by disclosing information so that you can brainstorm about alternatives with the other party. Yet, establishing a problem-solving atmosphere in a

Box 4.8: Resolving a Tangle during Presidential Campaign[28]

It is the final lap of a hard-fought campaign for the presidential election in the United States. A campaign team has planned to clinch the crowd's votes by distributing an elegant brochure with a nice photograph of the presidential candidate on the cover. Three million copies are printed and are ready for distribution. At the proverbial last minute, a campaign team member notices that the photograph is copyrighted, and the copyright is with a studio in Chicago. The team quickly realises the enormity of the problem because this would mean a three million dollar payout to the studio, at the rate of one dollar per reproduction. The campaign budget would be unable to afford this. At the same time, there is not enough time to reprint the pamphlet with a non-copyrighted photograph.

The team realises that if the campaign does not use the pamphlets at all, it would damage the president's election prospects. The choice of ignoring the copyright simply does not exist, since this would expose the campaign to a liability for an unaffordable sum, and a real possibility of a scandal erupting very close to the election.

The team concludes that there is no option other than negotiating with the studio owner, and reach a quick and reasonable settlement. As preparation for the negotiation, the team members at Chicago are contacted to get some background information on the owner of the studio. But the news received from Chicago turns out to be highly disturbing: the studio owner is a person likely to be singularly focused on making money. In a state of desperation, the campaign team members approach the campaign manager and nervously explain the problem. What would you do if you were the campaign manager?

Professor James Sebenius has written about the incident described above, which actually occurred in 1912. Theodore Roosevelt was the presidential candidate; the copyright was with Moffett Studios, Chicago; and the campaign manager was George Perkins. As it turns out, when Perkins learnt of the problem, he lost no time summoning his stenographer to dispatch the following cable to Moffett Studios: 'We are planning to distribute millions of pamphlets with Roosevelt's picture on the cover. It will be a great publicity for the studio whose photograph we use. How much will you pay us to use yours? Respond immediately.' Apparently he received a quick reply from Moffett: 'We've never done this before, but we'd be pleased to offer $250'. Reportedly, Perkins accepted—without bargaining for more!

bargaining situation is not easy and depends on the level of trust that you can create in yourself.
5. *What are the roadblocks to potential agreement and how can they be eliminated?* There could be behavioural, psychological or interpersonal barriers to agreement. Behavioural barriers may include inappropriate negotiating strategies by both parties to the negotiation. The other party may not be willing to concede anything in the hope of getting maximum benefits, which could frustrate you and lead you to terminating the negotiation. You could also be not willing to concede much, which in turn could frustrate the other party. Interpersonal barriers include lack of trust or communication difficulties. Both parties may get very emotional during negotiations leading to defensiveness and hostility, which is a psychological barrier. There could be organisational barriers as well. Those higher up in the organisation may question your agreement or deal. The agreement may violate some aspects of your company policy.
6. *How much power and influence does each party have over the negotiation process and its outcomes?* Negotiation researchers suggest that you can answer this question by looking at the architecture of a negotiation. Can you, for instance, redefine the parties to the negotiation? Can you bring people from the top to enhance your power? Can you negotiate directly with the other party's boss? Another aspect of architecture is time. Can you set deadlines for agreement? Another way to exert power is to make credible threats. Can you convey to the other party that not supporting the change may, in fact, diminish their interests? This is risky and will invite retaliation by the other party and should be considered as a last resort.
7. *What is the right thing to do in the negotiation?* Morality and ethics are important in all aspects of management. As we discussed earlier, you need to be both practical and ethical. Ethical aspects involve honesty, equity, force, impact on others and conflict of interest. Honesty relates to the extent to which you are willing to disclose your interests and options to the other party. Even if you can't be totally

honest, do not lie to the other party. Equity relates to the fairness of the agreement. What would be a fair deal for the other party? Force relates to the potential use of threats and sanctions in the negotiation. While some amount of pressure is legitimate in negotiations, you need to be aware of the limits to the potential use of force. The key question here is, what are the alternatives that the other party has? Impact on others relates to how the agreement will affect others in the organisation. Will the agreement benefit or disadvantage others? This is again related to the fairness issue and you need to include the concerns of others who are not party to the negotiation. The last issue of conflict of interest relates to the dilemma between what you think is fair and what the organisation requires you to do in the negotiation. You may be sympathetic to the other party's concerns but may have no choice other than implementing change that will disadvantage the other party. These ethical concerns have no easy answers. They make the negotiation process hard but they also help you to redefine your values and principles.

These questions provide a rigorous framework for principled negotiation but as Wheeler states[29]:

Rigorous negotiation analysis is necessary for success, but it alone is not sufficient. Strategy must be implemented with skill and insight. The ability to listen and persuade is highly valuable. So is patience (and sometimes even humour). Moreover, because negotiation is interactive, success is also contingent on your counterparts' attitudes and creative ability. Thus your own negotiation strategy should encourage constructive behaviour from the people with whom you deal.

SOME TIPS ON MOBILISING SUPPORT FOR CHANGE MANAGERS

Despite using the principles of influence, social networks and negotiation, change efforts in an organisation can falter for different reasons. There has been a great deal of interest in finding out why people are so unwilling to step out of their comfort zones and accept change. What are some of the major impediments to change?

1. *People believing that the change effort is yet another fad:* Over a period, many employees have come to perceive different change programmes as fads because they associate these with previously failed initiatives. As a result, they do not pay attention to the merits of the arguments. Change induces dissonance, and people often reduce the resulting stress by reverting to previously held assumptions, beliefs, and behaviours.
2. *People who believe that change agents are not credible or trustworthy:* Employees tend to view the strength of the change idea by associating it with the person who advocates that position. In other words, if the change manager is credible, the idea is seen as convincing. On the other hand, when the manager is perceived as untrustworthy, people tend to reject the change ideas.
3. *People who have difficulty unlearning old ideas and approaches:* Most often, people do not know how to stop what they have already been doing. When they are faced with uncertainty and ambiguity, they feel a sense of loss of control and this leads them to persist with their existing methods and approaches.
4. *People who have difficulty learning new patterns of behaviour:* When people face unfamiliar situations, they often fail to comprehend the complexities of the situation. They may also feel apprehensive that if they try out new behaviours and fail, they would attract criticism. Faced with a fear of failure and believing that change would make little difference, they may refuse to invest in learning new methods and approaches.
5. *People who feel that change threatens their identity:* When faced with crises or threats, people tend to uphold their pride rather than appreciating the learning challenge that it offers. There is great comfort in existing belief structures, as these constitute one's personal identity. Any attempt to

change behaviour may be seen as a challenge to that identity. As a result, it generates resistance to change.

Mobilising support for change requires a blend of logic, emotions, and values. The change manager should keep the following points in mind:

1. *Developing clarity about the target audience:* In an effort to achieve acceptance of any change idea, it is very important to clearly understand who the relevant stakeholders are, what are their identities, their aspirations, their values, and their influence in the organisation. The target audience is never a homogeneous group. There would be people who may be ready to support the change ideas quickly, people who oppose change no matter how sensible the ideas are, and people who are willing to listen but should not be taken for granted. A change manager should identify the real interests of these sub-groups and should tailor the communication and persuasion effort accordingly. In other words, the change manager should be sensitive to the fact that there would be multiple views and perceptions in an organisation and it is important to be clear as to what these are.
2. *Getting people involved:* When a change manager begins the change campaign by making a strong presentation and supporting it with huge data, there is a danger that employees at the receiving end may become mere spectators and sceptics. At the same time, it is not realistic to expect that people would volunteer themselves to engage in defining a change initiative. What is most useful in such a situation is a 'foot-in-the-door' approach. This involves asking people to make a small initial commitment, which may be in the nature of asking their views on the present situation and discussing possible courses of action. Over a period of time, these small commitments could be extended to sustain larger change objectives. This approach is particularly useful to attract sceptics to the change programme.
3. *Crafting the message:* A primary process in the influence effort is not change in attitude towards an object, but change

in definition and meaning of the object. Once meaning changes, attitudes change accordingly. A change manager should present the idea in such a manner that it evokes sufficient curiosity among members to explore it further. The message should be simple, but clear enough in its scope. Rather than a conclusive statement, it should invite people for a dialogue. People tend to be more attracted towards stories and symbols than hard numerical data. A change manager should be able to make use of these soft dimensions of relationships to gain attention to the change idea.
4. *Timing the campaign:* Many ideas are rejected because they are presented at a wrong time. A change manager should first use informal meetings to generate the need for improving present levels of performance and make people receptive to new suggestions. Change ideas should be presented only when people are willing to engage in a dialogue process. This is very similar to a gardener first preparing the soil before sowing the seeds.
5. *Sustaining the momentum:* Mobilising support for change is never a one-time activity. It takes considerable amount of time to get people involved and committed to the change idea. It would be best for people with high expertise and credibility to lead the change. People listen to those who have expertise while framing their position. Then those people should be identified who favour the change idea and they should be helped to articulate their views in public. People tend to stick to their positions that are made in public.

It is equally important to create situations where people, who believe in potential benefits of the idea, interact with others at the same level. When people from the same level praise an idea, it has greater persuasive power than seniors pushing it from the top. In the whole process of change implementation, it is important to make people feel significant and enhance their sense of control over the situation.

To conclude, people do accept new ideas and commit themselves to change when they genuinely believe in it. Hence, it is important to relate the idea of change to realities of the employees with as much clarity as possible. To be effective as a change manager, you have to have firm faith in the idea of change. The idea has to be pursued continually and consistently with a sense of optimism to gain the acceptance for new ideas in the organisation.

NOTES AND REFERENCES

1. Axelrod, R. H. (2000). *Terms of Engagement: Changing the way we change organisations.* San Francisco: Berrett-Koehler Publishers.
2. The word paradigm is another one of those overused expressions in management. It means a set of assumptions, concepts, values, and practices that constitutes a way of viewing reality for the community that shares them, especially in an intellectual discipline (www.thesaurus.com)
3. For economic arguments on this perspective, see Sen, A. (2001). *Development as Freedom.* New York: Alfred A. Knopf; Stiglitz, J. E. (2002). Participation and development: Perspectives from the comprehensive development paradigm. *Review of Development Economics,* 6(2): pp. 163–182.
4. Glidewell, John C. (1970). *Choice Points: Essays on the Emotional Problems of Living with People.* MIT Press: Cambridge, Mass.
5. Conger, Jay, (1998). The Necessary Art of Persuasion. *Harvard Business Review,* May.
6. Gladwell, M. (2000). *The Tipping Point: How Little Things can make a Big Difference.* Boston: Little Brown and Company.
7. Ibid., p. 67.
8. http://www.nuce.boun.edu.tr/glossary.html
9. Baum, D. (2000). *Lightning in a Bottle.* Chicago, IL: Dearborn.
10. Cialdini, R. B. (1993). *Influence: The Psychology of Persuasion.* New York: William Morrow and Company; Cialdini, R. B. (2000). *Influence: Science and Practice* (Fourth ed.). Boston: Allyn & Bacon.
11. Cialdini, R. B. (2001). Harnessing the science of persuasion. *Harvard Business Review, October,* pp. 72–79.
12. Francis, D. R. (July 8, 2003). Moves afoot to curb CEO salaries. *Christian Science Monitor.*
13. Larkin, T. J. & Larkin, S. (1996). Reaching and changing frontline employess. *Harvard Business Review, January–February,* pp. 24–42.

14. Cialdini, R.B. *Harnessing the science of persuasion.* Ibid. 2001. October: pp. 72–79.
15. This is often the reason why most of us despise politicians who fail to honour their public commitments.
16. Yates, J. (2001). Persuasion: What Research Tells Us. Unpublished manuscript, MIT, Sloan School of Management.
17. A detailed account of the case is given in: V. Nilakant & S. Ramnarayan (1998). *Managing Organisational Change.* Delhi: Response Books, pp. 326–333.
18. Ibid.
19. Bashein, Barbara J. & Markus, M. Lynne, (1997). A Credibility Equation for IT Specialists. *Sloan Management Review*: Summer.
20. Ibid., p. 37.
21. This section is based on Watkins, M. D. (2000). *The Power to Persuade.* Boston: Harvard Business School. Teaching Note #9-800-323.
22. Jick, Todd, (1991). Implementing Change, Teaching Note. Harvard Business School: 9-491-114
23. Beckhard, Richard & Harris, Richard, (1987). *Organisation Transitions*, second edition. Reading, MA: Addison-Wesley, pp. 94–95.
24. Ghosn, C. & Ries, P. (2005). *Shift: Inside Nissan's Historic Revival.* New York: Currency Doubleday, pp. 93–94.
25. http://www.pon.harvard.edu/main/home/index.php3
26. Wheeler, M. (2002). *Negotiation Analysis: An Introduction.* Boston: Harvard Business School. Teaching Note # 9-801-156.
27. Fisher, R., Ury, W., & Patton, B. (1991). *Getting to YES: Negotiating Agreement Without Giving In* (Second ed.). New York: Penguin.
28. Sebenius, James K. Six Habits of Merely Effective Negotiators. *Harvard Business Review*, 79, No. 4 (April 2001): pp. 87–95.
29. Wheeler, M. (2002). *Negotiation Analysis: An Introduction.* Boston: Harvard Business School. Teaching Note # 9-801-156; p. 14.

CHAPTER 5

Executing Change

OVERVIEW

This chapter deals with one of the most critical aspects of change management—implementing change. No matter how well a certain change is appreciated and planned, if it is not executed competently to produce results then the change effort would end up as a failure—irrespective of how well it is supported by the organisation. Many change programmes flounder at the implementation stage. We begin with a case study, by looking at the causes of implementation failure. Then, we present a framework for executing change based on two key assumptions. We identify three critical tasks for change leaders to ensure focus and energy during execution: (a) creating cross-functional linkages in the organisation; (b) aligning policies, procedures and removing structural impediments to performance and change; and (c) creating new routines for continuous improvements and innovations. In attending to these critical tasks, change leaders should create the right context for the human aspects of change to be effectively addressed. Our simple execution framework is based on literature and case studies of change. It offers practical guidelines for implementing change in organisations.

CHALLENGES OF EXECUTION

In terms of our model, a successful change effort requires: (a) adequate appreciation and planning, (b) sufficient support by employees, (c) competent execution by managers, and (d) change managers with appropriate skill sets and capabilities. In a classic paper published in the *Harvard Business Review*, the change management guru John Kotter[1] makes a similar point. Based on his experience, Kotter claims that less than one-third of all organisational change efforts are successful in producing anticipated results. He offers eight reasons for this low success rate. According to him, organisations that fail to produce results after undertaking change do so because managers in these organisations do not:

1. establish a sense of urgency among employees,
2. form a powerful guiding coalition for implementing change,
3. create a powerful vision to energise employees,
4. communicate their vision effectively to employees,
5. empower employees to act on their vision,
6. plan for and create short-term wins,
7. consolidate improvements and produce still more change, and
8. institutionalise new approaches.

Kotter's eight reasons are consistent with our model of change management. His first four reasons deal with appreciating change and mobilising support in our model and the last reason relates to creating capability for change. Remaining three reasons concern the implementation of change. Kotter argues that there are three prerequisites to effective execution of change, relating to *empowerment, motivation* and *consolidation*.

Let us understand the three factors in some detail. First, employees need to be *empowered* to act on the vision that has been created. They need to be freed from existing constraints, both mental and structural, that produces under-performance. Second, any organisation-wide change effort is likely to be long-drawn and can sap employee energy. Therefore, employee energy levels need to be continually sustained through constant *motivation*. According to Kotter, one method to sustain motivation in long-term changes is to celebrate the achievement of milestones along the way. Third, in an organisation-wide change process comprising multiple initiatives, it is easy to lose focus by losing track of the big picture. Therefore, it is necessary to *consolidate gains* and maintain the momentum of change. Kotter's reasons for low success rate of change efforts and his prescriptions for effective implementation of change are eminently reasonable, but they are rather general. We need a more in-depth understanding of the challenges of execution.

Professor Todd Jick has written extensively on organisational change. His research conducted on change management in 93 organisations identified the following pitfalls in implementation of change[2]:

- Implementation took more time than originally allocated
- Major problems surfaced during implementation
- Coordination of implementation activities was not effective enough
- Competing activities and crises detracted attention from implementation
- Capabilities and skills of employees involved in implementation were not sufficient
- Training and instruction given to lower-level employees were not adequate
- Uncontrollable factors in the environment had an adverse impact on implementation

In other words, organisations are almost always underprepared for change. They underestimate the time and resources needed for change implementation. They do not pay adequate attention to coordination and integration of activities. They fail to invest in building capabilities for change execution. We shall consider the last point, on capability building, separately in the next chapter.

For now, try to imagine a typical change management scenario in most organisations. Employees are exhorted to change but not enough resources are provided to them. Managers in charge of implementing the changes are under-resourced in terms of time, money, people and capabilities. They are under pressure to both keep current activities going and to implement change. After a while, they are in—in change management jargon—the *fire-fighting* mode. Most of their time and energy is wasted in dealing with crises created by faulty implementation of change. It is not surprising that both managers implementing change and employees experiencing change under such conditions feel exhausted and fatigued. Over a period of time, they may become cynical and may feel demotivated.

Lawrence Hrebiniak of the Wharton School at the University of Pennsylvania offers a simple yet elegant framework to conceptualise the challenges of executing change. According to him, the nature of change effort depends on two factors: (a) size of the change problem or content of change, and (b) time available for change.[3] The size of the problem could be large (enterprise-level change) or small (changing a unit/system/procedure). The time available could be short or long, giving rise to four change scenarios (Figure 5.1).

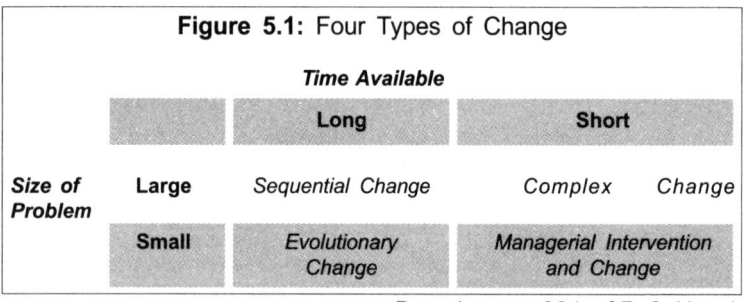

Figure 5.1: Four Types of Change

	Time Available	
	Long	**Short**
Size of Problem — **Large**	Sequential Change	Complex Change
Small	Evolutionary Change	Managerial Intervention and Change

Based on p. 231 of Ref. No. 4

Managerial interventions and changes are relatively easy to execute compared to sequential and complex changes. Evolutionary change, as the term implies, occurs by itself. The real challenge in change management is when the size of problem is large. A large change agenda coupled with short timeframe is the most difficult type of organisational change that managers can face. *Complex change*, as the term implies, is the most difficult challenge in change management. We now examine this challenge in some detail.

Repetitive Change Syndrome: Before we examine the specific challenges posed by complex change, let us look at a popular myth that leads to simultaneous elimination of old routines and establishment of new routines. We'll also see why this complex change tends to actually put organisations in great peril. Complex change runs into problems when chief executives and senior managers initiate it without carefully thinking about how to manage and implement such change effectively. They may base their approach on a faulty assumption that *change is good and more change is better.*

One of the most critical voices against the 'change is good, more change is better' logic is that of Eric Abrahamson, a Professor in Columbia University's Business School in the United States. He argues that this logic has led organisations to engage in what he calls the 'repetitive change syndrome.'

According to Abrahamson, this logic has had three outcomes. First, it leads to the motto of 'creative destruction', which argues that effective organisational changes need to be discontinuous by renouncing the past. Second, it justifies this by arguing that the only way to survive is to undergo destructive change, and that incremental change is never enough. Third, the increased stress and pressure on employees is justified by the motto 'no pain, no change.'

This logic has been repeatedly reinforced in a surfeit of popular books on change management. For example, *Who Moved My Cheese?* became a bestseller by claiming to offer 'an amazing way to deal with change in your work and in your life' through the parable of four mice. The moral of this story is: be eager and willing to adapt to all changes. While this advice may be valid under certain circumstances, the unthinking extension of this logic to human beings in organisational settings can have disastrous consequences. As Abrahamson brilliantly argues, this logic has led many organisations over the last 20 years, particularly in the United States, to engage in repeated and revolutionary changes *and therefore perish.*

Abrahamson[5] identifies three symptoms of the repetitive change syndrome: (a) *initiative overload,* (b) *change-related chaos,* and (c) *employee cynicism and burnout.* Initiative *overload* refers to the launching of more change-related initiatives than the organisation can handle. *Change-related chaos*, according to Abrahamson is 'the state of upheaval that results when so many waves of initiatives have washed through the organisation that hardly anyone knows which change he or she is implementing or why.'[6] Managers and employees tend to lose sight of the big picture. In other words, the change focus becomes diffused. *Employee cynicism is often a symptom of burnout* – where employees experience both low and negative energy. Repetitive change syndrome has corrosive effects on both individuals and the organisation. Individuals experience burnout and become cynical about management and change. The organisation's capacity to engage in further changes is severely eroded with every additional episode of change. In simple terms, it is not possible for burnt out managers and employees to produce effective change.

Dynamic Complexity: Let us return to the issue of what makes complex change difficult to manage. The challenge arises from a phenomenon called *dynamic complexity*—an idea we examined in chapter 3, where we noted that when a manager faces a large number of variables and factors, he/she is facing *static* complexity. Dynamic complexity arises in a system that has the following three characteristics: *feedback loops, time lag* and *non-linearity in the system.*

Let us look at a simple illustration of *feedback loops*. Imagine that a business firm has lowered the price of a product to enhance market share. However, this has led competitors to react and lower the prices of their products too. Thus, the original goal of enhancing market share has been nullified. Thus actions have both intended and unintended effects. When managers react and take corrective actions, a feedback loop may be set up that prevents the actions from yielding the desired results. In a complex system, there would be multiple feedback loops operating. Sometimes decision makers initiate actions and assume that the intended effects would occur. When they fail to monitor the effects of their actions in a systematic way, the realisation that their actions have not worked out may come too late.

Time lags refer to time intervals between when managers take decisions and when the results are achieved. In other words, a manager may do something today but the results may not be visible immediately. For example, an organisation may increase the amount it spends on advertising but there may not be any immediate effect on sales. The sales increase may occur many months later. During the intervening period, decision makers may not be able to determine if the advertising is working as intended.

Let us examine what *non-linearity in the system* refers to. Sometimes the relationship between cause and effect is not linear. In other words, constant increases in one factor (cause) do not result in proportionately constant increases in another factor (effect). In non-linear relationships, a small increase in one factor can result in a disproportionately large effect on another factor. For example, when a firm prices its product slightly over its competitors' prices, it may experience a small drop in market share. However, another small increase may result in a disproportionately large drop in market share. People think in linear terms, and so non-linearity poses considerable cognitive challenges.

The three characteristics—feedback loops, time lag and non-linearity—make a system or an organisation dynamically complex.[7] Such systems are challenging because they are difficult to understand and predict; specifically, they pose three problems for managers. First, since too many things are happening simultaneously, dynamically complex systems are difficult to coordinate and control. Second, such systems are difficult to understand and, therefore, cause-effect relationships are difficult, if not impossible, to predict and perceive. Third, because cause-effect relationships are difficult to predict and perceive, managers are unable to learn effectively from their experience. Dynamic complexity is what makes complex change most challenging. We illustrate the challenges of execution with a case study of unsuccessful change in an Indian organisation.

CASE STUDY OF A FAILED CHANGE

To illustrate the problems and challenges in executing complex change, we present a case of a large Indian organisation in the public sector—we refer to it as PSU. To cope with a deregulated environment, this large engineering organisation constituted new Business Planning Teams (BPTs) in each of its three major plants located across India. A group of line managers were selected from different operations departments and finance and accounts, and transferred to the newly formed department. The new groups were expected to initiate business planning for the respective plants. Each of these managers had spent about 20 years in his or her function, and was at the level of assistant general manager. An individual at the level of deputy general manager was made the leader of the team. This was an important corporate initiative, and so the initial formation of the group received wide attention at the top levels. We examine the experience of one of the three BPTs to draw lessons on execution.

In a sellers' market prior to deregulation, the PSU had largely been involved in optimising its facilities and planning the production. In such a scenario, there was minimal interface with functions like marketing and costing. There was little attention to development of new products and value-added products. BPT was expected to address all these problems and help the organisation gear up for the emerging competitive scenario. The newly formed group was assigned separate office space. The members felt quite enthusiastic about taking up the challenge. Unfortunately the initial euphoria did not last too long. The group started running into one hurdle after another with unerring regularity.

In the PSU, traditionally it was the production-planning department that was considered very powerful. This was a large department, headed by a general manager. The production-planning department did not take kindly to the newly formed BPT. The new group just was not able to get any information or support from the larger department. While even a large department like the production-planning department reported to the executive director (ED), who was the head of operations, the BPT reported directly to the managing director (MD), who was the overall head of the plant. This was done to ensure that business planning received attention at the highest levels. It was also done to clearly signal that business planning involved interface among all key functions of the organisation. While the underlying concept was good, it created enormous difficulties for the new group in practice.

The PSU had a strong hierarchical culture. Given the yawning gap in the status between the deputy general manager (DGM) heading the BPT and the MD, there were huge social difficulties in getting an appointment with the boss. While someone like the ED could walk directly into the boss's office, the DGM seemed to be waiting forever outside in the secretary's office to meet the MD. This created a number of roadblocks in doing work.

A few vignettes from the functioning of the new system illustrate these roadblocks. For example, the DGM in charge of the BPT wanted formal approval to buy a copying machine. When he sent a proposal, the MD returned the note with a query. Typically such small approvals did not go to the MD, but the DGM did not have an alternative within the existing working arrangement to obtain approval from any other senior executive. To address the MD's query, the DGM put together some analysis for his proposal. But when he went to discuss the matter, the MD pointed out that his query was different and that it had not been answered. The ball was back in the DGM's court, yet neither the problem nor the solution was clear to him. Thus, with decisions getting delayed, the work of the group became increasingly complex and frustrating.

The BPT put together a proposal for a new product, but when it was presented, the MD remarked that it was not practicable. Then he loudly wondered as to whether the group should be doing such projects in the first place. Actually the MDs themselves were somewhat unclear as to how to utilise the new function. When the nervous DGM asked him as to what he would suggest as a project, the MD did not openly share the haziness in his thinking. As he had participated in some deliberations pertaining to social forestry a few days earlier, he remarked that they could possibly explore a social forestry project. The DGM and his group did not have any background in this area. They had little clarity with regard to the nature and extent of details that would make sense for pursuing such a project at that time. Nevertheless, they all worked long hours for a couple of weeks, and prepared a report based on some secondary sources and submitted it. The report was ignored and the group did not know how they could follow up the matter. In any case, they had not come up with any concrete ideas in the report and were themselves not too convinced about their report.

Then the BPT started on a proposal for value added products, and needed some market data. When they sought market-related data from the marketing function, they were informed that the market research reports were confidential and could not be shared. The group considered approaching the MD to intervene to persuade the marketing department to release the data but did not pursue that path, as they were unsure if the MD would have the patience to listen to their problems and then offer support. Instead they had a team meeting to think of a way out of the organisational and social barricades erected by the absence of inter-functional and inter-level communication and co-ordination.

During the team meeting, a member remarked that a customer meet had been organised a year earlier by the finishing department of the plant. In that meet, the participants had completed a feedback questionnaire that the department had prepared. The questionnaire responses had not been worked on after the customer meet. As the team had ready access to the data, these were obtained. It was felt that a statistical package was required to analyse the data and a group member got busy with searching for the package. This was a poor solution as the data had only been gathered from a rather small sample of customers in only a couple of market segments. But these limitations were ignored and the team members busily pursued their pseudo-solutions.

In the meanwhile, the individual from the Finance and Accounts function was becoming concerned about continuing in the new group. He felt that he would lose his professional edge and might be sidelined in future promotions. Quietly, he spoke to the head of finance and moved back to the parent function. The group did not get a replacement.

When reviews were organised, the group put together presentations based on the analysis of whatever market and cost information they had access to. It was very easy for others in the group to pinpoint flaws in the analyses and in the proposed actions. Given the culture of the organisation, the real concerns and difficulties were not voiced in the review meeting. With real issues not getting surfaced and dealt with, there was little progress resulting in a crisis of credibility. The group became increasingly anxious and de-motivated. At senior levels, there was some concern that the change was not progressing well. The feeling was that the managers chosen for the function were not adequately skilled and motivated; and that it may be necessary to train them on the advances in strategic planning methods and motivate them to perform their new roles effectively. As is quite evident, these were also wrong solutions for the problems being confronted.

WHY DID THE CHANGE FAIL?

Let us now analyse the factors that led to the failure of the change effort. The PSU had initiated the change effort to prepare itself to face greater competition. The objective was to strengthen interface management among different functions to develop a pipeline of new products and value-added products. Commitment to this direction was established in the form of setting up cross-functional business planning teams for each of the plants. It would appear that there was perfect clarity on the goal to be achieved and the broad process to be followed to reach the desired future state. But did all the managers have the same understanding of the destination to be reached? Why did the change journey run into so many roadblocks and ultimately get derailed?

We can identify the following reasons for failure of change at PSU:

1. As the strategic direction had not been elaborated in terms of clear sub-goals and assignments, there were confusing and conflicting interpretations of both the goals and the processes for reaching those goals.

2. Certain structures, systems and processes were impeding the implementation of change and yet the organisation did very little to diagnose those roadblocks quickly and remove those impediments.
3. As communication did not flow freely across levels and functions, even simple problems became extremely complicated and so were either not tackled at all or wrongly tackled.
4. Without an overarching purpose and integrating mechanisms across levels and functions, the dysfunctional organisational routines persisted and so the execution of change suffered.

In the following paragraphs, we discuss these reasons for failure in some detail.

Conflicting and Confusing Interpretations of the Destinations and Pathways: Despite what the leaders may have assumed, the future remained misty to the key actors in the PSU system. As a part of the larger goal, the importance of development of new or value-added products was clearly articulated by key decision makers. But it was widely known that efforts for development would necessarily divert a certain amount of organisational resources and capacity from routine production without providing any returns in the short run. Development was also expected to pose short-run problems such as higher rejections, extra costs and time to be spent, loss of production, and so dip in both the top-line and the bottom-line.

Thus the two sub-goals—new product development and maximizing production of existing products—pulled in different directions. How could we expect these sub-goals to be balanced? Balancing effort would mean lowering the aspiration with regard to one or more sub-goals to avoid jeopardising others (for instance, lowering production expectations to release some resources for developmental initiatives). Given the realities of shop floor incentives being tied to production volume or specific quarterly targets being assigned to organisational members for production, sales and profits, different actors in the PSU had very different views on how far the existing production should be curtailed. Different actors in the system occupied different systemic positions and so were more or less committed to the different sets of sub-goals. As a result, there were different views on where the 'balancing line' had to be drawn.

The journey of change involves sailing in the stormy seas of uncertainty and complexity. There is ambiguity surrounding the definition of the final destination and the terrain to be traversed to be successful in reaching that visualised future state. In such a context, differences are inevitable. In the PSU, for example, organisational members across different levels and different functions were quite likely to have very different views on a number of issues:

> What aspects are the most important to analyse and act upon to achieve the goal of value added products and new products?
> How things would develop over time—for example, how long would it take to sort out technology issues to manufacture new products of consistent quality, how the competitors would respond to the PSU's moves, or when PSU's products would gain customer acceptance and support?
> What barriers are likely to be confronted on the way and what are the ways in which they should be managed?
> What aspects of the problem are more important and so need greater attention?
> How detailed should the analysis be at different stages?
> Which coordination mechanisms would be the most effective in helping achieve the goal?

In other words, while there was articulation of the broad aspiration or direction in the PSU, that direction—in terms of clear sub-goals—had not been concretised. More important, the linkages among the different sub-goals had not been explored to clarify how trade-offs among some of the sub-goals were expected to be resolved. Without a proper understanding of the linkages, having a long list of sub-goals or part goals tends to be more confusing than helpful. This is because organisational members may still have no clarity on 'what is really important', as compared to 'what is only urgent'.

Not Removing the Impediments to the Journey: It may be argued that the leaders should clarify all issues pertaining to the future state right at the start. Such an argument ignores the inherent uncertainties and complexities of change. When business planning team was constituted, the top managers could not have anticipated and provided for all the contingencies such as: how would the new team work with production-planning department to prepare the annual business plan; how information sharing would occur between marketing and business planning; how the Executive Director and also the other departments involved in the process of new product development would get involved; or how routine requests for additional office facilities made by the newly constituted team would be handled.

Even though the mission of business planning was clear, the specific roles (both what the new group would do and what it would *not* do) could have become clear only by starting specific activities that seem to be headed in the right direction, examining the outcomes that result from such organisational initiatives, analysing the roadblocks which may be confronted on the way, and deriving appropriate lessons. Given the uncertainty associated with change, organisational actors had to get things started with a general plan and then iterate as things proceeded. Inevitably, there had to be some 'learning by doing'.

The key actors also needed to develop a clear mental map of their existing state and the terrain they were required to pass on their way to the goal. For instance, decision makers at PSU had to clearly identify the key aspects that should be analysed and acted upon to achieve new product development. In the PSU there were several variables that were important to achieve progress towards the goal of accelerating new product development. Some of these have been listed below:

> ➤ New product development required active inputs from Research and Development, operations, marketing and finance sections. The interface of business planning with these functions and also among those functions themselves was an important factor but this was left to chance in the change process

- The organisation was driven strongly by the annual business plan. Production-planning department put this plan together but this department's interface with the BPT did not receive attention. There was need for clarity on where production-planning department's role would end and where the BPT's role would begin. In addition, given the realities of annual plan, some attention had to be given as to what the mechanisms would be to generate plant interest in new product development
- There were product development cells in the plants. It was not clear as to what role they would play
- In assessing the plant performance, there had to be attention paid as to how the developmental costs incurred by the plant would be taken into account. Otherwise the plants would have little incentive to incur those costs
- At some stage, the requirements to implement new product ideas should also have been linked to the human resource planning. Skills to develop applications and market research were in short supply at PSU
- Guidelines were required for the pricing of products made during developmental trials. Otherwise there would be difficulties in getting trial orders
- Development of certain new products posed major technological issues. Systems and processes had to be developed to address those issues on a priority basis. There had to be clear accountability for coordination of this agenda
- Projects directorate did the investment planning. As new product development may require capital budgets for additions, modifications and replacements, ways and means had to be worked out to have their involvement and contribution

Apart from the above, there were also other 'soft' aspects such as those pertaining to information sharing, interactions across lateral and hierarchical boundaries, and risk taking. All such factors determined the final outcome. Through processes of reflection and interaction, it was important for decision makers to identify the major factors influencing the outcome and their inter-relationships. In the absence of a clear map, decision makers were unable to anticipate potential hurdles and roadblocks. As a result, there were no preventive actions to avoid needless crises.

Absence of Linkages across Levels and Functions: Differences in views and perspectives can paralyse the organisation into inaction or they can lead to a cacophony of pointless arguments. But when they are channelled into a constructive force, they can also become a rich source of ideas and viewpoints and this can lead to high quality decisions.

In the PSU, people at junior levels did not talk freely and publicly about their concerns. Even when things were slipping badly, business planners continued to make presentations in meetings as if satisfactory progress was being achieved. The other group members attending the meeting perpetuated the ritual by merely making a few superficial comments but not raising any hard probing questions on the basic assumptions or premises underlying the approach to new product development. No new or unconventional ideas were raised at any stage. In both, individual relationships and in-group meetings, people tended to remain silent rather than talk of differences.

In several organisations, there is probably a strong assumption that seniors would not be open to candid discussion of potentially threatening and embarrassing issues and that open dissent could invite sanctions from senior levels. There is often a fear that dissent destroys relationships and could lead to loss of status and even expulsion from the group. When such fear operates, people do not deviate from group norms and merely conform to directives from the top.

At the same time, at senior levels, there was hesitation to admit past mistakes. When dilemmas arose, top managers persisted with their answer-giving mode rather than state honestly that they had no one clear answer to offer. For example, during an interaction with the MD, when the DGM asked what the business planners should focus on, the senior officer gave a snap response. Though the MD had not intended it that way, his off-the-cuff remark became a directive for the BPT.

During meetings, seniors rarely encouraged subordinates to question or challenge strategic assumptions. It is possible that there was a strong belief at senior levels that the boss should be all-knowing. Often superiors think that if they say, 'I don't know; I would rather listen to your views and suggestions', it would make people nervous, de-motivate them or even compromise their authority to lead. With such a mindset, leaders are likely to feel vulnerable when they are forced to listen to feedback that brings out newer dimensions of the issue under consideration.

The decision-makers at PSU started with a very limited view of the situation and did not sharpen their mental map during the journey through 'learning by doing'. Learning requires honest feedback and effective conversations, which were missing in the organisation.

A limited view tends to reduce all the complexities of the system to one factor or axiom (for instance asserting that 'if we have the right managers in business planning, we would be able to achieve our goal of new products and value-added products'). Such narrow perspectives tend to degenerate into dogmatism. All contradictory evidence and insights are ignored or rejected. In such a situation, too many aspects are left to chance or to the resourcefulness or relationships of the concerned actors to work out some solution within the artificial constraints imposed by a constricted mental map.

Therefore—when faced with complex problems—decision-makers apply straightforward solutions. Such simple-minded solutions only end up treating symptoms and leave the basic issues unresolved. When underlying conflicts are not resolved, repressed feelings of frustration, anger, anxiety or resentment remain potent, and shape people's relations and perceptions. As emotional distancing and disconnections occur in relationships, problems mount, and people become even more secretive and isolated.

When such patterns of relationships persist, something important is lost in the organisation. People lose hope and become passive. Paradoxically, teams that most need corrective actions tend to become the least likely to have a free and frank conversation to diagnose issues with an open mind and come up with appropriate steps to deal with the basic problems.

Status Quo in Chosen Approaches and Organisational Routines: Larry Hirschhorn and Thomas Gilmore[8] argue that the absence of linkages leads to status quo in organisational routines. In their view, the lack of integration is not always apparent on the organisational chart. Hierarchies, multiple functions or units spread across multiple locations are traditionally seen as 'villains' leading to the common problem of excessive differentiation, but inadequate integration. Yet the basic underlying problems exist in the *boundaries* that are found in the minds of people.

Hirschhorn and Gilmore list four psychological 'boundaries': authority boundary, task boundary, political boundary, and identity boundary. They list the necessary tensions at each of the four boundaries as:

- *Authority boundary:* How to lead but remain open to criticism? How to follow but still challenge superiors?
- *Task boundary:* How to depend on others that we don't control? How to specialise yet understand other people's jobs?
- *Political boundary:* How to defend our interests without undermining the organisation? How to differentiate between win-win and win-lose situations?
- *Identity boundary:* How to feel pride without devaluing others? How to remain loyal without undermining outsiders?

We saw how the development of new and value added products at PSU involved individuals and teams at different levels from several functions: R&D, operations, marketing, costing, projects, product development cells, and a few others. In terms of organisational routines, people had to depend on others with completely different sets of skills and resources. While focusing primarily on their own tasks, each group was required to take interest in the challenges and problems facing others. But did the different functions and different levels work together effectively to achieve the organisational goal? How did the boundaries affect the functioning of the organisation?

In the PSU, *task boundaries* were excessively differentiated but inadequately integrated. There was little information and interest in the problems facing others. With members unable to develop an overall conceptual understanding of the challenge, issues of interdependence were dealt with awkwardly and in a sub-optimal fashion. There was a strong 'silo' mentality. The following behaviour patterns were typical:

- Different functions not only worked with different priorities, but also different time frames on the same issue. Each function worked with a different 'control panel', and so agreements became enormously difficult. There was constantly the game of, 'if only the other function had acted responsibly, we could have achieved the goal'
- Accountability was experienced only for completing specific tasks or obtaining discrete outcomes, not for achievement of the overall objective
- People only sent information to their bosses within their own functions but not to colleagues across functions/groups. For example, operations had no idea of market feedback or technological challenges being tackled, or costing had little information on what was happening to rejections on the shop floor or the process that marketing was following to work out prices

Without an overarching sense of purpose and effective integrating mechanisms and processes, people developed narrow *identity boundaries*. They began thinking in terms of 'us' versus 'them' and tended to devalue the potential contributions of other groups to rationalise their own lack of a sense of accomplishment. As a result, most situations at the *political boundaries* were seen as 'win-lose' games. With groups unable to define their interests broadly, people became highly protective of their departmental or group boundaries. Obviously there were no healthy conversations to discover mutually beneficial solutions.

When different groups/functions pursue different interests in a healthy manner, it mobilises different interests and perspectives, which add up to a comprehensive view of the entire situation. Such diversity of perspectives can be extremely helpful to senior managers. But when lateral relations are characterised by squabbling and petty politics, top managers receive no useful feedback, perspectives or insights from operating levels. When asked to send their best players to cross-functional teams or task forces, departments may only nominate less competent individuals or appoint people who are already over-committed. When seniors see such behaviour, they conclude that juniors are poorly motivated apart from being lowly skilled. This makes them suspicious and over-controlling. When seniors become critical and controlling, the lower levels become even more cautious and excessively dependent. As a result, the quality and quantity of interactions suffer at the *authority boundaries*.

In summary, when social climate tends to be fear or blame oriented rather than learning oriented, conversations end up being characterised by lack of trust, openness and support. There is great deal of self-censoring and very little willingness to discuss issues openly. As a result, people at operating levels don't hear a coherent story that explains the changes in the outside world, strategies to meet the new demands, and the rationale for new ways of working together. Lack of coherent story also undermines effective upward and lateral communication. When employees are not sure of where the plans are supposed to be heading, they would neither be able to help realise the plans nor warn those at decision–making levels when plans go off-course.

As we have seen above, different groups seemed to be at loggerheads with each other at the PSU. For example, individual members of the BPT tended not to engage with the real problems of trying to develop win-win partnerships with production-planning department or marketing. They did not take initiatives with the MD or the ED to obtain clarity with regard to their roles and assignments. In review meetings, they chose to give an impression that they were achieving progress and faced no serious constraints. It is possible that they behaved this way because they considered the transaction costs of influencing their colleagues or their superiors to be prohibitively high. When the cost of surfacing views, negotiating workable arrangements or implementing agreements is too high, individuals may simply not engage with the problem.

The PSU case illustrates the nature of challenges facing change leaders in executing complex change. Change leaders need a framework that will enable them to address the challenges of effectively executing change. In the following section, we offer such a framework.

A FRAMEWORK FOR EXECUTING CHANGE

In this section, we discuss a framework for executing change in organisations. It draws on the first basic assumption underlying our change management model (discussed in Chapter 1). It states that *solutions to an organisation's problems cannot be found outside the organisation. An organisation possesses the potential and the capability to solve its own problems.* This assumption is also a value, in that it asserts that change is most successful and effective when people in an organisation act collectively to generate solutions and implement actions. In other words, solutions that are *imposed* on an organisation from outside have little chance of success. The role of leadership in change is to *expose* the organisation to challenges and problems faced, to mobilise support for change and to create the right conditions for people inside the organisation to generate ideas for improvement.

If organisational change is to be generated from within, how do people go about changing the organisation? What do they change? To answer, we repeat our second assumption (from Chapter 1) that states that *organisational change, in its essence, is about bringing a change in an organisation's routines.* To restate the concept of a routine, the term routine refers to the ways in which people perform their activities in an organisation. It includes rules, procedures, policies and conventions. It includes both the formal (written) aspects of an organisation's architecture and its informal (unwritten, tacit) aspects. An organisation's policy for recruiting staff is a routine. Its procedure for evaluating quality is a routine. The way in which employees in an organisation actually respond to customer complaints is another routine. For a specific behaviour to be an organisational routine, it must be both repetitive and widely shared.

210 Change Management

Our second assumption is based on both empirical and theoretical ideas in organisation studies.[9] Activities that are performed to carry out day-to-day tasks of an organisation are also referred to as *operational routines*. Some organisations also develop special kinds of routines, developed with the explicit objective of *modifying existing operational routines* in order to enhance the organisation's effectiveness.[10] These are referred to as *dynamic capabilities*.[11] If an organisation already has well-defined dynamic capabilities, there is little need for anyone to manage change. However, the need for change arises because many organisations lack such dynamic capabilities.

What do we mean by changing a routine? Organisations can change their routines in three ways: First, they can *modify* an existing routine. A modified routine is different but not fundamentally different from the original routine. Second, they can *discard or eliminate* an existing routine. Here, the organisation stops performing a particular task or activity. Third, they can *establish a new* routine. This may take the form of introducing a new policy, procedure or task to perform a new set of activities.

Thus effective change management involves modifying existing routines, eliminating some old routines and introducing a few new routines. Why do we need to change a routine? An organisation may under perform if its routines are dysfunctional or inappropriate. If an organisation has an elaborate routine for decision-making that requires considerable time, then the organisation is in trouble if its environment begins to demand quick decision making. In another example, an organisation may be shipping out products with too many defects because its quality control routine is ineffective. If this leads to customer complaints and loss of market share, then the organisation needs to examine and change its quality management routines. In other words, environments impose demands on an organisation in terms of costs, speed and quality. An organisation's routines need to change to match these demands.

In the execution phase of our model of change management, routines that are ineffective, inappropriate and dysfunctional need to be identified and changed i.e. modified, eliminated or replaced with new routines. Who should identify and change such routines? Using our framework based on our first assumption, we suggest that people inside the organisation should do the identification and change of routines. However, this is not an easy task. First, identification of dysfunctional routines is difficult for insiders. Second, even if the routines are identified, modifying or changing them is even more complicated. Routines are shaped by and, in turn, shape the mindsets and mental models of people inside the organisation. Therefore, it is difficult for insiders to identify dysfunctional aspects of their routines.

Modifying or changing a routine requires the cooperative effort of different people in an organisation. In the absence of formal authority, managers and employees at middle and lower levels find it hard to generate the requisite cooperation and willingness from others at their level. Therefore, four things need to happen to facilitate modification of routines by insiders in an organisation:

1. They need to be exposed to alternative perspectives to free them from the dysfunctional constraints of their mental models.
2. Organisational arrangements need to be created to enable people from different functions to work together.
3. Roadblocks and barriers to modifying existing routines need to be identified and removed.
4. New routines need to be created to focus the organisation's attention on continuous improvement.

The role of top management in execution is to establish a context that facilitates the four requirements outlined above. The context is to be created by altering the existing roles, responsibilities, systems and procedures of the organisation. In other words, change leaders can facilitate the execution of change by creating an appropriate architecture that is made up of roles, responsibilities, systems and procedures. We refer to this important role of change leaders in executing change as that of a *systems architect.*

As a systems architect, change leaders need to set up integration and coordination mechanisms to enable people to work together and learn from each other. This will facilitate both exposure to new mental models and focus of different functions on common goals. Second, they need to ensure that organisational policies, procedures and incentive systems are all *aligned* towards the common goals. This will also involve removing structural impediments to change. Third, they need to establish new routines to focus organisational efforts towards change. To summarise, these three crucial tasks in executing change are: (a) creating cross-functional linkages in the organisation; (b) aligning policies, procedures and removing structural impediments to performance and change; (c) creating new routines for continuous improvement.

The framework emphasises the role of the change leader as a systems architect. Therefore, it focuses on creating cross-functional linkages, removing structural hurdles and creating new routines. However, the emphasis on architecture and structure should not detract managers from paying attention to human aspects of change. The human aspects of change are also crucial in ensuring that the architectural and structural changes deliver the anticipated results. A key human aspect is the articulation of a clear sense of purpose that gets people to move from preoccupation with 'problems of yesterday' to focusing on 'plans for tomorrow'. Otherwise giving up old routines would become enormously difficult.

We discuss the three aspects of strengthening cross-functional linkages, removing structural impediments, and creating new routines in some detail in the following sections. Then we examine what would be required to pay attention to human aspects of change. To begin with, we present an illustration of a successful case study of execution.

THE NISSAN TURNAROUND

In March 1999, the CEO of Renault, the French car manufacturer, asked Carlos Ghosn to lead a turnaround of Nissan, the Japanese auto giant. Renault and Nissan had just entered into a strategic alliance with Renault taking a 37 per cent equity stake in the Japanese company. In 1999, Nissan had been struggling to make a profit for the previous eight years. It lacked brand power; its margins were low and it had excess plant capacity. The company's mounting debts had reached a staggering $11 billion. As Ghosn puts it, it was a do-or-die situation. Nissan would have ceased to exist if it hadn't been turned around.

Ghosn was very familiar with the auto industry. He had joined Michelin, the French tyre company, as an engineer and had risen to become the chief operating officer of its Brazilian subsidiary and subsequently the CEO of Michelin's operations in North America. After joining Renault, he had led a turnaround initiative in the company facing the after effects of its failed merger with Volvo. Ghosn spent considerable time talking to people both inside and outside the company to understand the change issues facing the company. As he puts it:

To tell the truth, I never met anyone in Nissan who could give me an exhaustive analysis of what had happened to it. I never went to a single place where anyone could speak about the company articulately. No one was able to offer me a summary of the problems listed in the order of their importance. Management was in complete and obvious chaos. This, I believed, was the primary cause of Nissan's difficulties.[12]

Based on his conversations, analysis and reflection, Ghosn identified five problems that were the basis of his roadmap for change: (a) Nissan wasn't really engaged in the pursuit of profit; (b) There was a lack of customer orientation; (c) There was a lack of urgency although the company was facing a crisis for survival; (d) The company was highly compartmentalised into different functions; (e) The company had no strategy.

As an industry insider, Ghosn clearly understood that the key success factor in the auto industry is brand image or brand identity. Brand identity, in turn, is based on product design. Nissan had cut back on product development and had no new models since the early 1990s. Therefore, Ghosn's objective for change involved simultaneously cutting costs *and* stimulating growth through new product introduction. His roadmap was based on a clearly articulated sense of purpose that was based on a guiding philosophy and values. According to him[13]:

> In corporate turnarounds, particularly those related to mergers or alliances, success is not simply a matter of making fundamental changes to a company's organisation and operations. You also have to protect the company's identity and the self-esteem of its people. Those two goals—making changes and safeguarding identity—can easily come into conflict; pursuing them both requires a difficult and sometimes precarious balancing act.

Ghosn's roadmap for change was underpinned by this guiding philosophy to safeguard Nissan's identity and the self-respect of its people. The lessons from the Nissan case were clear. Although, the sense of purpose is part of the appreciating change phase, it gets articulated and developed in the mobilising support phase as the roadmap for change. By the time the company enters the execution phase, it should have a clearly focused roadmap that addresses its unique problems and is simple enough for everyone to understand. The roadmap should also clearly articulate the underlying philosophy and values driving the change.

Effective leaders develop a very clear understanding of the drivers of success in their respective organisations. As we shall see later in this chapter, they also follow similar approaches to executing changes within the framework of their roadmaps. For now, the most important lesson for managers leading change in their organisations is that they need to have a clear sense of purpose that gives rise to a roadmap for change. This should be based on sound diagnosis, explicit values and a guiding philosophy. Otherwise, they are not ready to execute change. But a roadmap alone is not sufficient to bring about change. They also need to pay attention to an organisation's architecture.

ROLE OF ARCHITECTURE IN EXECUTION

An organisation's architecture includes its structure in terms reporting relationships (hierarchy), functions, departments, and roles. It also includes rules, procedures and policies and most importantly decision making processes. The architecture of an organisation can significantly shape an employee's focus and energy. Architectures that promote compartmentalisation of functions and roles tend to promote rivalry and conflict between departments, divisions and individuals. Many large organisations, over a period of time, develop such architectures. There is little collaboration between departments and individuals tend to focus on their own and their department's interests. Typically, projects or decisions that require individuals from different departments to work together tend to get delayed. Individuals become highly protective of their turf or territory and there is little information sharing. In worst-case scenarios, such as Nissan prior to 1999, this architecture can lead to a culture of blaming others. As Ghosn notes in the case of Nissan:

> *The compartmentalisation inside Nissan was well known to people outside the company. We had the feeling that everyone was protecting his own territory, hiding information about it from his neighbours. Such a lack of communication is extremely dangerous. When you are in a company that doesn't work cross functionally, every one feels satisfied with his own performance and assumes that bad results are someone else's fault.*[14]

Employees in such organisations lose both focus and energy. Changing anything seems to be a huge task beyond any individual's capacity. A culture of 'learned helplessness' seems to creep in.[15] To convert this learned helplessness into learned optimism requires altering both the architecture and the culture of the organisation. The architecture and culture of an organisation are closely related, reinforcing each other to produce supportive or dysfunctional dynamics. The situation that Ghosn found in Nissan is not unique. You will find it prevalent to a lesser or greater extent in most large companies.

We'll draw on the above case of successful execution of change to elaborate our framework. As we have seen earlier, our framework has identified certain tasks of top management that would ensure the sustenance of employee focus and energy during the execution phase. In the following sections, we examine the execution tasks of creating cross-functional linkages in the organisation, aligning policies, procedures and removing structural impediments to performance and change, creating new routines for continuous improvement, and attending to the human aspects of change.

DEVELOPING CROSS-FUNCTIONAL LINKAGES

The Institute on Governance (IOG) has carried out research on enhancing the effectiveness of public policy formulation, regulation and provision of services to citizens in Canada. Their study has indicated that a major problem pertains to inability of departments to work together arising from turf consciousness and absence of incentives to support collaboration. While some competition is inherent in government and is in fact a reflection of democratic process in action, the study revealed that conflict had gone well beyond the level needed to reconcile legitimate interests.[16] The unhealthy pathology that had crept into the culture was hurting the overall organisation.

FACTORS CONTRIBUTING TO NON-COLLABORATION

The analysis of turf carried out by IOG was aimed at identifying the causal factors. Certain factors were found to be the most influential drivers of the situation under analysis. The IOG Study has categorised these as root or fundamental factors (Figure 5.2) causing turf issues. There were some other factors of secondary importance. These were not to be overlooked, but they were found to work together with the first order factors and to be affected by them. The study found that greater energies were being expended on the visible symptoms of the bigger problem, and not enough attention was being given to the root causes.

According to the IOG study, the root or fundamental factors contributing to the 'turf' problem were:

1. *Reward System that Fails to Encourage Collaboration*: In the organisations studied by IOG, there was little recognition

Figure 5.2: Factors Contributing to Non-Collaboration

Fundamental Factors Contributing to the Problem: Reward System, Performance Expectations, Vision, Leadership

Contributory Factors of Secondary Importance: Skill Sets, Mindsets, Culture & Values, Structures and Mechanisms

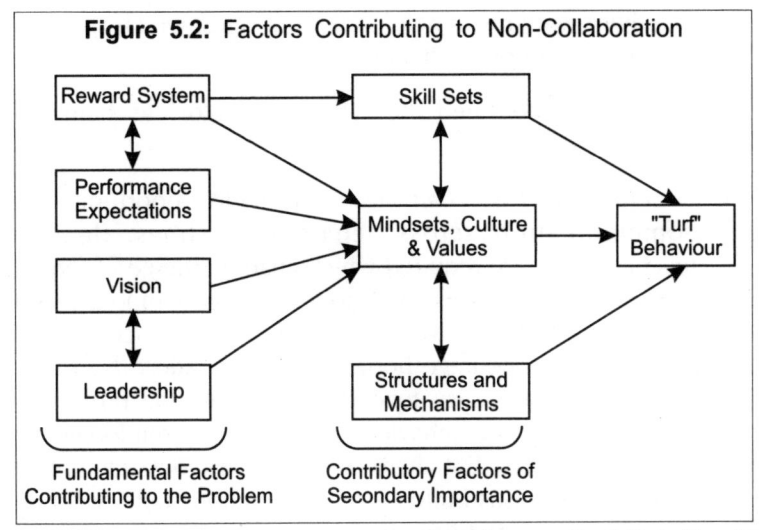

"Turf" Behaviour

Based on p. 9 of Ref. No. 16

of collaboration and cooperation across departmental lines. The general perception was that the real rewards came from winning something for one's own department or function. As a matter of fact, the collaborative act of giving up something or sharing power for a larger goal was generally perceived as a sign of weakness.

2. *Performance Expectations*: These were found to encourage behaviour and priorities that are oriented 'upward'. There was little or no emphasis on interdepartmental collaboration. Goals tended to be more department-specific.

3. *Signalling Behaviour from the Leadership*: The leadership did not communicate through their words and actions that cooperative approaches across departments were a priority. As a matter of fact, certain leadership actions were found to transmit some wrong messages—for instance, to be ranked as high-fliers, people should aggressively pursue departmental goals rather than being concerned about larger goals.

4. *Lack of a Sense of Coherent and Collective Purpose*: A common 'vision' acts as a rallying point for a new spirit of cooperation. The study found that people did not believe

that there were meaningful larger priorities, which speak to the need for more collaboration.

The research identified the following factors as being of secondary importance:

1. *Structures and Mechanisms*: To provide opportunity for communication across departmental lines, flexible mechanisms were required which span the range of formal and informal, structural and non-structural, temporary and permanent. But there were hardly any such structures and processes to encourage horizontal coordination. Narrowly defined mandates also tended to aggravate the problem.
2. *Skills*: The existing behaviour patterns were reinforced by current skill sets. But there was no conscious attempt to develop consensus-building or cooperation skills. Without new capabilities to trigger the change process, the unhelpful mindsets and values tended to persist.
3. *Mindsets, Culture and Values*: With low risk tolerance, collaborative approaches were generally seen as unusual and therefore risky. Command and control attitudes, absence of a strong client-focus and lack of trust were also contributors to mindsets and attitudes discouraging collaboration. Short-term orientation and perceived resource constraints also intensified turf battles.

The analysis revealed that to 'trample the turf' action would be required on several fronts. Greatest impact would come from tackling all the root factors as well as the second order contributing factors in combination with the first. The factors should not be considered in isolation and a systematic approach would be required to achieve success.

ATTENDING TO CROSS-FUNCTIONAL LINKAGES FOR EXECUTION EXCELLENCE

As an organisation, Dr. Reddy's Laboratories (DRL) is quite unlike the government departments where the IOG conducted its research. It operates in the pharmaceutical sector that has been undergoing far-reaching changes in technological, market, legal and regulatory environments. Just about thirty years ago, India was struggling to make the most basic drugs. Now the country has emerged as the leading manufacturer of low cost pharmaceutical ingredients and generics for the world.[17] With its consistent focus on innovation, DRL has been one of the pioneers in this industry. The company markets its products to over 100 countries worldwide.

Given the nature of the environment and its own aspirations, change management has been an important priority for the company. To devote special attention to executing change, DRL has started a new initiative termed as 'Execution Excellence'. To improve execution, the company has decided to focus efforts on better managing the interfaces among the different functions. Why the special attention to cross-functional linkages? The company felt that it is at the interface between functions that implementation starts to deviate from intentions.

Like most organisations, DRL operates with a functional structure and strong departments. In the old paradigm, individuals did their jobs and passed on their outputs to other functions. Whenever a slippage occurred in meeting the larger goal in terms of quality, delivery or costs, there was the familiar explanation of 'We did our work, but the other function failed', and 'Though the other function may have delivered on time, what they gave us didn't quite meet our requirements and yet no support was available'. The company found that when the teamwork across functions was effective, even complex assignments worked out smoothly and achieved success. On the other hand, weak teams seemed to make even simple projects very complicated, and consequently failed in meeting the end goals.

With goals becoming stringent in a competitive environment, there was realisation that very little leeway was available for slippages on quality, delivery or cost parameters. Under the new circumstances, the chemists working on technology development for example, could not stay within their comfort zones of being concerned only with scientific parameters. They had to learn to think about the issues of the ready availability of cost-effective raw materials or whether the process would suit the engineers.

Apart from bringing about such mindset changes, the organisation had to move from tacit emphasis on vertical relations to strengthening lateral relationships across functions so that different functions don't steer in different directions.

The evaluation of the effectiveness of an individual, team or function can be made on the basis of four yardsticks: a) *inputs* made in terms of efforts, energy or time invested or resources consumed; b) *outputs* generated, for example results achieved or services provided; c) *outcomes*—that is whether the results or services satisfy the requirements of the relevant stakeholders; and d) *Impact* in terms of the achievement of the larger goal of the organisation through the combined effect of different outcomes. In the absence of cross-functional dialogue, the different functions have little or no feedback on how well they are progressing towards *outcomes*, what factors are contributing or impeding the achievement of needed outcomes and ultimately whether the combined actions of different functions would have the desired *impact*.

The cross-functional teams at DRL helped in superior execution by sensitising different groups to the outcomes they were accomplishing and the impact they were having. This awareness helped the organisation move from crisis-induced learning to anticipatory, participatory learning. The different groups were able to more clearly understand the other functions' requirements. Each group had opportunities to give and receive valuable feedback on what was required to meet the larger goals of the organisation. The teams developed ground rules and norms for how the interactions would be managed, how decisions would be made and how the exceptions would be handled. The people at operating levels could directly communicate with their counterparts from other functions and improve the work processes.

The DRL managers who had worked on cross-functional teams (CFTs) felt that the leadership had an important role in setting the right context for creating and sustaining the enthusiasm of operating personnel as well as senior managers. For example, it was observed in DRL that operating levels enjoyed getting involved in the exercise of strengthening processes. But the work required heavy time commitments, so employees were concerned about implications for the appraisal of their performance. It was important for leaders to provide clarity on how the work on CFTs would be evaluated and how it would affect the careers of the personnel working on these assignments.

Senior managers were expected to give up their role as evaluators and become enablers—a transition was not always easy to make. When operating personnel made presentations on the limitations of existing processes, the seniors found it difficult to accept the diagnosis. The DRL managers found that when leadership creates a context that is focused on aspirations rather than on the limitations of the past practices, it becomes easier in generating acceptance of the current realities and making well-considered decisions on the improvements and innovations.

Box 5.1 and Box 5.2 illustrate that the leaders also set the right context by constantly reinforcing the *impact* and *outcome* dimensions.

The spirit of Sanjay Jaju's communication (Box 5.2) was not any different when he went about empowering citizens, through the use of information technology in rural India.

Box 5.1: Reinforcing Commercial Focus in Day-to-Day Interactions

Sir David Simon, Chairman of British Petroleum is widely regarded as an outstanding leader. He considers it important to give quality time to interactions with his people. In his interactions, he does not lose an opportunity to communicate the message that a performing culture has to understand and emphasise the commercial aspects as much as it understands the technical merits. For example, he may ask: 'How much money do you make in this factory?' An employee may reply: 'I can tell you how much oil we produce.' Simon's response would be: 'I am not interested in how much oil you produce. Where is the money? Oil is only relevant in terms of money for the shareholders, not in terms of barrels.'[18] The purpose of this interaction is to signal to the employees the importance of not remaining within the confines of own inputs and outputs but to pay attention to whether the intended outcomes are being achieved.

> **Box 5.2: Unlearning Mindset of 'Beneficiary' and Learning to be 'Entrepreneur'**
>
> As the District Collector of the West Godavari district in the state of Andhra Pradesh, India, Jaju initiated a rural e-Governance project to provide efficient, transparent and responsive service to citizens in his predominantly rural district. It was planned that the service delivery would be provided through rural kiosks run by local unemployed youth drawn from economically backward sections of the society.
>
> The kiosks had been set up with subsidies and low interest loans from the government. Jaju knew that the government support would be available to the unemployed youth only for a very limited time period. So they had to learn quickly to operate with an identity of 'small scale entrepreneur' rather than remain entrenched in a mindset of 'beneficiary of a government aid programme'.
>
> On the basis of some back-of-the-envelope calculations, he figured out that unless the kiosk operators reached a certain level of income per month, there was little likelihood that they would be able to continue the operations after the initial support period. In his personal interactions with them, he kept focusing on the overall billing that they had been able to achieve and what new work areas they should initiate to enhance their earnings. He kept emphasising the importance of taking initiatives to reach a critical size of operations as fast as possible. Without this sensitivity to the larger goal of sustaining the kiosks, the change could have ended up as a mere 'flash-in-the-pan' that only lasts as long as the government aid continues.

CROSS FUNCTIONAL TEAMS

In recent years, cross-functional teams (CFTs) have become an indispensable part of an organisation's strategy for competitive success. There is growing interest in studying the factors that make CFTs effective. Typically, business organisations employ CFTs to speed up new product development. CFTs are an integral part of a change management process, embodying the parallel organisation concept that we discussed in the previous chapter.

In simple terms, a cross-functional team is made up of people from different specialisations or functional areas. For instance, a product development team may consist of managers from marketing, engineering, manufacturing and finance. A cardiac surgical team in a hospital may consist of surgeon, the surgeon's assistant, a scrub nurse, an anaesthetist, and technician.[19] A cross-functional team pools the diverse resources of its members to achieve objectives that cannot be achieved by the functional departments acting on their own.

Requirements for an Effective CFT: Creating and managing effective CFTs requires attention to two factors. First, the selection of people and the composition of CFT is a crucial factor in its success. CFTs must not be too big. Size of a CFT should preferably not exceed 10 to 12 individuals. There is a common tendency in organisations to establish a CFT by asking for nominations from different functional departments. This is not a good idea. CFT members should preferably be selected on the basis of the following criteria. They should be: (a) competent in their functional areas with a high level of credibility and respect among their colleagues; (b) able to work with others i.e. they should be friendly and demonstrate openness and behavioural flexibility; (c) confident and energetic in their outlook. Membership of a CFT should be fixed for the duration of the project or assignment. Departments should not be allowed to nominate substitutions for an existing member.

Second, leadership of a CFT is crucial for its success. Top-level managers need to be selected to lead CFTs in an organisation. This will ensure that the CFT has credibility and access to resources. The selection of team leaders is also a crucial issue in the effectiveness of CFTs. Team leaders need to be more than technically competent. They must be able to enhance focus and energy levels in their teams. Research on high-performing CFTs in cardiac surgery provides some interesting insights into characteristics of team leaders who are likely to be effective.[20]

It was found that successful teams in this study were engaged in real-time learning, i.e. analysing and drawing lessons from the surgical process as it was unfolding. Teams that were successful in learning were also high-performance teams; the design and management of CFTs significantly contributed to their effectiveness in learning. This study also suggests that team leaders in CFTs need to: (a) be accessible, (b) explicitly ask for input by inviting suggestions, and (c) be willing to admit their mistakes. These three behaviours create psychological safety for team members and encourage them to experiment with new ideas and behaviours.

The research has also found that team leaders who reframe the task of the group as responding to an organisational challenge are likely to be more effective than those that view the task of the group as a technical one. Reframing technical problems as organisational issues creates a higher sense of purpose that can make team members more focused and energised.

The Nissan Experience with CFTs: CFTs were the centrepiece of the successful turnaround of Nissan between 1999 and 2002. Ghosn put together nine CFTs to address the key drivers of Nissan's performance. Each team was given 90 days to review the company's operations and come up with recommendations for profitability and growth. The teams reported directly to Nissan's nine-member executive committee. The CFTs had no decision-making power, but—unlike in the case of PSU discussed earlier in this chapter—they had access to all aspects of the company's operations. According to Ghosn, *'nothing was off limits.'*[21]

There were about ten members in each CFT. These members were drawn from the middle management of the company. Each CFT formed a set of sub-groups, consisting of CFT members and other managers selected by the CFT. Each subgroup was also limited to about ten members. The manufacturing CFT, for instance, had four subgroups focusing on capacity, productivity, fixed costs, and investments. According to Ghosn, about 500 people in Nissan worked in the nine CFTs and their sub-groups.[22]

Each CFT had two leaders drawn from the executive committee, who acted as sponsors to remove roadblocks and provide resources. According to Ghosn, *'Having two such senior voices made it less likely that the team would focus its efforts too narrowly. For instance, we decided that Nobuo Okubo, Nissan's executive vice president for research and development, and Itaru Koeda, the executive vice president of purchasing, would lead the purchasing team. Their voices would balance each other, so no single function's perspective would dominate.'*[23] The team leaders, however, did not play an active role in the team's work. They attended few of the meetings and were mostly in the background.

The actual work was carried by the regular members; one of the members acted as the team's 'pilot', taking the responsibility for driving the agenda and discussions. Nissan's executive committee selected pilots; leaders and pilots of the CFTs selected the rest of the team. According to Ghosn, *'Typically, the pilots were managers who had frontline experience with Nissan's operating problems and the credibility with the rank and file. I took a personal interest in their selection because it gave me a chance to have a close look at the next generation of Nissan leaders.'*[24]

For example, Otani was the purchasing group manager chosen to head the CFT on purchasing. His CFT made recommendations to the Executive Committee that would have resulted in 10 per cent savings in purchases over three years. But Ghosn rejected their recommendations outright, saying that they were not aggressive enough. The team was devastated but they realised that they had no alternative other than to challenge the Engineering Department to achieve the targets given to them. According to Otani:

We went back to work. We all knew that the biggest barrier would be the Engineering Department. To achieve the new goal would require bringing about a fundamental change in the long-cherished values. The Engineering Department was large, cohesive, and all-powerful. They viewed Purchasing merely as a supporting function. It was unthinkable at old Nissan for Purchasing or for that matter anyone to challenge the Engineering Department. We now knew what Ghosn meant when he said that there would be no sacred cows.

The next two weeks were literally hell. Even my own people in the Purchasing Department told me in no uncertain terms that they wanted no part of the unrealistic recommendations. Our team leaders, two executive vice presidents, helped us in convincing the Engineering Department to support the steps that were necessary to achieve the 20 per cent reduction in the next three years. I also relied heavily on my personal network in the Engineering Department. After a wrenching two weeks of hard work and tough negotiations, we finally came up with recommendations that met Ghosn's expectations.

After we made the final presentation it really dawned on us that although our recommendations sounded radical, they were not at all. They were pretty straightforward and obvious. This project made me realise that Nissan's problem in the past was our inability to implement what was so obvious.

CFTs are only one element of successful execution of change. During execution, it is also necessary to identify roadblocks that may be slowing down the change process. In most organisations, aspects of structure can become barriers to change. In the following section, we examine structural impediments to change and discuss how these can be minimised or eliminated.

ALIGNING POLICIES AND REMOVING STRUCTURAL IMPEDIMENTS TO CHANGE

The structure of an organisation includes the vertical levels in terms of hierarchy of authority, horizontal linkages in terms of departmentalisation and division of labour, formal rules and coordination mechanisms. Organisations have choices in terms of the structures they can adopt; and their structure reflects the organisation's preferences and mindsets. More importantly, a structure also reflects what the organisation values and the dynamics of power inside the organisation.

Over time, the structure of an organisation evolves due to technical, political and cultural factors. In many instances, the structure fails to respond to the current challenges facing the organisation. In a worst-case scenario, the structure becomes highly dysfunctional leading to loss of focus and energy throughout the organisation. In most instances, where the structure is ineffective or inappropriate, decision-making slows down. The organisation seems to take an inordinate amount of time to launch new initiatives. In such situations, the structure is clearly a roadblock to change. In Nissan, the board was made up of 37 directors before its alliance with Renault and was reduced to ten members as a result of the alliance. As Ghosn puts it, in Nissan's case:

> ... the board didn't represent the shareholders but rather the company's bureaucracy. One gained a seat on the board of directors through mere length of service rather than because of any ability to conceive and carry out an effective strategy. The huge size of the board served as a screen for the ironclad supremacy of the CEO and the small circle of people around him.[25]

One needs to examine whether the structure reflects current priorities. For instance, in the Nissan case, Ghosn realised that one of the problems facing Nissan was its weak design. Its design was less innovative and creative compared to its competitors and reflected the dominance of its engineering function. In fact, the design function was subordinated to the director of engineering. Ghosn reorganised the design function, putting it under product planning. He also hired a Japanese outsider, Shiro Nakamura from Isuzu, to head the critical design function in Nissan.

Let us examine a case illustration from a totally different situation. When plans were formulated to set up the Delhi Metro Rail Corporation (DMRC) within ambitious cost and time targets, very few would have nursed much hope of the project getting even anywhere close to achieving its objective. After all, the precedent of Kolkata Metro was there for all to see: that project of much lesser complexity had taken 22 years to complete and the cost had gone up almost 12 times.

E. Sreedharan assumed charge as the MD of DMRC in November 1997. With his intimate understanding of the ills of the functioning of Indian government organisations in general and Kolkata Metro in particular, he was aware that unless the structural impediments to performance were removed and policies were aligned to the strategies, the fate of DMRC would be no different from that of the Kolkata Metro. The Delhi Metro project was technologically complex and politically sensitive. There would be a large number of decisions that would be required to be made at every stage of the project. Unless decision-makers had the freedom and autonomy to act in the best interests of the project, the organisation would inevitably get mired in intractable difficulties.

Sreedharan was able to convince the policy makers that the effective completion of the project demanded certain structural arrangements for approval and sanctioning that would have to be radically different from the usual government style of functioning.

The organisation created two-level sanctioning authorities: the first one was the Empowering Committee, headed by the Cabinet Secretary. As the Cabinet Secretary is the head of the bureaucratic set up, this mechanism was able to ensure that the DMRC proposals received the attention from all the concerned secretaries without any delay. Delhi Metro has enormously benefited from the Empowering Committee as the process of considering the proposals from different perspectives and then moving to approval stage happens very quickly. The second mechanism that was created is termed as Group of Ministers presided by a senior Cabinet Minister. This body takes up the matters that are required to be approved at the Cabinet level. The Group of Ministers has been authorised to make appropriate decisions relating to the project without referring it to Cabinet, thus saving valuable time. Consequently the corporation is not required to run in circles for getting approvals from one department to another and from one minister to another.

Both these approval mechanisms have helped significantly in enhancing the timeliness of decisions and their acceptance by key stakeholders despite their large financial outlay, complexity and uncertainty. This is a far cry from the scenario in other government organisations where people wait for years together to get even small decisions made.

Apart from the structure for effective strategic decision-making, policies and procedures pertaining to land acquisition and dealings with contractors were also significantly changed to be able to meet the project's stretch goals. It was realised that the land acquisition in Delhi would not be easy, and it would get drowned in controversies unless an effective communication campaign and more importantly fair, transparent and customer-oriented policies and processes backed it. This required moving away completely from the precedents for handling this task in the governmental systems. In a similar vein, there had to be an entirely different approach to contractors on whom DMRC would be heavily dependent for its success. The dealings had to be built on bedrock of careful selection based on clear criteria and performance record, trust-based procedures, free and frank sharing of progress and problems, and commitment and mutual support to achieve stretch goals.

How much did these policies and structures help? The following quote illustrates the accolades that the project has been receiving from a wide variety of stakeholders:

Everybody laughed when plans to build a metro rail in Delhi were announced. All of us knew the chaos even a small, one-line metro in Kolkata had caused for a decade and a half... It is now built, ahead of schedule, in spite of the setback of the Japanese sanctions after Pokharan and without making a tenth of the mess the construction of an ordinary flyover creates in Delhi.[26]

Another important aspect of alignment is to ensure that incentive systems in an organisation are aligned with the goals of change. Given the nature of the organisation, DMRC did not offer any financial incentives to its employees. But for the professional workforce of DMRC, the challenge of handling a major challenge of national importance with a fair degree of autonomy was itself a significant intrinsic reward.

Designing appropriate controls and incentives is part of the task of aligning policies and procedures. Managers need to be aware that the role of incentives is to *encourage* specific types of behaviour. Incentives alone cannot be expected to create motivation for the desired behaviour. The role of incentives is primarily to facilitate change by reinforcing behaviours that will lead to change.

The need to achieve results and demonstrate competence is a fundamental driving force in all human beings. An incentive system should build on this fundamental need. Therefore, as Hrebiniak points out, managers should first ensure that the incentive systems in place do not *de-motivate* people.[27] The most effective way to do this in change situations is to first clarify responsibilities and accountabilities. There is nothing more de-motivating for managers than having to operate in a context where responsibilities and accountabilities are ambiguous or unclear.

In his book, Hrebiniak identifies the characteristics of an effective incentive system. Good incentives systems, as he points out, target the 'doers' and performers. Such incentive systems also target desirable behaviours. These systems are tied to the overall purpose and roadmap for change. Not only is it important to reward the right behaviours, any incentives, even if unintentional, that encourage wrong behaviours must be eliminated. If an organisation wants to foster cross-functional collaboration, providing team-based incentives will reinforce cooperative behaviour. In such a scenario, providing incentives for individual performance can undermine cooperative behaviour.

Hrebiniak points out that some organisations have put in place what he calls 'all-or-nothing' objectives. For instance, if a manager achieves 100 per cent of the set objectives, he or she is considered a success but a 99 per cent achievement of goals is considered a failure. These 'all-or-nothing' systems can be de-motivating and can potentially lead to dysfunctional behaviour. Good incentive systems are based on objective appraisals where managers are encouraged to negotiate their objectives. Such systems are also brutally honest in reviewing performance so that managers can learn from their mistakes and take corrective actions.

A common mistake that most organisations make during change is, they either develop or retain multiple performance criteria. Some of these criteria may be inconsistent with the goals of change and, therefore, may be inconsistent with other criteria that are oriented to change.[28] Such appraisal systems can lead to confusion and under-performance particularly when top management insists that middle managers 'do their best.'

Good incentive systems need equally good control systems to make them work. The characteristics of good control systems are that they provide a good corrective mechanism for the organisation by facilitating learning and change, providing feedback on performance, and reinforcing execution methods.[29] In other words, a good control system is a routine for learning and improvement. This crucial task for change leaders is discussed in the following section.

DEVELOPING NEW ROUTINES FOR INNOVATION AND IMPROVEMENT

Setting up routines to encourage learning and continuous improvement is another important aspect of change execution, which requires routines to generate and generalise ideas with impact. New ideas may be generated from four activities[30]:

1. Benchmarking—Seeing what others have done and adapting to it.
2. Experimentation—Trying out new things to see if and how they work.
3. Acquisition—Hiring or developing people with new skills and ideas.
4. Continuous improvement—Carrying out process analysis or implementing suggestion systems.

After the right ideas have been generated, they need to be generalised for deriving the maximum benefit. This would require routines for moving ideas from one leader to the next, from one geography to another, or from one business unit to another through Knowledge Management initiatives.[31] We show the approaches to generate and generalise ideas through a few illustrations; beginning with the examination of the Manthan initiative of Tata Chemicals, widely regarded as a phenomenal success. As on December 2004, after three years of practice, the actual cumulative savings from innovations and improvements resulting from this initiative have been more than Rs. 2.1 billion.

Prior to the mid-90s, Tata Chemicals thrived in a sellers' market within an insulated economy. But the economic liberalisation brought the earlier regime of import restrictions and huge tariff barriers to an end and the nature of the company's business environment changed dramatically. The import duty came down progressively from a high of 150 per cent to 10 per cent. Additionally, the organisation was confronted with the adverse impact of overcapacity in the industry, threat from imports and price-cost squeeze. For its sheer survival, new routines had to be instituted for learning and continuous improvement. It was realised that creating these learning routines would be quite challenging in an organisation that had been established in 1939 and that functioned as a closely knit community in Mithapur, a small town quite distant and detached from the outside world.

The initiative of bringing in innovation and learning was termed as *Manthan*—a Sanskrit term for churning, and a powerful metaphor to describe the processes that ensue when the difficult task of self-evaluation is undertaken. In the Hindu mythology, s*amudra manthan* (churning of the ocean) was aimed at attaining the nectar of immortality. In Tata Chemicals, it signified churning of minds and ideas to produce fruitful results in terms of significant operational improvements in different areas ranging from manufacturing to purchasing to supply chain management. It was expected that the innovations and improvements would occur with little or no investment of funds.

Manthan sought to institute and sustain the following three critical routines for making improvements and innovations through CFTs[32]:

a) A tightly time-based problem solving process oriented to a clear purpose,
b) A bottom-up idea generation process with middle management and staff cooperation, and
c) Stretch targets for cost reduction in each unit and a detailed idea implementation process.

As a part of the initiative, small teams were expected to get involved in the process of challenging prevailing assumptions about the 'way we have always done things' and come up with ideas for improvements. More than 100 employees were initially trained on these new routines. In these training workshops, organisational members were educated on analysing operational processes, developing databases, working out priorities, reviewing and evaluating ideas, obtaining sign-offs from key actors, planning implementation steps and so on. There were, for example, specified routines for categorizing costs into compressible, semi-compressible and non-compressible categories.

The initiative was championed by a steering committee. The steering committee roles and responsibilities were clearly specified. Different teams were constituted to carry out improvement activities and it was expected that the programme leader and programme coordinator would carry out the coordination of these teams. They were expected to link the teams with the higher management, select team leaders and facilitators, and actively remove barriers to quick and effective implementation. There were detailed role descriptions for team leaders, senior facilitators and facilitators. Thumb-rules were also outlined for selecting the operational issues to work on, target setting and so on.

The elaborate role definitions, clear specifications for choosing improvement areas or analysing costs helped provide clear criteria in terms of *who, what, how and when* at different stages of problem solving to guide thinking and action. They deconstructed the broader goal into specific aspects and provided clear rationale for choices and thus contributed to speed of decision-making and action. Thus they helped the new routines for learning to take root. In the words of one of the participants, 'The project created a new vocabulary that was shared among the team members. The use of business and financial language helped us perceive and deal with aspects that we had not even thought of earlier'.

As we have seen above, tools and techniques had been clearly spelt out for different processes such as small group idea generation, recommendation development, gaining approvals and so on. There were clear ground rules relating to getting away from precedent or hierarchical orientation, looking at the issue from a process or customer perspective rather than from one's own functional angle, and concentrating on making things better in future, rather than being preoccupied with allocation of blame for past problems.

The clearly defined purpose and well-thought out processes ensured that the approaches followed by team members were appropriate for effective problem solving and their actions added value. When the sense of shared purpose and effectiveness of processes are both low (Figure 5.3), people tend to fritter away their energies in adversarial relations. When people are highly preoccupied with processes but don't share a strong sense of common purpose, they become bureaucratic. High sense of purpose, but without corresponding attention to processes leads to well-intended actions, but under-utilisation of potential resulting from factors like uncoordinated initiatives. When a unit is high on both purpose and processes, people become both 'Trained and Knowledge-Able' and so add value.[33]

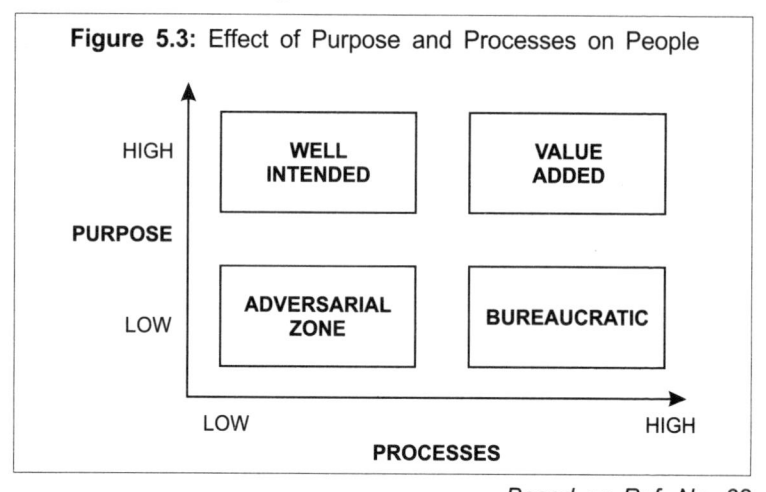

Figure 5.3: Effect of Purpose and Processes on People

	LOW PROCESSES	HIGH PROCESSES
HIGH PURPOSE	WELL INTENDED	VALUE ADDED
LOW PURPOSE	ADVERSARIAL ZONE	BUREAUCRATIC

Based on Ref. No. 32

Box 5.3 illustrates changes resulting from the *Manthan* initiative, by presenting a sample of new behaviours and team-based approaches that emerged in the organisation and how they changed the outcomes.

GE's Workout methodology, introduced in 1989 is quite similar in the sense that it is built on two major pillars: a highly structured approach to solving operational problems quickly and simply; and team-based solutions through knowledge sharing. As a part of the Workout approach, several tools, formats and checklists

Box 5.3: New Behaviours Resulting from *Manthan*[34]

- The project members searched for best practices by paying direct visits to other organisations and scanning the literature. To their utter surprise, they found that even certain organisations close to Mithapur had superior processes and technologies in certain areas. Spurred by these comparisons, a team working on brine path project ran experiments in the pilot plant to test some ideas. They elicited the involvement of a retired employee who had valuable insights on the subject and worked out an improved method.
- A team working on fuel purchase project examined the idea of using pet coke as a substitute for coal in a boiler but was initially stumped by the problem of neutralising Sulphur. A team member undertook a search to see if any organisation had tackled this problem. It was discovered that this had been done in a related industry. A team from that organisation was invited. Their presentation and subsequent interactions gave a very good lead to the project team. Discussions with boiler manufacturers and experts followed, and then experiments were initiated using 2 per cent pet coke with coal. After trials, the percentage of pet coke in the fuel mix was gradually increased. On the purchase front, the total requirement was consolidated and fresh terms were negotiated. This project led to a cost saving of Rs. 230 million.
- When differences of opinion persisted among team members on the extent of possible improvement from the induced draft fan for the boiler, the matter was resolved by taking the fan to the boiler and then measuring the efficiency first internally and then by a third party to arrive at a conclusion.
- A project team realised that it had insufficient expertise on port management and so was unable to understand the cost structure. To quickly gain this understanding, the members visited a port and went on a boat to mid-sea to understand ship loading and unloading processes.
- For the team members, review meetings were no longer 'boring waste of time'. They were now keen to get an update on how the other teams were doing, what approaches they had adopted so that they could pick up some new ideas that they had not considered.

have been developed as useful and practical frameworks for effective problem solving.[35] For example, RAMMPP matrix is a tool to remove extra steps that take time but don't add any value.

In this step, group members assess, analyse and remove the clutter in Reports, Approvals, Meetings, Measures, Policies, and Practices (RAMMPP). Specific routines are specified for using this technique to remove wasteful work practices.

When team members get to the stage of formulating steps to address problems, they are provided with a worksheet to strengthen an action plan or evolve a communication plan (summarised in Box 5.4). The checklist to strengthen an action plan is expected to ensure effective self-monitoring and self-regulation, by including important items that tend to be ignored during routine problem solving. In a similar vein, a workout communication checklist ensures that the right information with right levels of details go to the right audience.

Box 5.4: Summary of Points for 'Strengthening Action Plan' and 'Evolving Communication Plan'

Strengthening Action Plan

The following hard-nosed questions on the checklist would help the team improve an action plan before it is presented for approval:

- What can be done to enhance the probability of success of the proposed action plan?
- Are the dates realistic, given other commitments and priorities?
- What can be done to build steps to address key risks and weak spots in the plan?
- Who are the individuals/groups with whom you have to share the plan?
- How will you communicate with those affected?
- Are there people who should be asked to help with some parts of your project?
- How can you create enthusiasm for the change effort?

Evolving Communication Plan

To evolve a workout communication plan, some questions are recommended along with a format for organising the work of communication to different individuals and groups. The questions include:

- What messages should be communicated?
- Who should receive it?
- What is the appropriate time frame?
- How should the message be communicated?

The workout methodology also specifies certain common struggles of teams working on improvement projects, such as: *dividing the work among small groups too quickly; not being sharp and clear enough in describing the recommended action plan; losing sight of the goal; wanting to work on too many ideas; staying with an idea too long; and including too much detail and preparing too lengthy presentations.* Such a checklist serves a useful purpose by clearly identifying 'fail points' and warning actors in advance so that they can watch out for and avoid those traps.

The methodology also notes that the buzz that starts at the workout meeting to generate ideas and evolve action plans would last only few days. The energies would ebb soon after the hard work of implementation kicks in. The workout process, therefore recommends specific interventions to sustain energy. Thus the reality is squarely faced and the important issue of sustaining people's energies is not lost sight of in the excitement of creating new ideas and working out novel action plans.

The experience of Mittal Steel in turning around Imexsa also serves as an interesting illustration of developing new routines for making improvements. After the take over by Mittal Steel in 1992, Imexsa won numerous international awards for quality. It is also one of only two companies to earn the British Standards Institute's award for quality. According to Rafael Mendoza, the Quality Director at Imexsa:

> *In the steel industry these days, all companies have access to good ideas through customers, suppliers and consultants. The difference is who can implement them successfully. Traditional quality programmes such as ISO 9000 provide excellent statistical tools for documenting your current processes, but they are not as useful in accelerating continuous improvement. For this we introduced benchmarking, Top 10s and internal agreements.*

As part of benchmarking operating processes, the quality teams identified the best practices within the Ispat network, the steel industry as a whole and also in related processes in companies like Ericsson and General Electric. In the Top 10 programme, each department first identified projects to either cut costs or improve quality, developed quantitative indicators for likely financial impact and rank-ordered the projects based on financial impact. Each project was implemented by a CFT that developed an action plan and monitored progress. In 1996, Imexsa initiated a systematic programme of establishing service agreements between various departments in the company. Each department would meet with its supplier department and specify targets and explicit measures of service delivery. The service provider was allowed to specify prerequisites necessary to guarantee delivery. According to Piramal and Ghoshal:

The maintenance department might agree to provide preventive maintenance on time, for instance, provided that they were notified at least one week in advance of the scheduled downtime. The head of the department providing the service was responsible for monitoring performance on a daily basis and reporting to the head of the internal customer on a monthly basis, who would sign off on the performance evaluation. If a service provider repeatedly failed to meet goals, the failure would be elevated for discussion in the daily meeting, but this had occurred only once in the programme's first two years. In 1998 Imexsa had 140 internal service agreements across 28 production and service departments and sub-departments in the plant. 70 per cent of the agreements fulfilled 100 per cent of the requirements, 11 per cent of the agreements met between 95 per cent and 99 per cent, with the remainder fulfilling less than 95 per cent. These internal agreements yielded significant improvements in operations.[36]

This case illustration highlights common features of change processes that aim to improve quality. These are: enthusiastic commitment from top management, participation and involvement of all staff, exposure of all employees to continuous improvement training, ensuring that the change is value-driven and extending the change to all functions and activities. Improving quality is a long-drawn process requiring commitment, patience and hard work at all levels. There are no short cuts to either quality or success.

Knowledge sharing and integration across the organisation is another way to promote continuous improvement. Mittal Steel has instituted a Knowledge Integration Programme (KIP) to share the best practices and learn from one another in the organisation. According to Piramal and Ghoshal:

> *A few representatives from each operating and staff function (twelve in total) at each Ispat plant would meet twice each year. These KIP meetings lasted two to four days, and rotated among the plants in the Ispat network.*
>
> *Prior to the meeting, the department heads would send their suggestions for discussion topics to Ispat group headquarters in London, where the agenda would be set and then distributed to each of the participants in advance.*
>
> *During the meeting, the participants would review their performance against targets, including major accomplishments and disappointments, discuss common technical problems, update each other on developments in their plant and commit to future targets.*

ATTENDING TO HUMAN ASPECTS OF EXECUTING CHANGE

For a process to be repeatable, and successful, it cannot merely remain concerned with systems; it has to concentrate on people.[37] A change leader has to make sure that all fears are known, all ideas are heard, and a safe, non-disruptive plan is created. Once the hearts and minds of the people are involved, the systems obediently follow.

Executing change requires focus and energy. Change leaders need to sustain focus and energy throughout the organisation during the execution phase. Human aspects of change are as important in executing change. Therefore, managers need to build a behavioural climate that emphasises hope and optimism. By initiating actions that sustain hope and optimism, change leaders contribute significantly to addressing the need for control and maintaining sense of competence. We discuss this aspect in greater detail in the next chapter. Here, we summarise key ideas that can be used for executing change:

CLEAR SENSE OF PURPOSE

People need worthwhile purposes to direct their energy. For this, goals must be clear, specific and realistic. People must be able to see how their goals contribute to the larger mission of reinvention. As we saw earlier, the goals assigned to CFTs challenged the members to think beyond their boundaries and question the traditional ways of doing business. Specific goal-setting enables people to focus on the task rather than groping in the dark. When people are able to visualise the larger picture and yet at the same time be clear about their assigned tasks, they become hopeful and optimistic. This also makes them committed to the change process.

DECONSTRUCTION OF COMPLEX CHANGE

It is important to break the complex goals down into manageable sub-goals. Individuals tend to get paralysed when the problem is too huge to tackle. To maintain our sense of competence, we must feel that our problems are controllable at our level (illustrated in Box 5.5).

Obviously each of the sub-goals (Box 5.5) would have to be further broken down. Once this is systematically done, the challenge does not appear impossible any more to the organisational members. Deconstruction scales down the magnitude of the problem, and this has a positive effect on the quality of thought and action because the emotions such as

---

Box 5.5: Deconstructing the Goal of 'Reduction in Purchase Costs' at Nissan

The larger goal of reducing 20 per cent purchasing costs at Nissan was broken down into specific manageable sub-goals, such as:

- Reduce the number of suppliers by 50 per cent
  - Reduce suppliers from 1145 to 600
  - Reduce service providers from 6900 to 3400
- Forge partnerships with competitive global suppliers
- Form an alliance with Renault and purchase jointly to reduce costs (enhances bargaining power)

frustration, arousal and helplessness are kept at bay. When people are able to identify a series of controllable opportunities of modest size that produce visible results, they feel stretched and challenged. This evokes emotions of moderate intensities, where its contribution to performance of complex tasks is most beneficial.

PSYCHOLOGICAL SAFETY

Complex change can create anxiety and stress. If employees do not experience psychological safety in such a scenario, they would become excessively preoccupied with maintaining their sense of competence. While the task at Nissan was large, employees felt empowered. They had the decision-making authority; they could question old habits and beliefs and even challenge powerful departments. They were now part of a group navigating an uncharted territory; they were not struggling alone. The leadership was very demanding but highly committed and supportive. Ideas were not imposed from the top. People felt themselves to be in control of their own and their organisation's destiny. All these factors enhanced psychological safety and enhanced their levels of hope and optimism.

ENHANCING PREPAREDNESS

People are more hopeful when they feel confident of managing the unexpected. Contingency planning, scenario analysis and alternate courses of action all instil a sense of readiness for multiple possibilities. If people have visualised multiple alternatives to handle the challenges, they feel sure of their decisions and actions. On the other hand, if they consider their preparation as far from satisfactory, they suffer pangs of self-doubt. Some groups use a technique known as mental rehearsal. Individuals visualise important upcoming events, anticipate possible obstacles, and mentally picture alternative pathways to overcome obstacles. When there is hope and optimism, execution challenges are perceived as opportunities for growth as opposed to worrisome hurdles. The subjective world of organisational members is what determines what they see and how they would think and act. It is too important to be left to chance.

CHANGE LEADER AS A SYSTEMS ARCHITECT

In this last section of the chapter, let us briefly review the key ideas we have discussed. We saw that executing change presents major challenges. Studies have found that many organisations underestimate the time and resources needed for change; do not attend sufficiently to coordination and integration of activities; and fail to build capability for change execution. Typically, change managers get into a fire-fighting mode, waste precious time, energy and resources on dealing with crises, and then over a period of time get cynical and de-motivated.

This chapter presents a simple typology of change and noted that complex change (where the size of the problem is large and time available for execution is short) presents the greatest challenge. The challenge arises from dynamic complexity. Dynamically complex systems are difficult to understand and predict given three factors: (a) feedback loops that blunt the actions and prevent them from yielding the desired results; (b) time lags between actions and results; and (c) non-linearity in relationships between actions and effects.

Implementing Complex Change with Inappropriate Mindset: As seen in the PSU example, several organisations and managers make the mistake of attempting to execute *complex change* with the mindset of *managerial intervention* or *sequential change*. In such a scenario, organisations run into problems with unerring regularity. To start with, people at different levels and functions end up having conflicting and confusing interpretations of what has to be done and how, even though the larger direction has been clarified. So people start pulling the change in different directions.

Given the uncertainty associated with complex change, it is not really possible to plan out all the details of execution right at the start. Leaders have to get things started with a general plan and then iterate as things proceed. There has to be some 'learning by doing'. This would have to be in terms of identifying what the impediments to effective execution are and taking quick corrective actions.

But *learning by doing* becomes difficult when the 'boundaries' harden around authority, task, political interest and identity. This prevents healthy conversations and consequently discovery of mutually beneficial solutions. In the process, organisational actors are unable to sharpen their mental maps of the execution issues confronting them. A limited view tends to reduce the complexities to one factor or axiom and soon narrow perspectives tend to degenerate into dogmatism. Then contradictory evidence and insights get ignored and change execution becomes a victim of social and organisational difficulties.

Critical Tasks for Change Leaders: Effective change execution requires a change leader to understand and address these challenges. Organisational change, in its essence, is about bringing a change in organisational routines. The routines that are ineffective, inappropriate and dysfunctional need to be identified and changed. This requires exposing people to alternative perspectives to free them the dysfunctional constraints of their mental models. This would happen when people are exposed to customers and people from other functions and have the possibilities of working together with them. Roadblocks and barriers to modifying existing routines need to be identified and removed. And new routines need to be created to focus the organisational attention on continuous improvement.

Thus change leaders have to assume the important role of systems architect and create an appropriate architecture of roles, responsibilities, systems and overall context that facilitates effective execution. Without an appropriate context, employees lose both focus and energy, and this would create a culture of learned helplessness. To convert this learned helplessness into learned optimism, change leaders have to attend to some key areas of organisational architecture, as outlined below.

The first task is one of setting up integration and coordination mechanisms to enable people to work and learn together. The mindset of collaborative functioning requires the leaders to set the right context by developing a larger purpose that makes a compelling case for people to work together. The context in terms of performance expectations, rewards and skill sets should facilitate cross functional teams to discover pathways to reach the organisational stretch goals that cannot be achieved by the different functions acting on their own without attention to issues of interdependence.

During execution, it is also necessary to identify factors obstructing the process of smooth, quick and effective change execution. Sometimes there are structural impediments; at other times, incentive systems may not be aligned to the organisational goal. Change leaders should create a favourable context where even weak signals pertaining to structural and systemic impediments get quickly identified and then actions are taken to minimise and eliminate these.

A third important aspect of change execution is one of setting up routines to learning and continuous improvement. This requires attention to generating ideas through different methods. To derive the maximum benefit from the ideas, there should be attention to moving ideas to different leaders, different geographies and different businesses by utilising Knowledge Management initiatives.

Finally, change leaders cannot merely restrict their concerns to structures and systems. They should concentrate on people aspects of executing change. There should be a behavioural climate for people that creates and sustains hope and optimism. This would give individuals the much-needed sense of control and competence as they embark on the journey of uncertainty through complex change. Having attended to the strengthening of roles, systems, linkages and procedures, they should create a context that addresses the subjective world of organisational members. It is this subjective world that determines what people see and how they would think and act. We explore this aspect in greater detail in the next chapter.

NOTES AND REFERENCES

1. Kotter, J. (1995). Leading change: Why transformation efforts fail. *Harvard Business Review*. March-April: pp. 59–67.
2. Jick, Todd, (1991). *Implementing Change*. HBS Note, 9-491-114.
3. Hrebiniak, L. G. (2005). *Making Strategy Work: Leading Effective Execution and Change*, New Jersey: Wharton School Publishing.
4. Ibid.
5. Abrahamson, E. (2004). *Change Without Pain: How Managers Can Overcome Initiative Overload, Organisational Chaos, and Employee Burnout*, Boston: Harvard Business School Press.
6. Page 94 Abrahamson, E. (2004). Avoiding Repetitive Change Syndrome. *MIT Sloan Management Review*, Winter. 45(2): pp. 93–95.
7. Sastry, A. M. (2001). Understanding Dynamic Complexity In Organisational Evolution. In A. Lomi & E. R. Larsen (Eds.), *Dynamics of Organisations: Computational Modelling and Organisation Theories*. Menlo Park, Ca: AAAI Press.
8. Hirschhorn, L. & T. N. Gilmore. (1992). New Boundaries of the Boundaryless Company. *Harvard Business Review*. May–June: pp. 104–115.
9. Nelson, R. (1991). Why Do Firms Differ, And Why Does It Matter? *Strategic Management Journal, 12*, 61–74; Nelson, R., & Winter, S. (1982). *An Evolutionary Theory Of Economic Change*. Cambridge, Ma: Harvard University Press; Zollo, M. & Winter, S. G. (2002). Deliberate Learning and the Evolution of Dynamic Capabilities. *Organisation Science*, 13(3): pp. 339–351.
10. Zollo, M., & Winter, S. G. (2002). Deliberate Learning and the Evolution of Dynamic Capabilities. *Organisation Science,* 13(3): pp. 339–351.
11. Teece, D. J., Pisano, G., & Shuen, A. (1997). Dynamic Capabilities and Strategic Management. *Strategic Management Journal,* 18(7): pp. 509–533; Eisenhardt, K. M., & Martin, J. A. (2000). Dynamic Capabilities: What Are They? *Strategic Management Journal,* 21: pp. 1105–1121.
12. Ghosn, C. & P. Ries, (2005). *Shift: Inside Nissan's Historic Revival*, New York: Currency Doubleday, p. 97
13. Ghosn, C. (January 2002). Saving the Business without Losing the Company. *Harvard Business Review*, pp. 37–45.
14. Ghosn, C. & P. Ries, (2005). *Shift: Inside Nissan's Historic Revival*, New York: Currency Doubleday, p. 100.

15. Peterson, C., Maier, S. F., & Seligman, M. E. P. (1993). *Learned Helplessness: A Theory for the Age of Personal Control.* New York: Oxford University Press.
16. Institute On Governance (April 3, 1996). *Trampling the Turf: Enhancing Collaboration in the Public Service of Canada.* A Study Prepared for the Deputy Minister Task Force on Horizontal Issues; and the Deputy Minister Task Force on Service Delivery.
17. Reddy, K. Anji, The Future of Medicine in 25 CEOs and Thought Leaders on India in the Year 2020. *Business Today.* January 16, 2005, pp. 192–198.
18. Manfred F.R. Kets de Vries & Raoul de Vitry dAvaucourt, (1997). *Transcript of Video Interview with Sir David Simon and John Browne.* INSEAD Case. 497-013-3.
19. Edmondson, A., Bohmer, R., & Pisano, G. (October, 2001). Speeding Up Team Learning. *Harvard Business Review*, pp. 125–132.
20. Ibid.
21. Ghosn, C. (January 2002). Saving the Business without Losing the Company. *Harvard Business Review*, pp. 37–45.
22. Ibid.
23. Ibid., p. 41.
24. Ibid., p. 41.
25. Ghosn, C. & P. Ries, (2005). *Shift: Inside Nissan's Historic Revival.*, New York: Currency Doubleday, p. 96.
26. From *Hindustan Times,* New Delhi December 18, 2001.
27. Hrebiniak, L. G. (2005). *Making Strategy Work: Leading Effective Execution And Change.* New Jersey: Wharton School Publishing.
28. Ibid.
29. Ibid.
30. Yeung, Arthur K., Ulrich, David O., Nason, Stepehen W., Von Glinow & Mary Ann, (1998). *Organisational Learning Capability.* New York: Oxford University Press.
31. Ulrich, Dave & Brockbank, Wayne, (2005). *The HR Value Proposition.* Boston, Massachusetts: Harvard Business School Press.
32. Gopakumar, M. G. (2005). *Project Manthan at Tata Chemicals Limited: Case,* Tata Management Training Centre, Pune.
33. Buckman, Steve (June 29–July 2, 2003). *How to Succeed in a Changing Marketplace and Business Culture.* Presidents' Panel of the 84th Annual International Management Conference—PIMA, New York City, New York.

34. Gopakumar, M. G. (2005). *Project Manthan at Tata Chemicals Limited: Case*, Tata Management Training Centre, Pune
35. For a detailed description of the Workout methodology, refer to Ulrich, Dave, Kerr, Steve, & Ashkenas, Ron (2002). *'The GE Work-Out'*, McGraw-Hill Professional Publishing.
36. Piramal, G. & Ghoshal, S. (March 17, 2005). The Extraordinary Story Of Mittal Steel. *Www.Rediff.Com (Http://Www.Rediff.Com/ Money/2005/Mar/17mittal.Htm)*
37. Buckman, Steve (June 29–July 2, 2003). *How to Succeed in a Changing Marketplace and Business Culture.* Presidents' Panel of the 84th Annual International Management Conference—PIMA, New York City, New York.

CHAPTER 6

Building Change Capability

OVERVIEW

This chapter discusses the fourth critical task in change management, of building change capability. This aspect is not given enough emphasis in current models of change management. We first present an overview of building capability and discuss the key ingredients of this process. In the following sections we expand on the specific ingredients of building change capability. Self-efficacy, focus and energy are key elements for building capability. Change managers build capability by setting challenging goals, creating ownership, structuring activities to facilitate reflection and action, initiating processes to accelerate unlearning and learning, and fostering a behavioural context that is positive and learning-oriented. The basic leadership task in building capability is to develop people's confidence by demonstrating *faith* in their capabilities. To put it simply, effective leaders build capability by making people believe in their own abilities to achieve challenging goals.

BUILDING CHANGE CAPABILITY

This section examines the notion of capability and how it is built. We advance four propositions to capture the process of building capability in organisations. But before getting down to defining capability and advancing the propositions, we present an overview of the remarkable journey of Tata Steel over the last 10 to 12 years. The story provides a concrete illustration of the capability building process.

INDIA'S TATA STEEL: THE WORLD'S LOWEST COST STEEL PRODUCER

For a company that is almost 100 years old, Tata Steel[1] has shown remarkable agility since the early 90s. When the forces of liberalisation were set in motion, the business environment for this steel company changed dramatically. It became quite clear that the company would no longer enjoy the luxury of cost-plus government-determined pricing and seller's market. To prepare for global competition, the organisational leaders put in place myriad processes.

Over a hundred teams were mobilised to bring about improvements in different areas. Cumulatively, over 5000 people were entrusted the challenge of carrying out various initiatives for modernising mindsets of the company's 40,000 employees, enhancing quality, bringing about radical performance improvements through 'Total Operational Performance' (TOP), creating a market-oriented organisation, de-bottlenecking facilities, phasing out technologically obsolete plants, adding new facilities for manufacturing value-added products, capacity expansion and so on. The entire workforce of 40,000 people was trained in certain improvement techniques to change patterns of thinking. A major change initiative called ASPIRE (Aspirational Initiatives to Retain Excellence) was launched to use teams as an instrument and source of innovation in the company. The idea was to get people to look at existing operations with new eyes, be innovative and translate the ideas into effective ground-level implementation.

Box 6.1 presents a small sample of the significant performance improvements that the company was able to bring about, thanks to the unleashing of the energies of individuals and groups working on challenging projects in the new environment.

> **Box 6.1: Sample of Performance Achievements Resulting from ASPIRE**
>
> ➤ The new cold rolling mill with a capacity of 1 million tons per annum was completed in a world record time of 28 months and a world record lowest cost of Rupees 16 billion, beating the previous record held by Pohang Iron and Steel Company (Posco), Korea
> ➤ The total revamp of a blast furnace was completed in a record time of 105 days and at a cost of Rupees 2.1 billion, against best offers from foreign contractors for 210 days implementation and Rupees 5 billion cost
> ➤ With very little additional investment of financial resources, but considerable investment of innovative energies of workers and managers, a run-down mill to make reinforced bars that the consultants had recommended to sell off, has consistently been a star performer in the company, significantly exceeding design capacity and generating record profits
> ➤ Raw material consumption per ton of saleable steel has dropped from 4.52 tons in 1994 to 3.20 tons in 2003
> ➤ There has been a sharp drop in specific refractory consumption from 20.6 units in 1996 to 7.9 units in 2003

The company's revenues have steadily increased to $3.7 billion in 2004–2005 compared to $800 million in 1990–1991. The profit after tax was about $800 million for 2004-2005 against a figure of $50 million in 1990–1991. The World Steel Dynamics (WSD), a US-based independent agency that monitors and ranks the performance of global steel manufacturers, has rated the company among the top five steel producers in the world for the last four years. With its consistent cost rationalisation and impressive record of doubling labour productivity in the previous five years, Tata Steel has emerged as the world's lowest cost producer of Hot Rolled coils. As a vindication of the success of the company's sweeping and radical changes, Tata Steel has been ranked the best steel company in the world in WSD's 2005 ranking.[2] For a company that was considered by many as uncompetitive even in the Indian market as early as in the early 90s, this has been a spectacular resurgence.

FOUR PROPOSITIONS ON CAPABILITY BUILDING

The remarkable story of Tata Steel conveys certain valuable insights on the notion of capability and how it is built. Capability or the quality of being capable refers to a talent or ability that has potential for development or use; the capacity to be used, treated, or developed for a specific purpose.[3] We say that an individual has developed his/her capability in a specific area when he/she can execute existing tasks more effectively and can also carry out new tasks successfully. In the specific context of change, employees who have developed change capability are: able to psychologically cope with change more effectively, less resistant to change, able to generate new ideas and able to execute changes more effectively. Building change capability of employees enhances an organisation's future prospects for survival, growth and transformation. Enhancing change capability of employees facilitates ownership of change leading to a more proactive organisation. Therefore, building capability or capacity for change is an integral aspect of change management.

How can managers and organisations build capability? We advance four propositions to capture the process of building capability in organisations. First, *capability is built by individuals and groups*. Organisations don't learn; people do.[4] But not all people are learning oriented. About 10 per cent of the population tends to comprise active learners who are perennially curious, tuned into the external world, and picking up what is going on around them.[5] As a result they are highly effective in new or challenging situations. About 60 per cent tend to be random or passive learners; they learn as a matter of happenstance rather than habit. In the right environment, their learning process is kindled. Blocked learners seem to lack the facility for learning. About 30 per cent people in organisations are usually in this category and are resistant to change and learning. Tata Steel provided the active learners numerous opportunities for their natural inclinations by setting high aspirations. The random or passive learners had an inviting context to get involved and contribute. There were opportunities for individuals to come together, reflect and act in order to build capability.

Second, *individuals and groups build capability when they successfully execute challenging projects.* In other words, in order to build capability, individuals need to undertake a task that is slightly beyond their present capacity. Capability is built when they successfully complete the task and reflect on their success. In Tata Steel, over 5000 individuals worked on challenging improvement and innovation projects. There were groups pursuing a variety of goals pertaining to cost rationalisation, greater sense of identification with the customers, and development of value-added products. At the run-down merchant mill, managers and workers worked together on the almost-impossible goal of not just saving the mill, but bringing about dramatic performance improvement. Learning was required to achieve each of these goals, and in the process capability was built.

Third, *building capability involves paying simultaneous attention to both action and reflection.* Individuals and groups need to act in order to build capability but mindless action does not lead to increased capability. There may be successes or failures; but it is necessary to study why things succeed and why things fail. It is the inquiry into 'why' that constitutes organisational sense making, and that is the only path to consistently generate new ideas and effective performance. Reflection or learning from experience is crucial for building capability.

Fourth, *leaders and organisations can help individuals and groups build capability by providing a context that aids action and reflection.* In particular, organisational contexts that promote a positive behavioural climate tend to encourage building of capability. For a number of years, Tata Steel languished as one of the mediocre players in the steel industry till the leaders set a powerful vision to align the people in the organisation and unleashed a whole set of learning initiatives. In the new context characterised by challenges, support for initiative, role models and ready outlets for innovative spirit, processes were put in place for people to gain necessary knowledge and insights and apply them. There were systematic approaches to develop new methods of working. Most important, the change programme also became a process of modernising mindsets and of changing the way people are motivated.

SELF-EFFICACY, FOCUS AND ENERGY FOR CAPABILITY BUILDING

An organisation's change capability is enhanced when individuals in that organisation enhance their own capabilities. There are three related aspects to capability building by individuals. First, they must have confidence in their abilities to learn and enhance their own capabilities. They must have positive expectations that their efforts will lead to increased capabilities. We refer to this sense of confidence as *self-efficacy*. Second, they must be clear about the ways in which they can increase their capability. They must be able to set goals and develop an action plan to expand their capabilities. This provides *focus*. Third, they must exert the necessary effort and energy to achieve their goals. This *energy* is required to drive capability building.

Thus the process of building capability requires paying attention to individual attributes such as self-efficacy, focus and energy. Capability building occurs by achieving challenging goals through processes of learning and change. It requires paying attention to learning processes and behavioural contexts that promote learning. We expand on these ideas in the following sections.

SELF-EFFICACY

Learning requires being prepared to venture into areas that are new and different, and to deal with the unexpected. It requires individuals to deal with ambiguity, and be optimistic and persistent even when initial efforts fail to achieve results. They have to get into inquiry mode, examine the root causes, and take actions to prevent the recurrence of difficulties or tap the benefits of opportunities. On the other hand, if individuals feel uncomfortable with the complexity and uncertainty inherent in ambiguous situations, they are more likely to avoid those situations. They would respond in a manner that merely gets rid of the immediate difficulties. In such cases, there would be little or no adaptation to change.

Ambiguity has at least two faces. When connected to confusion, it is seen as negative. On the other hand, when it is associated with richness, it would be interpreted as positive.[6] Whether or not they are aware of it, organisational members make choices in dealing with organisational situations. One option for them is to stick to established routines and avoid dealing with uncertainty. The other is to choose to engage with the richness of greater ambiguity. This choice has a significant impact on their learning and capability development. To quote the French novelist Marcel Proust, 'The real voyage of discovery consists not in seeking new landscapes, but in having new eyes.'

Let us review the Tata Steel experience to examine the nature of choice points in dealing with ambiguity. In the organisational routines prior to early 90s, most employees largely operated from a 'spectator' stance, rather than behave like 'actor' in the system. With a spectator orientation, people may see what is happening, but they do not feel capable of exercising positive influence to move the decision in the right direction. Several individuals may have worried about the persistent difficulties or the lack of excitement. In private conversations they may even have discussed the futility of their limited approaches and blamed the other functions. But they did not venture outside their set routines. Perhaps they perceived the choice of trying out ideas and initiatives as posing unacceptable levels of ambiguity or even as 'impossible' given the nature of their organisation or their status and influence in the system.

When individuals don't engage with ambiguity for whatever reason and remain highly selective in trying out different approaches, they do not gain too many new experiences. Only a new experience can serve as a basis for new learning. When the experience and exposure are restricted, the supply line of basic inputs for learning and capability building gets choked. In such a situation, individual and organisational capabilities tend to stagnate or even decline.

Research done at the Centre for Creative Leadership and elsewhere indicates that people grow and develop only when there is greater exposure and greater variety of experiences.[7] As we have seen above, even when there are opportunities to be exposed to new experiences, people need to be confident about their abilities to learn and enhance their capabilities. Albert Bandura of the Stanford University refers to this concept as self-efficacy.[8] According to him:

> A strong sense of efficacy enhances human accomplishment and personal well-being in many ways. People with high assurance in their capabilities approach difficult tasks as challenges to be mastered rather than as threats to be avoided. Such an efficacious outlook fosters intrinsic interest and deep engrossment in activities. They set themselves challenging goals and maintain strong commitment to them. They heighten and sustain their efforts in the face of failure. They quickly recover their sense of efficacy after failures or setbacks. They attribute failure to insufficient effort or deficient knowledge and skills, which are acquirable. They approach threatening situations with assurance that they can exercise control over them. Such an efficacious outlook produces personal accomplishments, reduces stress and lowers vulnerability to depression.
>
> In contrast, people who doubt their capabilities shy away from difficult tasks which they view as personal threats. They have low aspirations and weak commitment to the goals they choose to pursue. When faced with difficult tasks, they dwell on their personal deficiencies, on the obstacles they will encounter, and all kinds of adverse outcomes rather than concentrate on how to perform successfully. They slacken their efforts and give up quickly in the face of difficulties. They are slow to recover their sense of efficacy following failure or setbacks. Because they view insufficient performance as deficient aptitude it does not require much failure for them to lose faith in their capabilities. They fall easy victim to stress and depression.[9]

According to Bandura, self-efficacy has four major effects on people. First, it affects their thinking and analytical ability or what is known as cognitive ability. Second, it affects their motivation. Third, it shapes their emotions. Finally, it also affects the activities and task people choose to pursue. Building on the ideas of Bandura, Conger and Kanungo[10] list four context factors leading to potential lowering of self-efficacy belief: organisational factors, supervisory style, reward systems and job design. A summary of the factors that tend to lower self-efficacy is given below:

1. Organisational factors such as bureaucratic climate, poor communication, centralised control of organisational resources.
2. Poor quality of relationship with superiors—e.g. absence of feelings of autonomy, emphasis on failures, lack of consideration such as, not providing reasons for actions, etc.
3. Perceived absence of rewards based on competence, performance or innovative behaviour.
4. Nature of jobs characterised by lack of role clarity, absence of meaningful goals/tasks, low discretion, high rule structure and rigid work routines.

In managing change, self-efficacy is a major determinant for success. Employees with higher levels of self-efficacy can overcome obstacles and challenges that are inevitable part of any change effort. Change leaders can shape their employees' self-efficacy by setting them challenging goals and then helping them to achieve those goals. However, this aspect of change management has not received a great deal of attention in the change management literature.

As can be seen from the Tata Steel experience, for capability building to occur, individuals need to be willing to take on challenging tasks. This implies facing up to complexity and uncertainty. But managers may not be comfortable with complex uncertain situations. A research group at the University of Bamberg in Germany has conducted several studies on cognitive aspects of dealing with problems characterised by uncertainty and complexity.[11] Their studies clearly demonstrate the important role that efficacy (or sense of competence as this research group refers to it) plays in enhancing the effectiveness of complex problem solving.

Often, there is a tendency for people to create a superficial sense of competence to shield them from confronting the real challenges of complexity and uncertainty. For example, individuals may focus on activities that are not so important but which can gratify the psychological need to feel competent. Even when far more important challenges are waiting to be dealt with, they may clean office desk tables, deal with inconsequential correspondence or perform tasks that get some quick and favourable attention from colleagues or co-workers. They may even 'invent' some problems to solve to gain a sense of control. This may include reassigning roles to people, introducing new reports, or getting a study initiated. Such behaviour keeps them away from challenges that they need to really face up to. Obviously this can prove to be highly dysfunctional.

Efficacy is demonstrated when individuals feel secure in avoiding such pseudo solutions. The Bamberg researchers have identified certain factors as contributing to a sense of competence or self-efficacy. Their insights have been summarised in Box 6.2 below.

Box 6.2: What Factors Contribute to Self-Efficacy?

➤ Being exposed to a range of experiences most of which end with positive outcomes
➤ Apart from initiating actions to get things done, pausing to reflect and inquire into one's understanding of the changes and developments (What are we really trying to accomplish here? What is the best route?) and developing a valid mental map of the change (sense making) to be able to find plausible explanations for things that happen
➤ Feeling of mastery related to the job arising, for example, from performing complex tasks on one's own, tasting success and testing one's efficacy
➤ Managers acting as role models—this motivates team members to behave in a like manner
➤ Words of encouragement, verbal feedback that individuals possess the capabilities to master given tasks; support to overcome self-doubts or personal deficiencies
➤ Trusting group atmosphere that provides emotional support and fosters risk taking associated with venturing into new areas
➤ Work processes that encourage decision autonomy and provide due consideration to views and ideas that are expressed
➤ Operating in a work environment that accepts genuine errors as chances for learning and improvement and encourages self reflection, feedback, and constructive criticism rather than look for scapegoats

EFFICACY IN HIGH UNCERTAINTY ENVIRONMENTS

In a prize-winning paper, Eisenhardt[12] studied feelings of efficacy in high uncertainty environments. She points out that emotion is integral to high stakes decision-making. Factors like complexity, uncertainty and limited information tend to cause anxiety, loss of confidence/impetus to act and urge to procrastinate. Confidence and anxiety are key factors that influence the pace of decision closure. Her studies show that fast and effective groups demonstrate certain interesting patterns of behaviour to accelerate decision-making. They achieve this by protecting the feelings of efficacy against the uncertainty posed by high velocity environments. Eisenhardt found that fast and effective groups followed certain approaches to make decisions. A summary of her research findings is presented in Table 6.1.

Table 6.1: Accelerating Decisions in High-uncertainty Environments

Practices of Quick and Effective Groups	Outputs Achieved
Extensively track and discuss real time information	Build familiarity and friendship among team members. Encourage frank conversations. Develop collective intuition that helps superior grasp of changing dynamics
Incorporate frame-breaking tasks into routines	Establish and reinforce the desirability of constructive conflicts as norm
Consider each decision as part of larger context; Norm of 'Consensus with Qualification'	Reduce emotional stakes associated with choices; Achieve closure and timeliness of decisions.

First, rather than being pre-occupied with future trend projections (that tend to lag behind realities), fast and effective groups extensively track and discuss real time information. They keep a close tab on results in important areas and on external information. Frequent meetings build familiarity and friendship, and make frank conversations easier. Individuals are encouraged to organise themselves around their natural inclinations to consider different sides of the issue. This helps the teams build collective intuition. With superior grasp of changing dynamics, people see threats and opportunities sooner and more accurately.

Second, fast and effective groups employ an approach to conflict management that is better suited to the demands of an uncertain environment. Such environments inevitably lead to divergence of views and perspectives. These groups recognise that while conflict can be an energising force, it can also be highly dysfunctional if there is endless debate that can degenerate into paralysis by analysis at one end or tendency to centralise decision-making to avoid irreconcilable differences at the other.

To prevent dysfunctional conflicts (for example, people avoiding surfacing important issues or not being open to others' viewpoints or perspectives), these groups establish a strong norm that conflicts are acceptable and even desirable. Without adequate discussion of alternatives, decision-makers would not have the confidence in the final choice. That's why they constitute teams that are diverse in age, gender and functional background. They build frame-breaking tasks into their routines. For example, they resort to scenario planning and consider decisions in light of several possible future states. They play roles from different perspectives including their competitors' perspectives. They test well-crafted arguments by raising unexpected and occasionally fanciful concerns, and even structure the conversation to foster debate.

Third, having considered a multiple array of possibilities, they achieve closure on issues to meet time deadlines by resorting to 'consensus with qualification'. In this process, while the decision process is conducted with the goal of consensus in mind, there is a ready back-up if consensus does not emerge. The groups break the deadlock by using voting or allowing manager with the largest stake in the outcome to make the decision. These groups also consider each decision as a part of a larger context to reduce the emotional stakes associated with single decisions or choices.

Such approaches help fast and effective groups achieve three important outcomes:

1. Accelerated cognitive processing,
2. Smooth group process, and
3. Confidence to act.

Accelerated cognitive processing implies collective intuition to recognise and process information in patterns or blocks and to gain superior grasp of changing dynamics. Smooth group process allows consideration of different views and ideas without sacrificing timeliness of decisions. Most important, the groups retain their impetus to act despite the high level of uncertainty because their decision-making approaches are better suited to the demands of high velocity environments.

FOCUS AND ENERGY

Enhancing self-efficacy, while important, is only one of the three aspects for building change capability at an individual level. The other two are focus and energy. Focus implies that individuals and groups have clear understanding of the goals to be attained, requisite capabilities to be acquired, and the specific steps to be taken for this purpose. Energy signifies that actors are determined to do what is required to achieve the goals. If an organisation is aimlessly pursuing learning, it cannot be considered a learning organisation. Such an organisation may be learning things, but it is not in pursuit of a well-defined vision or set of business goals.[13] Learning is valuable only when it is geared to a well-defined agenda.

Let us examine both the elements of focus and energy together in this section. In a co-authored paper published in the *Harvard Business Review*, the late Sumantra Ghoshal, who was a Professor at the London Business School, offered a remarkable insight into what makes managers effective. Based on case studies of corporations in Europe and the United States, Bruch and Ghoshal[14] identified two key elements of successful change. These are *focus* and *energy*.

Focus refers to concentrated attention defined as zeroing in on goals and seeing them to completion, weighing options before acting and concentrating on key projects. Energy refers to the vigour that is fuelled by intense personal commitment. According to Bruch and Ghoshal, 'energy is what pushes the managers go the extra mile when tackling heavy workloads and meeting tight deadlines.'[15] Both focus and energy are positive qualities that are required to bring about effective change in organisations. Neither is sufficient by itself. Bruch and Ghoshal offer an interesting matrix (Figure 6.1) of four possible typologies by combining these two essential elements.

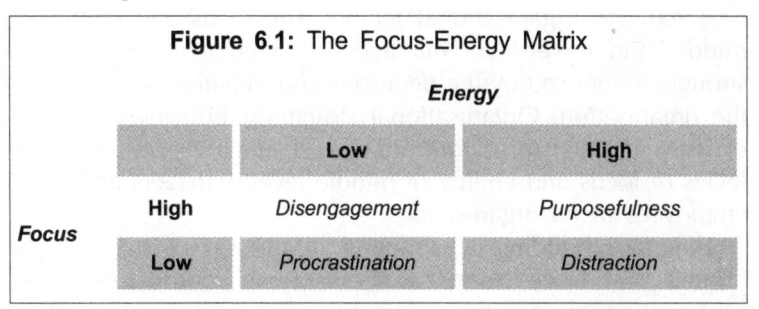

Figure 6.1: The Focus-Energy Matrix

Focus		Energy	
		Low	High
	High	Disengagement	Purposefulness
	Low	Procrastination	Distraction

The matrix, in simple terms, identifies four types of behaviour. All managers can be seen to belong to one of the four cells in the matrix in terms of their behaviour. Managers who are high on both focus and energy are *purposeful*. Those that are high on energy but low on focus are *distracted*. Managers low on energy but high on focus are *disengaged* and those that are low on both focus and energy are *procrastinating*. You don't need to be a genius to figure out that purposefulness is the most desirable behaviour for bringing about effective change. What might surprise and alarm you, however, is the distribution of managers across the four typologies.

According to Bruch and Ghoshal, less than 10 per cent of all managers are purposeful. About 30 per cent are procrastinators while another 20 per cent are disengaged. The remaining 40 per cent are distracted i.e. they are high on energy but low on focus. Brusch and Ghoshal's data provides an insight into why organisations engage in meaningless repetitive change. Imagine a scenario, where the top management is largely made up of managers with high energy and low focus—a typical scenario is many large organisations. Their high levels of energy will result in an initiative overload while lack of focus will turn it into change-related chaos. The effect of this behaviour on middle managers is interesting. The competent middle managers will be disengaged while others unable to cope will be procrastinating.

Effective change management is characterised by behaviour that is *purposeful*. In other words, managers at all levels must be highly focused and energetic. This is not an easy task because the natural tendency of most managers is to be low in either focus or in energy and sometimes in both due to a variety of personal and organisational factors. The focus and energy of middle and lower-level managers in a large organisation is strongly influenced by the decisions and initiatives at the top of the organisation. Organisational structures, policies and rules, or what we refer to as *routines*, can significantly influence the levels of focus and energy of middle level managers and other employees in an organisation.

Therefore, building capability is all about understanding the factors that lower focus and energy of employees in an organisation so that these can be minimised or eliminated. However, before enhancing the focus and energy of employees, top managers need to evaluate their own levels of focus and energy. Generally, one can expect to find high levels of energy among top managers. Therefore, the critical issue is to ensure that they are also highly focused. Distracted managers driving change from the top can unleash a wave of initiatives that can lead to disengagement, procrastination, burnout, cynicism and despair at lower levels. How can top managers act purposefully during periods of change?

PURPOSEFULNESS AMONG TOP MANAGERS

For a top manager, the key to understanding how to be purposeful lies in knowing how to move from being distracted to being purposeful. However, we cannot move from a present state to a future state unless we identify the precise features of each. In other words, what are the distinguishing characteristics of purposeful and distracted managers? Table 6.2 presents the characteristics of each type of manager.

Purposefulness is an indispensable quality for a manager at the top of an organisation. In fact, this is one key distinguishing feature of people who have been very successful in initiating and managing change. Carlos Ghosn, who achieved one of the most remarkable turnarounds in corporate history by transforming a nearly bankrupt Nissan in 1999 into the most profitable automobile company in the world in less than three years, embodies this quality of purposefulness. Lakshmi Niwas Mittal, the chief executive of Mittal Steel, is another exemplar of purposefulness. There are numerous others, perhaps not so well-known, in different industries and in different countries who exemplify this quality of purposefulness. The managing director of the Delhi Metro Rail Corporation in India, Elattuvalappil Sreedharan,[16] is one such exemplar. Later in this chapter, we examine one of his achievements in leading the completion of ambitious projects before deadlines and within budgets—a rarity in politics-plagued Indian public systems.

Table 6.2: Distinguishing Features of Purposeful and Distracted Managers

Distracted Managers	Purposeful Managers
► Well-intentioned ► Highly energetic ► Feel a desperate need to do something when under pressure ► Tend to be aggressive and unreflective ► Have trouble developing strategies and adjusting to new requirements ► Tend to be short-sighted ► Over-involved in multiple projects ► Mostly in fire-fighting or crisis-management mode ► Are largely reactive (feel constrained by the external environment)	► Highly energetic and highly focused ► High levels of self-awareness ► High levels of clarity about their own intentions, values and beliefs ► Are very careful in picking their goals and battles ► Feel personally responsible for company's fate ► Welcome opportunities to pursue new goals ► Are good at generating and using their energy ► Are skilled in finding ways to reduce stress and refuel themselves ► Are proactive (They first decide what they must achieve and then manage the external environment)

Source: Based on Bruch and Ghoshal, 2004

PROCESSES OF CAPABILITY BUILDING

We have discussed the three elements for building capability—self-efficacy, focus and energy. We also advanced four propositions to capture the capability building process. As we noted, capability is built by individuals and groups successfully executing challenging projects and during the process paying simultaneous attention to reflection and action in a favourable context. Thus the capability building process involves setting *challenging goals*. Not only are challenging goals to be set, but there also has to be *ownership by organisational members* and their willingness to engage with the problems in achieving those goals. *Structuring of activities* should be able to foster reflection and learning. There should be initiatives to *promote learning* and *facilitate unlearning*. And there should be a *positive behavioural context* in the nature of a facilitative organisational architecture. We discuss each of these processes in some detail in the following sections.

ROLE OF CHALLENGING GOALS

The most effective way to build capability is to challenge managers and employees in an organisation to achieve goals that are just slightly beyond their capacity. As Ghosn puts it:

You have to solicit their collaboration, you have to demand a lot from them, and you have to give them challenging goals. If not, they'll gradually waste away. One may have a beautiful physique, but if it's not put to work, it atrophies.[17]

Setting unrealistic goals destroys a person's self-efficacy because it will lead to a failure experience. For instance, while Ghosn was aggressive in setting targets and pushing people towards higher performance, he was also sensitive enough to know when not to push. In his own words:

In purchases, we knew that we had a price discrepancy with Renault—it was between 20 per cent and 25 per cent. And we knew that was something we wouldn't be able to fix in six months. We pushed the team to raise its goals higher, but once we achieved a reduction of 20 per cent—after three years—I felt that we'd reached the limit. This wasn't a scientific conclusion. It was based on experience, on real life, and on talks with team members. There comes a time when you have to know when to stop. I'd wanted to achieve at least a 20 per cent reduction in purchasing costs. Reaching that goal was the result of what was already a major effort, so we decided it was best to stop there.[18]*

Ghosn's views are quite similar to those of Sir David Simon, Chairman of British Petroleum who was able to bring about a successful organisational transformation with the same broad strategy that his predecessor had tried to implement, but failed. Simon felt that the primary shift had been from behavioural to performance parameters. According to him,

We made slow progress when we were more or less obsessed inside the company with cultural change, behavioural change and how to treat each other differently... (Later) all I did was to say the outcome of change must be that certain targets are achieved. It was to take a behavioural process into a performance process. The only way you get things to perform in my view is to set targets and measure progress. Picking the right targets is a skill in itself.

This principle that Ghosn and Simon used successfully was also the basis of turnaround in the companies acquired by Mittal Steel. In the early 1980's, the Mexican government built a new steel mill based on the DRI technology adjacent to an existing steel mill. Built with an investment of about $2.2 billion, this was a state-of-the-art facility that was intended to produce steel pipes for the booming oil industry. However, the end of the oil boom coupled with a failing Mexican economy forced the government to devalue the Peso. Investment in the new plant was slashed and the company had to turn to the open market to procure iron pellets at a high cost. A planned plate mill was also abandoned and the company was forced to sell lower value steel slabs rather than finished steel plates. It operated well below its capacity of 2 million tons a year, incurring heavy operating losses. The Mexican government blamed the management and workers of the company for its losses and decided to privatise both the old and the new steel mills. Based on the reputation LNM had acquired by turning around a steel mill in Trinidad, his company, Ispat, was invited to bid for the Mexican company, Imexsa.[19]

Mittal sent a CFT consisting of 20 managers representing all line and staff functions from Ispat's Trinidad and Indonesia plants. The team was instructed to develop turnaround plans. The team discovered a factory consisting of a young but demoralised workforce, running at 20 per cent capacity, producing low quality slabs and overwhelmed with technical problems. Ispat took control of the plant on the first of January, 1992 in the midst of a global recession in the steel industry. The furnaces had to be shut down briefly because of lack of demand and inadequate storage capacity for the finished slabs. Despite this economic downturn, only 70 people were made redundant and another 270 were hired. Mittal recalls his first steps at Imexsa:

In Mexico we did what we do with every business . . . we sat down with management of the acquired company to discuss various options for improvement and we developed the business plan. We sat down with each of the departments to understand their problems and viewpoints and gave our input based on international experience and our 'due diligence.'

Together we set very aggressive targets because we don't benchmark companies based on local standards, but on international standards. If the management of the acquired company is willing to commit to these targets, they stay. If they have any problems following our business plan and vision, they go. The Imexsa managers stayed.[20]

A production planning manager at Imexsa recalled his experience with Mittal:

In our first meeting, we presented two alternative production plans, one for 600,000 tons—it was conservative and based on our past experience—and another plan for 1.2 million tons. Mr Mittal saw both and said, 'forget the small plan, just let me know what you need to implement the second plan.' We expressed concern that we might not find a market for the additional slabs, but Mr Mittal said, 'You will have the volume because I'm going to take care of that for you.'

In 1992, Imexsa increased its shipments from 528,000 tons to 929,000 tons and earned a small profit. Between 1992 and 1998, the annual shipments increased from 929,000 tons to 3 million tons. While there were other factors that improved Imexsa's performance, a significant factor was the way in which Mittal empowered people by challenging them to set higher goals and ensuring that they had the resources to achieve the goals. As one of the managers at Imexsa put it:

I feel the need to constantly improve performance every day, but the management does not force it upon me. I'm not fighting against somebody else's budgets—I agreed to the goal, and the best way to reach a goal is not with a big gun to your head. I set stretch goals because I want Imexsa to win.

At first, I wanted Imexsa to be the best steel plant in Lazaro Cardenas, then the best steel plant in Mexico, but now I ask 'why can't we be the best steel plant in the world?' We always wanted to be the best, but we couldn't because the old management put up too many limitations.[21]

In conventional change management literature and programmes, empowerment is seen as delegating authority and resources. That is a very limited view of empowerment. By merely providing people authority and resources, we cannot ensure that they are empowered. Empowerment is not only a structural feature but also a state of mind. People feel truly empowered when they have a belief in their ability to achieve challenging goals. It is the role of the change leader to foster this belief and, thereby, enhance people's self-efficacy. Leaders can do this by: (a) providing people with success experiences associated with achieving challenging goals, (b) being a role model, and

(c) persuading them that they have the ability to achieve the goals set for them.

Whether it is the case of Tata Steel, Nissan or Ispat, leaders created an environment where certain aspirations became real to people. How do the challenging goals or aspirations help build capability? To start with, shared aspirations create demands for ideas that can lead to higher performance. To develop new ideas and implement those effectively, new routines are required. New routines spur the need for acquiring or developing new capabilities. In both Tata Steel and Nissan, new organisational arrangements like special task forces, learning workshops and cross-functional teams emerged to realise the challenges. These made it possible to engage with the problem differently. For example, the processes helped focus attention on improvement agenda, incorporate multiple perspectives in analysing issues, make quick and innovative decisions, and follow these up with prompt and proactive steps to achieve results.

The new organisational arrangements created to achieve challenging goals provided employees a very different kind of exposure. For instance, they were working closely with colleagues from other functions for the first time to evolve action plans within challenging time frames to achieve dramatic improvements in results. Such exposure helped them gain different experiences and so acquire newer capabilities. In the same organisations, in the earlier milieu, individuals had not chosen to pursue the less trodden path. But they behaved differently in the new context. The pattern of engagement with ambiguity was clearly different. By exhibiting willingness to chase challenging goals, people tackled difficult tasks and in the process built capability.

FRAMING OF CHALLENGES

Do challenging goals always energise people? Tucker and her associates state that this is not necessarily the case.[22] Sometimes people may perceive the new demands as unfair burden and lose even their existing levels of enthusiasm. Why does this happen? Tucker and her associates contend that the way leaders '*frame*' challenges has a vital bearing on how people perceive the challenges and how they respond to them. Their research identifies two frames that leaders tend to adopt—'*Learning*' frame and '*Performance*' frame.

A learning frame casts new challenges or situations as collaborative opportunities to learn and make worthwhile contributions. Leaders adopting a learning frame help their organisations break through the insularity that all too often accompanies success. They are far more successful in engaging others in a rewarding collaborative effort to confront new and challenging situations and achieve effective implementation and superior results.

A project or challenge that is viewed through a learning frame has three characteristics:

- The project is seen aspirationally—as an opportunity to help team members accomplish compelling goals for themselves and their stakeholders
- The leader emphasises his or her dependence on the help and input of other team members
- The other team members see themselves as partners, essential resources for overcoming the challenges that lie ahead

On the other hand, when a project or challenge is viewed through a performance frame, the results tend to be dismal. A performance frame has a different set of characteristics:

- The project's purpose is seen defensively—as a burden, a necessary requirement for keeping up with the competition
- The project leader portrays his or her role as that of an essentially self-sufficient technical expert who is beyond the difficulties and problems of the group
- The other team members see themselves as subordinates, mere implementers of the leader's project

The implications of the framing studies are clear. The leaders should avoid articulating the goal as a burden or an inevitable necessity in the competitive environment. Instead, they should learn to communicate the challenges in a manner that captures the excitement of achievement and progress. They should help the team members perceive the challenges as presenting opportunities to excel and contribute. The leaders should communicate by words and deeds that they are actively involved in the process and the team would strive to realise the challenges in a collaborative mode.

It would be interesting in this regard to note the views of Sir David Simon: '*I spend a lot of time talking. And a lot of time, listening. It is dialogue... Part of the leadership role is generating excitement for other people. You should know how to give the buzz to other people. I would be very disappointed if people came to my room to chat about anything, they didn't go out feeling that this was an exciting business*'.

CREATING OWNERSHIP

Capability building requires making deliberate efforts. While challenges may exist, appropriate actions would follow only if employees own those challenges. Let us return to the example of Tata Steel to illustrate this aspect. Even prior to 1990's, the company faced challenges with regard to enhancing product quality, minimising costs, building customer orientation and so on. But employees did not seem to view these as 'their problems'. In other words, they did not *own* those problems. In such situations, there is no 'contact' between the organisational actors and the richness posed by the ambiguity arising from the challenges. Consequently no learning occurs.

But after Tata Steel instituted a number of change and learning initiatives, the patterns of employee engagement became different. A number of employees assumed ownership of specific challenges. They began to see opportunities for improvement and innovation in the same old situations. We notice that different patterns of engaging with ambiguity get manifested in terms what aspects people pay attention to, which phenomena in the chosen field are actually perceived, and how the information is interpreted.[23]

Thus it is important to examine whether people perceive the 'problem' in a given situation and whether they assume ownership of the problem. Sometimes the ownership gets limited to overcoming immediate obstacles. This is referred to as first-order problem solving. It is only in rare cases that ownership is also assumed for the higher order problem of diagnosing and altering the underlying causes to prevent recurrence. This is called second-order problem solving.[24] Depending on how the problem is perceived and responded to, capability building is enabled or prevented. When employees exhibit first-order problem solving, it effectively means that they have assumed ownership of only the lower order problem. In this case, they do not expend any more energy on a problem after obtaining the missing input needed to complete the task. They do not concern themselves with investigating and seeking to change the underlying causes. Studies have shown that as high as 90 to 95 per cent of the responses to problems could be of the first-order problem solving kind.[25]

Thus it is important to study the processes underlying people's recognition of problem and assumption of ownership. Here Maurice Landry's ideas provide some interesting insights. Landry[26] suggests that four interrelated conditions signal the presence of problem:

1. Past, present or future occurrence within an organisational context, which is judged as negative by an individual or a group—in other words, the situation is judged by an individual or a group as negative, and so it is seen as a crisis or opportunity.
2. Preliminary judgment on intervention capability—that is, individuals or groups feel some sense of control over the situation or event and conclude that something can be done about it.
3. Expression of a prima facie interest in doing something and committing resources—in light of limited time, attention and energy to deal with different issues, organisational actors conclude that they want to deal with this issue
4. Uncertainty as to appropriate action and how to implement it—in other words, individuals or groups feel that available readymade solutions are not acceptable and therefore systematic reflection is necessary.

Thus problem solving cannot be separated from the organisational actor's mindsets. According to Landry, the judgments and choices that organisational members make on the four factors determine whether or not they see a problem and whether or not they feel that some action is necessary for adaptation. Table 6.3 lists the four factors that can help create ownership.

Table 6.3: Factors that Lead to Recognition and Ownership of Problem

Creating Ownership
1. Help people perceive crisis or opportunity
2. Enable them to view issue as controllable at their level
3. Generate interest in allocating time, attention and resources to the issue.
4. Get people to reject existing solutions and undertake systematic reflection.

Let us begin with the first factor of *getting people to perceive a crisis or opportunity*. To be able to perceive crisis or opportunity, organisational members require feedback from service users and other stakeholders. But when the unit operates almost like a closed system, barriers to feedback remain high. That's why even when others see a crisis or opportunity, people inside the unit may conclude that the situation is not so negative. Sometimes, in organisations faced with serious difficulties, employees may see the need only for some 'fixing'. As we have seen above, this is first-order problem solving. By resorting to superficial solutions, organisational members effectively ignore the underlying symptoms.

It is therefore important for leaders to ensure that employees receive relevant feedback. There should be regular benchmarking and peer comparisons. A culture needs to be created that motivates and encourages people to report problems or near-misses, without being labelled as cynics or complainers. Certain leaders determine in advance what feedback they would need on the way change initiative is progressing and when they would get it. They utilise progress reviews and postmortems of change projects to identify, analyse and discuss the root causes of the problems and what needs to be done.

The second factor pertains to *enabling organisational members to view issues as controllable at their levels.* This would be judged as low if individuals feel that they have no access to necessary information to engage with the problem. For some aspects of the problem, they may be dependent on others, but have no way of getting their assistance and support. When there are no easy and convenient methods for communicating with others about their views and ideas and obtain their assistance, people would perceive their intervention capability as low and find the issues uncontrollable at their levels. It is also possible that people consider their status or influence within the system to be too low for dealing with the issue. This is a particularly serious problem in large organisations.

To enhance feelings of controllability, a number of steps can be taken. First, it is necessary to break down the larger challenge into manageable components and assign clear responsibilities for different parts. Organisational arrangements must be created for communication and coordination so that there are convenient forums and methods for sharing information, views and ideas and obtain assistance. It should be ensured that members have necessary resources, information, assistance and support to solve problems. Last but not least, leaders should generate optimism and hope that improvements can result from the initiatives taken by the employees.

The third factor relates to *generating interest in allocating time, attention and resources to the issue.* Organisational actors would be hesitant to commit resources when they feel that there is lack of acceptance of risk inherent in problem solving. In many organisations, role expectations are defined narrowly, and people may feel that they would 'cross wires' by initiating steps to diagnose the root causes. Commitment to resources may also not happen if people are preoccupied with routine urgencies. Problem solving and making improvements require expenditure of time, energy and resources, and so may be accorded low priority.

To tackle this factor, leaders should energetically communicate the importance of change agenda. They should convey expectations that employees would address the change issues. Promotion, pay and status should be linked to development of new ideas and skills. Conscious efforts should be made to move the culture and norms towards greater risk taking and acceptance of genuine mistakes as a normal part of learning. Work methods and assignments should be reviewed to create some slack for employees entrusted with certain responsibilities for change programme so that they can comfortably devote their time and energy. For example, unnecessary work should be eliminated when new responsibilities are added.

The fourth factor relates to *rejection of current ways of solving the problem*. This is unlikely to happen if the unit does not receive any direct external feedback that the solutions in vogue are unacceptable. When there are rigid boundaries across functions and hierarchical levels, people are more likely to stick to ready-made solutions. Any deviation from established routines may even be seen as invitation for trouble from other functions or from superiors.

A number of actions can help in getting employees to reject ready-made solutions and be willing to search for newer approaches. Role models in powerful positions who reject the status quo can change the perception of what is acceptable and what is not. People must be helped to reflect on how the usual ways of dealing with the situation would not be able to achieve higher aspirations, and what the long-term consequences of the actions could be. Cross-functional teams also help people realise the limitations of existing approaches. Successful change efforts should be publicised to encourage people to try newer approaches.

STRUCTURING ACTIVITIES FOR LEARNING

As we have noted earlier, demand for new ideas to achieve shared challenging goals spur emergence of new routines. These new organisational arrangements would be expected to help focus on improvements and innovations, incorporate multiple perspectives in analysis, decision-making and action taking. The field of Organisation Development (OD) has developed several interventions to systematically address problems and opportunities through effective participation and involvement of organisational members. The field has accumulated principles, rules of thumb and practical knowledge to guide managers on how to bring about change. OD interventions present valuable ideas for structuring activities in such a manner that individuals and groups can bring about improvements and enhance learning. French and Bell outline the design considerations that OD practitioners employ for structuring activities to maximise learning.[27] We present a summary of these thumb rules:

1. Include the people affected by the problem or the opportunity. If the goal is improved team effectiveness, have the whole team engage in the activities. If the goal is improved relations between two separate work groups, have both work groups present. Pre-planning the group composition is necessary for properly structuring the activity.
2. Ensure that the activity is not only problem or opportunity oriented, but also oriented to the problems and opportunities *generated by the individuals facing the issue*. People feel involved and interested when they have defined the issues. They are also then more likely to follow up with appropriate actions.
3. Set in motion processes to help people clarify the goals and ways to reach the goals. Don't assume that destinations and pathways are clear to every one. It would be highly de-motivating for people participating in a group process to not know what the group is working toward and how they can attain the goals.
4. Ensure that the expectations are realistic. Even if the tasks are hard, complicated and taxing, they should be attainable. After the experience, success or failure in accomplishing the goal should be examined for learning.
5. Involve both people strong on experience and those with good conceptual understanding to bring in multiple perspectives.
6. Shape the mood and climate in such a manner that individuals feel 'freed up' rather than anxious or defensive.

7. Design the process in a manner that the participants learn both how to solve a particular problem and 'learn how to learn'.
8. Individuals should learn about both *task* and *process*. The task is what the group is working on, i.e., the stated agenda items. The term *process* refers to *how* the group is working and *what else is going on* as participants work on the task, such as individual styles of interacting, behaving, and so on.
9. Ensure that individuals are engaged as whole persons, not segmented persons. It means calling into play role demands, thoughts, beliefs, feelings and strivings.

How to sequence activities? OD practice provides some useful guidelines[28]:

1. *Maximise diagnostic data.* Start with interventions that generate data needed to strengthen subsequent intervention decisions.
2. *Maximise effectiveness.* For example, this can be done by first developing readiness, motivation, knowledge or skills required by other interventions.
3. *Maximise efficiency.* Work out a sequence of actions to conserve organisational resources such as time, energy, and money.
4. *Maximise speed.* The sequence should also help enhance the speed with which ultimate organisational improvement is attained.
5. *Maximise relevance.* Deal first with the most immediate problems and the ones that have an impact on organisational performance so that the motivation to continue the efforts is maintained.
6. *Minimise psychological and organisational strain.* To maintain people' sense of competence and confidence and their commitment to organisational improvement, choose those interventions that are least likely to create dysfunctional effects such as anxiety, insecurity, distrust, unmet or under-met expectations, and unanticipated and unwanted effects on organisational performance.

What outputs would the OD interventions be expected to create that would have a bearing on capability building? French and Bell list the following points[29]:

1. *Feedback.* People learn new things about themselves, others, group processes, or organisational dynamics—data that either they did not know or did not previously take active account of. Awareness of new information tends to lead to change if the feedback is not too threatening.
2. *Awareness of changing socio-cultural norms or dysfunctional current norms.* People tend to modify their behaviour, attitudes, and values when they become aware of changes in the *norms* influencing their behaviour. Awareness has potential to lead to change because individuals seek to adjust their behaviour as per new norms.
3. *Increased interaction and communication.* When individuals and groups have an opportunity to communicate with people that they do not normally interact with, changes in attitudes and behaviour can result.
4. *Confrontation.* This term refers to surfacing and examining differences in beliefs, feelings, attitudes, values or norms to remove obstacles to effective interaction. Confrontation is a process that seeks to discern real differences that 'get in the way'.
5. *Education and participation.* Development of knowledge, skills and attitudes and increasing the number of people involved in problem solving, goal setting and generating new ideas increases the quality and acceptance of decisions, increases job satisfaction and promotes employee well-being.
6. *Increased accountability.* This results from activities that clarify people's responsibilities and that monitor performance related to those responsibilities.
7. *Increased energy and optimism.* Activities that energise and motivate people through visions of new possibilities contribute to effective problem solving and learning.

PROMOTING LEARNING

Capability is built through a process of learning that involves reflection and action. Learning is vital for building capability. There can be no increase in capability without learning. In Chapter 3, we discussed how mental models or mindsets can inhibit learning. The case of J & J cited by Finkelstein[30] (Box 6.3) illustrates this point, and throws light on the trappings of success.

> **Box 6.3: How Mindset Inhibited Learning at J & J**
>
> J & J revolutionised angioplasty procedures in 1994 when it introduced the stent in the United States, and its angioplasty surgery package had achieved more than 90 per cent market share and profit margins of nearly 80 per cent by 1997. Although a significant improvement, J & J's stent was still difficult to use. Feedback was available from key stakeholders on further innovations required. US cardiologists pointed to the superior products available overseas and urged J & J to introduce a new stent. There were constant requests for discounts from hospitals that were under intense pressure to control costs. The company's leaders could see their market share in Europe eroding. J & J was well resourced at the time. In operational terms, it was functioning at a high level. Yet J & J didn't respond. Intent on exploiting its dominant position, it continued to spend all its energy trying to keep up with demand and in the process lost sight of the need to continually innovate. When rival firm Guidant finally received approval for a product that better met customers' needs, the product captured 70 per cent of the market share within 45 days.

Finkelstein points out that formula that has contributed to past successes gets overused or misapplied, resulting in a seriously skewed view of reality. He points out that leadership role is critical in reframing the tacit assumptions and beliefs that team members have about specific challenges as well as their own roles in addressing these challenges. They should create openness to even unwelcome information. They should encourage discussions about making changes to better align the firm with market trends.

David Garvin, a professor at the Harvard Business School has written extensively on what really constitutes organisational learning. He states that for an organisation to be effective in today's dynamic environment, it should be *skilled at creating, acquiring, interpreting, retaining and transferring knowledge; and at purposefully modifying its behaviour based on new knowledge and insights.* He lists five main activities that promote learning[31]:

1. *Systematic problem solving.* Organisations must cultivate the habit of relying on the scientific method, rather than guesswork, for identifying and solving problems. They need to insist on data, rather than assumptions, for making decisions. Garvin argues that it is easy to train employees in problem-solving techniques but it is relatively more difficult to inculcate the appropriate mindset. Mental discipline is a prerequisite to systematic problem solving. Mental discipline is as much a value and attitude as it is a technique.
2. *Experimentation with new approaches.* This involves searching for and testing of new knowledge. It can take place in two ways: (a) Ongoing programmes, which involve a continuing series of small experiments to improve quality, yields, productivity and reduce costs. Ongoing programmes may also involve visiting other organisations to learn from them. Successful ongoing programmes require incentives for risk taking and skills to perform and evaluate experiments; (b) Demonstration projects are holistic, system-wide changes introduced in a single unit of the organisation for developing new organisational capabilities.
3. *Learning from their experience and history.* This is based on reflection and self-analysis. Garvin quotes the famous philosopher George Santayana, who coined the phrase 'Those who can not remember the past are condemned to repeat it.' Failure is the best teacher if one is willing to learn from it. IBM's 360 computer, Boeing's 757 and 767 planes were all based on learning from past failures. Garvin distinguishes between a productive failure and an unproductive success. An unproductive success occurs when something goes well and no one knows how or why. A productive failure is one that leads to insight, understanding and adds to the shared knowledge of the organisation.

Learning from failures requires tolerance and patience. Organisations must give up the common preoccupation with allocation of blame for failures.
4. *Learning from the experiences and best practices of others.* This includes benchmarking and learning from customers. This again requires open, attentive listening. Organisations must be prepared to face criticism. Customers can provide up-to-date product information, competitive comparisons, insights into changing preferences, and immediate feedback on products and services.
5. *Transferring knowledge quickly and efficiently throughout the organisation.* Learning becomes truly organisational only when it is spread throughout the organisation. Mechanisms that promote transfer of knowledge include written, oral, and visual reports, site visits and tours, personnel rotation programmes, education and training programmes, and standardisation programmes. Knowledge is more likely to be transferred when there are right incentives in place.

Garvin notes that most companies are reasonably skilled at creating and acquiring knowledge, but are much weaker on interpreting, retaining, and transferring knowledge, as well as on changing their behaviour based on their knowledge.[32] *Interpretation* problems occur because of very predictable biases in organisations arising from the tendency of looking at new realities through old mental models. For example, market research is largely used for purposes of confirmation. Organisational actors must be willing to accept surprising results.

According to Garvin, the most commonly assumed reason—that people are resistant to solutions that they did not create—is not the primary obstacle to effective transfer of knowledge.[33] As it turns out, the transfer and retention problems exist because it's far more difficult to specify a practice completely. As it is very difficult to articulate fully what goes into a best practice, transfers require a very intense period of hand-holding, in order for what is typically tacit, unwritten knowledge to be conveyed in all its richness. And what about purposefully *modifying behaviour* based on new insights? Garvin says that 'if you don't change the way people are motivated, it is very difficult to modify behaviour'.[34]

In light of the above discussion on quick and efficient transfer of knowledge, let us look at how General Electric transfers the best practices across its units.[35] This has been outlined in Box 6.4.

Box 6.4: Transfer of Best Practices at GE

If the GE appliances group has developed a good new technique, the GE's leadership education centre would invite a team of about seven members from that unit to the centre; the team might include people from finance, marketing, the union, human resources person, and purchases. Another 80 people from six other GE units would also be invited to learn from the appliance group. The learning process may be designed as follows:

1. Appliance team does a 15-minute overview. Not much is given away because the intention is to get people to learn how to learn, not just learn.
2. The seven appliance people go to separate rooms to answer questions from others in smaller groups. The 80 people from other units divide themselves up into smaller groups; they consult each other on what they would ask and the issues that they would explore. Each individual goes to two of the seven rooms for 45 minutes each. But collectively, each unit team would have gone to all seven rooms.
3. Teams from different units, then, meet in their respective groups and discuss what they have learnt, and how they can apply it in their units.
4. Then all the groups come into a big room, where each group presents what they think were the keys to the success of the appliances group.
5. Finally, the appliances group is asked: 'Which questions were not asked? What part of your transformation is a success that they did not figure out?' The group responds and gives useful suggestions. For example, they may say, 'There were hardly any questions on how we did the training. No questions were asked about the relationship with the suppliers, and that was the key'.

GE's approach (Box 6.4) is interesting because it is rooted in the philosophy that learning should be reflected in quality of action rather than in a mere understanding of a principle in abstraction. It is possible to identify several merits of the design that has been adopted:

- A multi-functional group is involved from each unit. It sends a powerful signal that the organisational challenge needs to be perceived in an integrated manner
- Despite a large gathering, there are opportunities for numerous conversations. Participants are put in an active rather than passive mode
- The multi-functional group has several opportunities to interact among itself. The group members have opportunities to learn from colleagues to examine issues from different perspectives. In addition, this helps adapting the practice to the needs of the unit and evolving plans for moving to action phase
- The members learn skills of 'learning to learn'. For example, inquiry involves questioning skills and integrating skills and also attitudes of curiosity, keenness to learn etc.
- The design involves an element of competition among different units. It puts the focus on learners. It has also a 'fun' element. All these facilitate learning
- There is also an element of feedback involved, which also helps learning process

It is not possible to create a learning organisation in a few weeks or even months. Attitudes, values and behaviour have to be cultivated slowly and steadily over a period of time. However, an organisation can take a few simple steps.[36] An appropriate climate for learning needs to be created. This includes training people in appropriate skills related to problem solving, brainstorming, statistical analyses, conducting experiments and so on. Learning requires contemplation and reflection. Crisis management, deadlines and other work pressures that focus on immediate problems are barriers to learning. Learning is facilitated and shared when boundaries between people and departments are broken down. General Electric has made *boundarylessness* a fundamental building block of its strategy. Creation of cross-functional teams, rotation of people across departments and rewarding collaborative behaviour are some of the ways to promote learning across departments.

Learning also implies tolerance and acceptance of mistakes and failures. Bennis and Nanus illustrate this idea beautifully in their book *Leaders*:[37]

Indeed, we can propose a general rule for all organisations: 'Reasonable failure should never be received with anger.' Spinoza announced a principle very much like this. He said that the highest activity a human being can attain is learning, or, in his language, understanding. To understand is to be free. He argued that those who respond to failure of others by anger are themselves slaves to passion and learn nothing.

Tom Watson, Sr. IBM's founder and its guiding inspiration for over forty years, put that Spinozan principle to work a number of years ago, probably without knowing the source of his action. A promising junior executive of IBM was involved in a risky venture for the company and managed to lose over $10 million in the gamble. It was a disaster. When Watson called the nervous executive into his office, the young man blurted out, 'I guess you want my resignation?' Watson said, 'You can't be serious. We've just spent $10 million educating you.'

LEADING LEARNING

To build capability in a dynamic global environment, managers need two special leadership qualities. According to Bossidy and Ram Charan[38]:

Two leadership qualities have become absolutely indispensable today, and they aren't on the usual lists. The first is business acumen, more commonly called business savvy. The second is a need to know—or, to put it another way, a refusal to take anything for granted, and insatiable curiosity about what's new and different.

Business savvy refers to the ability to understand how to make money in a given industry. People with business savvy, according to Bossidy and Charan, think in terms of business models. They are able to simplify complex details and achieve clarity. Need to know refers to *a relentless quest for the critical 1 per cent information that can make all the difference to your business prospects.*[39] According to Bossidy and Charan, 'several leadership qualities are more critical now than before. These include intellectual honesty, comfort with ambiguity, self-confidence, and courage. But if you have business savvy and the need to know, you're a good bet to have those other qualities as well: they come with the territory.'[40]

'Need to know' makes individuals perennially curious. They tend to indulge in a wide range of interests and pursuits, which prepares them for dealing with the unexpected when they venture into new areas. These individuals also learn from a host of sources such as conversations with various kinds of people and other people's successes and failures. It is said that Harry Truman was able to learn from the White House archives. He referred to what other presidents had done. He was, he said, consulting his 'Council of Presidents'.[41]

According to Garvin, leaders must master the art of questioning and listening to facilitate learning.[42] He echoes the view of Peter Drucker who has said that the most common source of mistakes in management decisions is the emphasis on finding the right answer rather than on asking the right questions. Good questions get to the heart of a matter; they force deep thinking and reflection. Questions can be used to frame issues, solicit information, probe for analysis, draw connections, seek opinions, and ratify decisions. Questions should be designed to draw out assumptions, lead discussion and allow participants to probe actively for the roots of differing positions. The most effective questions don't produce anxiety about not knowing; they create an excitement about learning. Andrew Finlayson, author of *Questions that Work*, writes that we should focus on seven elements in questioning[43] (Box 6.5).

While questioning generates the needed raw material, listening ensures that it is put to good use. Listening is a demanding process that requires attentiveness and genuine interest. There is an ancient oriental parable (Box 6.6) that illustrates the notion of listening and needing to know remarkably well.[44]

As the story points out, those things that are readily visible and are convenient to measure quickly grab attention. There are underlying processes of greater significance, but these are not easily discernible. In *The Little Prince*, Antoine de Saint-Exupery conveys this thought beautifully: '*It is only with the heart that one can see rightly; what is essential is invisible to the eye.*'

Box 6.5: Seven Elements in Questioning

1. *Awareness*: What are the most important things you need to know? Are you looking for feelings or facts? And how much information are you willing to share?
2. *Ability*: Make sure you are asking a person who has the expertise and authority to answer your questions.
3. *Atmosphere*: Give careful consideration to when and where you ask your questions.
4. *Attitude*: Tailor the phrasing of your questions to the respondent's personality—then really listen to the answers you receive.
5. *Answer*: Are the responses you have received verifiable? Did all your questions get answered?
6. *Appreciation*: Even if the answers you receive don't meet your needs, they demonstrate your gratitude anyway. Such appreciation can encourage others (especially shy people) to be more forthcoming. Moreover, be sure to explain your questions in a way that gives people a reason to help you in the future.
7. *Action*: Make sure your questions have real-world consequences.

Box 6.6: Hearing the Unheard

A prince is sent to the great sage to be educated on the basics of being a good ruler. The master sends his young student to the forest and tells him to return after hearing all the sounds of the forest. At the end of his assignment, the prince enthusiastically recounts the sounds of the cuckoos singing, the leaves rustling, the hummingbirds humming, the crickets chirping, the grass blowing, the bees buzzing and the wind whispering and howling. But the master is not satisfied with the answer and sends his student back to the forest to listen more intently. For days and nights on end, the young prince sits alone in the forest listening. But he hears no new sounds. One fine morning, he is able to discern some new sounds, and the feeling of enlightenment envelops him. He returns to the master and tells him about hearing the unheard—the sound of flowers opening, the sound of the sun warming the earth and the sound of the grass drinking the morning dew. The master nods approvingly and says: 'It is necessary for a ruler to listen closely to the people's hearts, hear their feelings un-communicated, pains unexpressed, complaints not spoken of, in short hear the unheard. States start to decline when leaders listen only to superficial words and do not hear true opinions, feelings and desires'.

FACILITATING UNLEARNING

Learning requires unlearning. Unless an organisation is able to unlearn by giving up old habits, attitudes, assumptions, behaviours and mindset, it can not embark upon change, particularly discontinuous change. There is an old story of a person who had come to visit a Zen master. The visitor claimed that he had read widely, but was interested in finding out if he could learn anything more from the master. The master offered him a full cup of tea, but continued to pour more tea into the cup from the tea jug. The visitor was intrigued, and pointed to the tea overflowing from the cup on to the ground. 'Just as the cup is too full to hold any more tea, you may be too full to learn anything new', said the master. 'For new learning to find space within you, you have to first give up the belief that you already know those things'.

Unlearning, however, is a difficult process that has received little attention in the literature on organisational change. *Unlearning is associated with strong negative emotions.* Giving up or letting go of habits, assumptions, attitudes and behaviour induces anxiety, stress and fear. People experience a loss of control. They may react to this loss by becoming inflexible and entrenched in their attitudes and behaviour. Facilitating unlearning requires sensitive and thoughtful management of emotions associated with a sense of loss. Todd Jick has described the complex psychological processes of passing through difficult, often conflicting, emotions.[45] He identifies three transition stages:

1. Ending phase and letting go. This involves letting go of the previous situation. This may involve dramatic emotions such as pain, confusion and terror. People experience a sharp break with a familiar past that had been taken for granted. There is disengagement. This is followed by a loss of identity or dis-identification. People may feel betrayed and deceived. Things fail to make sense. In other words, there is disenchantment
2. Neutral zone. This involves completing endings and building energy for beginnings. People may feel adrift and confused. They become ineffective and unproductive. They are

disoriented. They need to bury the past. The old mindset needs to be disintegrated. They begin to discover new possibilities.
3. New beginnings. This includes new possibilities or alignment with a vision.

These phases take time and cannot be accelerated. If an organisation tries to speed up the process, it risks carrying unfinished psychological 'baggage' from one phase to the next. Sufficient time needs to be spent on letting go and dwelling in the neutral zone.

Another way of looking at the different stages associated with unlearning is to view it as risk-taking.[46] Change requires people to adopt unfamiliar mindsets, attitudes and behaviour. This involves taking risks such as loss of face, appearing incompetent, seemingly unwilling or unable to learn and so on. People move from discomfort with risks to acceptance in four stages:

1. Shock. In this phase, people are threatened with change. They may become immobilised. They feel unsafe, indecisive, and unable to take any action. They may deny that any change is taking place.
2. Defensive retreat. This includes lashing out in anger at the change and holding on to familiar accustomed ways of doing things. People still feel uncomfortable and unsafe.
3. Acknowledgement. People eventually come to accept that they have lost something and mourn. They experience both grief and liberation. They begin to take risks and are gradually able to build their confidence.
4. Adaptation and change. People feel comfortable with change. There is greater energy for risk taking. The change in internalised. People move on and help others to change. They may also become advocates of change.

Jick also provides some guidelines for individuals and managers for coping with change.[47] First, individuals need to accept negative emotions as natural and acceptable reactions to change. Individuals experiencing change must accept their negative feelings and take time to work through these feelings.

This may take time and cannot be done instantaneously. It requires patience and tolerance. Individuals need to learn to nurture and nourish themselves. This process may also be unsettling and ambiguous for most people. They need to tolerate the unsettledness and ambiguity. Individuals also experience a loss of control. They need to be helped to establish a sense of personal control in other areas of their lives. Second, change is almost inevitably associated with stress. Individuals undergoing change need to learn to manage stress. Managing stress includes maintaining physical well-being, seeking information about the change, limiting other sources of stress, taking regular breaks and seeking support. Third, individuals need to develop a sense of objectivity about the change. Individuals undergoing change must be helped to identify their options and gains. They need to ask themselves, 'What have I lost, what am I gaining?' This is quite different from just looking on the bright side. It involves developing a sense of balance. Individuals must be helped to diversify their emotional investments to other contexts. If one has emotional investments in other areas of one's life like family, friends, social or community activities and religion, then it is relatively easier to accept change in the workplace because work ceases to be the only source of meaning.

Jick has three pieces of advice for managers who want to help their employees deal with change.[48] First, they must *not* consider resistance to change as an obstacle or something that needs to be overcome. Resistance must be seen as a natural process of adapting to change. Frequently, strong negative emotions that are evoked by change are labelled as resistance to change. Resistance may also be for rational reasons. Resistance to change needs to be considered as a healthy part of the change process. It must be seen as a positive step toward change. It provides energy to work with and gives information critical to the change process. Resistance must be accepted, acknowledged and managed instead of being brushed aside. Second, managers need to give emotional first aid to individuals experiencing change. This involves simply listening to their feelings and experiences without being judgmental. They need to be given information about the change, support and counselling. It also involves identifying what is not changing and uncovering the reasons for this. Third, managers must create the capability for change by providing safety and rewards. Jick observes[49]:

> *Co-operation, negotiation, and compromise are critical to the implementation of any change; it is difficult to get co-operation, negotiation, and compromise from people who are effectively ordered to change, never listened to or supported, and then faulted if they fail to change as expected... Creative managers who truly wish their employees to grow, who recognise the difficulties inherent in the challenge of change, and who support efforts to make change, are patient along the way; their reward, in turn, is the trust of their employees—and a potentially more flexible organisation.*

As we have seen above, this mindset is likely to emerge when the organisational factors are conducive to learning. For example, there is greater support for collaboration between different parts of the organisation, there is greater autonomy for action taking, the organisational goals motivate and encourage people to focus on enhancing performance and effectiveness, and culture emphasises risk taking.

ROLE OF POSITIVE BEHAVIOURAL CONTEXT

Capability building is facilitated by a positive behavioural context. If we use the metaphor of the growth of a plant, the plant grows and develops naturally when the soil conditions, moisture and climate are favourable. But when the environment is unsupportive, the same plant may stop growing, start withering away and even face threat to its survival. To facilitate capability building, we need to understand what kind of an environment or context helps accelerate learning and what factors obstruct learning. We can say that when appropriate factors are present, it is in the nature of living organisms to learn.

As we discussed in Chapter 5, the notion of organisational architecture is useful in identifying the features of such a context. An organisation's architecture includes its structure, procedures, policies and processes. Just as a mould determines the shape that jelly would take, the architecture of an organisation significantly shapes an employee's focus and energy. For example, architectures that promote compartmentalisation of functions and roles tend to promote rivalry and conflict between departments, divisions and individuals.

Sometimes architectures foster a mental paradigm that the boss should be on the critical path for fixing everything. We find this illustrated in a case on the Bose Corporation. Warren was a relatively new head of the Information Services department in the company. At one stage, he felt that he had tried several initiatives to improve service; but it always seemed as if he was trying to run uphill. One obstacle was getting the departmental staff to accept responsibility for problem resolution:

I always looked like I was in charge; I was responsible for fixing all the problems. We would get together in a group and we would brainstorm, and then they would 'wash their hands' and say, 'Now Warren knows all the problems and it is up to him to fix them'. And only if I really wanted to get involved, would I get involved fixing any of these. That was the kind of paradigm.[50]

Thus architecture and culture of an organisation are closely related reinforcing each other to produce supportive or dysfunctional dynamics. In the rigid steel frame of government bureaucracy, such a situation creates huge hurdles for any change initiative. E. Sreedharan had spent 36 years of his professional life in the Indian Railways. He had several ideas, but the strict procedures that were to be followed did not allow many of these ideas to be effectively implemented. When he was assigned the responsibility for taking the Konkan Railway project from the stage of conception to completion, he felt that the organisation to achieve this massive challenge should have a completely different architecture.[51]

The Konkan Railway project involved building a 760 km-railway line connecting Mumbai and Mangalore along the West Coast of India with as many as 93 tunnels aggregating to a total length of 835 km. Some of the tunnels to be built were more than 3 km in length, and the longest tunnel was 6.5 km in length. They had to construct as many as 179 major bridges, totalling a waterway of 21.1 km and as many as 8,000 minor bridges. About 300 bridges were road over-bridges and road under-bridges. It was expected that the project would be completed in five years time from the first day, when the word 'go' was given, till the first train started running. The complexity of the project arose not only from the difficulties of the terrain and the time schedule, but also from the necessity for using several front line technologies for the first time in India.

The project was of great strategic importance. For example, it reduced the haulage distance between Mumbai and Mangalore from 2,041 km to 914 km a saving of 1,127 km. The saving in travel time was also immense. Between Mumbai and Mangalore, it came down from 41 hours to 15 hours.

Sreedharan decided to organise the project based on radically different architecture to achieve the goal. He knew that the governmental method of working would not allow the stretch objectives to be accomplished. He created new systems, procedures and culture at the Konkan Railway Corporation (KRC) to help the new corporation rise up to the challenges and successfully reach the goal.

The project involved acquiring land from over 40,000 landowners. The land acquisition process in the government tends to be a very painful and slow process. Several projects languish for years because the process gets mired in grievances and litigations. As a result, land acquisition does not reach a closure leading to costly delays. KRC utilised a very pragmatic approach that combined selling the project to the people of that area and proactively addressing the problems of the landowners. A lot of spadework was undertaken to talk to people and motivate them. There was a communication campaign on what the project means, what benefit the project will give, how that area will gain from the project. Any difficulties faced by the landowners were promptly redressed. In many cases, they had to take over the houses and had them demolished. The house owners could move to any other house they wanted, and the Corporation paid the rental for that house for up to 12 to 18 months till they had built their own house with the compensation that they received. They could retrieve whatever they could—such as doors, windows, tiles, etc. for possible use in the new houses. Sreedharan adds:

> We even assisted them in transporting the household things to new locations, give advances for incurring expenses, and helped them get electricity and water. As a result there was not even a single case where a person refused to hand over the land. The entire land required for the project was in the Corporation's possession within 8 or 9 months, which is a mighty achievement.

KRC realised that its success depended on the success of the contractors. So contractors were seen as partners, and an environment had to be created for contractors to succeed. Great care was exercised in pre-qualifying the contractors. But once they were chosen, it was ensured that they did not run into cash flow problems or suffer the costs of the Corporation's indecision. For this, the organisation worked out procedures to ensure that contractors were paid 75 per cent of their bills within 48 hours and did not have to wait for decisions for more than 48 hours. In a complex project, with several tunnels and bridges, many decisions were required at every stage. For example, in the tunnel work, they may suddenly come across a difficult geological stratum and decisions may be required on how to deal with that particular area. But an assurance was given to the contractors that any decision they wanted would be given in 48 hours even if it meant that the top managers had to rush to the site for any major decision. To ensure that everybody knew how much time was available for that particular work, a reverse clock was part of every office, where each day the clock came down by one day, and persons were constantly reminded as to how many days were left for completion of the project.

In a radical departure from the government style of functioning, KRC did not feel constrained by the rigid boundaries of the contract document if it was felt that the contractor had a genuine problem. For example, the originally agreed rates may not be workable because of the general inflation in the country or the contractor may have run into a cash flow problem. The general approach was to find out what exactly were the difficulties and try to sort out those issues even if it meant going outside the terms of the contract agreement. Certain decisions were proactively made keeping in mind the demands of completing the work on time and the problems that contractors were likely to run into:

> As a number of tunnels were involved and all the tunnels had to be completed in such a short time, a number of highly sophisticated high-speed tunnelling equipments were needed for the work. We said that we will procure these equipments and give them to contractors free of charge. We only fixed the time needed for using it. If the contractor does not complete the work within time, yes, there would be a penalty.

In addition to periodic reviews of very difficult works for quick problem solving, there were weekly meetings of the heads of departments, where all the problems connected with the whole project were discussed. The team analysed the slippage in the previous week and then decided what was required to be done in the following week. On the first Monday of each month, the field engineers were also brought into this meeting, so that everyone could contribute and understand the priorities and issues. Sreedharan insisted that there was no paperwork in these meetings:

> I insisted that even the minutes of such meeting be not recorded, because I do not believe in this; it is a waste of time and paper work distributing the minutes of the meeting. After all, we knew what was happening every day and everybody was involved in this.

To make it possible for working with such systems, the organisational members were required to have impeccable integrity. So employees were selected with great care. They were given ample authority so that they did not have to depend on the corporate office at all for day-to-day work. Some very enterprising and very smart finance officers were entrusted the task of fine-tuning the role of finance department and the finance procedures to support transparent, accountable and innovative decision-making. In Sreedharan's words:

The whole work of administration was on the basis of trust. One of the first things that I did was to lay down the corporate objectives and ten items of corporate culture. All the organisational members should have the same work ethos, same approach and same objective.

The outstanding achievement of KRC arises from the behavioural context that Sreedharan was able to build for organisational members that allowed them to function at dramatically superior levels. According to Bartlett and Ghoshal, many large organisations have built a behavioural context with four characteristics: *compliance, control, contract* and *constraint*. Compliance refers to implicit obedience and absence of debate and dissent. Control means monitoring employees closely and holding them accountable for their individual performance. Contract refers to the nature of the relationship between an organisation and its employees. Contractual relationships emphasise impersonality and financial incentives. Employees distance themselves emotionally from the organisation and feel that they are 'employees of an economic entity' rather than 'members of a social institution'.[52] By constraint, Bartlett and Ghoshal mean the confinements and barriers created by strategies, goals and priorities. They cite the example of Westinghouse, an American corporation, to illustrate these characteristics. Westinghouse had gone through three radical, transformational changes in ten years with little results. The reason it was unsuccessful was that it failed to alter its behavioural context.

In contrast to Westinghouse, organisations like the Konkan Railway Corporation and other successful companies have a very different behavioural context. Their contexts are characterised by four common aspects: *discipline, support, trust,* and *stretch*. Discipline refers to self-discipline that is an alternative to compliance to authority or rules. As Bartlett and Ghoshal observe:

In disciplined organisations, people do more than follow directives and conform to policies; they also return phone calls promptly, come to meetings on time, refrain from questioning in the corridors decisions made in the conference room, and, above all, deliver on promises and commitments.[53]

Support implies coaching, helping and guiding which are alternatives to top-down control. Stretch refers to that aspect of the organisation that spurs employees to strive for more, rather than less, ambitious objectives. Bartlett and Ghoshal claim,

In a company in which people feel stretched, they are constantly encouraged to see themselves and the organisation not in terms of its past or present constraints, but in terms of its future possibilities.[54]

Trust is an alternative to contractual relationships. It implies transparent, open management reinforced by a sense of fairness in processes and practices. According to Bartlett and Ghoshal, 'In the end, trust is the most vital component of a management context for renewal because it is essential for risk taking'.[55] Their research highlights the importance of creating positive contexts in organisations.

COMPONENTS OF CAPABILITY

In this chapter, we have discussed self-efficacy, focus and energy as the three elements contributing to capability. We also explored the processes of capability building. We examined how challenging goals can energise learning and what could be done to build employee ownership for those goals and get organisational members to engage with the problems in a manner that fosters learning. We looked at interesting insights from theory and practice on how learning could be promoted, how activities should be structured, and what role leaders should play to accelerate the process. Finally, our discussion centred on the importance of creating a positive behavioural context for learning and capability building. In this closing section, we summarise these ideas and insights to identify the components of capability.

Management theorists have pointed out that learning capability is constituted by individual and collective capacities to learn. Mathias and Brand list six dimensions of learning capacity as: (a) individual capacity to learn arising from factors such as individual's questioning and listening abilities and openness of mind, (b) collective capacity to learn resulting from group spirit, capacity to dialogue and so on, (c) structural capacity to learn reflected in organisational characteristics such as decentralised structures and integration of line and staff functions, (d) cultural capacity to learn which refers to organisational norms and values, (e) capacity to learn resulting from the organisation of work that favours individual and collective learning through project groups, and effective information systems, and (f) capacity of the leadership to learn and promote learning through their styles and modelling of right behaviours.[56]

Adler and his associates studied performance improvement in hospitals to examine what elements constitute performance improvement capability.[57] The components of capability identified by them have some similarity with those listed by Mathias and Brand. Adler and his associates identify five components of capability: *Skills, Systems, Structures, Strategies and Culture*. Their study concludes that when the environments of organisations become complex and increasingly demanding, the organisation's capability assumes critical importance in determining competitive standing and ability to consistently deliver excellent performance. Table 6.4 presents how the five components of capability are expected to contribute and areas of possible interventions that progressive organisations attend to for enhancing capability.

As outlined in Table 6.4, *skills* enable people to acquire information, inquire into issues, and act effectively. With an appropriate skill-base, organisations are more capable of making quick and effective performance improvements. As we have seen in this chapter, progressive organisations intervene in a number of ways to hone skills of their employees particularly those with

Table 6.4: Components of Capability Building

Component of Capability and Expected Contribution	Areas of Possible Interventions for Enhancing Capability
SKILLS—Enable people to inquire into issues, disseminate learning and act effectively to make quick and effective improvements	Developing inquiry skills; Building mindsets of systematic problem solving; Making important skills more broad-based; Getting people in various leadership roles to act as role models to spur learning and innovation
SYSTEMS—Provide mechanisms to exchange ideas and reach quick and effective decisions. They support and guide individual efforts to deploy skills effectively	Building up systems for identifying improvement opportunities, rewarding knowledge sharing, communicating change priorities, filling employee skill gaps, searching for and testing new knowledge, effective action planning etc.
STRUCTURES—Clarify responsibilities and accountability mechanisms to channel attention to specific concerns and induce capacity for coordinated action	Strengthening linkage and integration to bridge organisational 'boundaries'; Enhancing discretion and flexibility; Assigning specific responsibilities for learning initiatives
STRATEGIES—Help build will by clarifying the learning agenda, and provide the demand for generation of capability	Developing stretch goals and expressing these in a manner that communicates excitement of achievement, progress and contribution; Articulating the capabilities required to effectively execute strategies
CULTURE—Ensures that the context is favourable for capability building	Creating a context characterised by *discipline, support, trust, and stretch*; Shaping a culture of free and frank dialogue, boundarylessness, risk taking and seeking to be the best

important change management responsibilities. Certain areas of possible interventions are outlined below:

- Develop inquiry skills of questioning, listening, facilitating discussions, creating excitement, constructive conflict management, self-reflection and learning to learn
- Build mindsets of systematic problem solving to enable individuals to view situations from multiple perspectives, think systematically and think critically
- Make important skills more broad-based, rather than narrowly concentrated in specialised staff groups or senior leaders
- Get people holding various leadership roles to pay conscious attention to the following: develop clarity about own intentions, values and beliefs; deconstruct the larger challenges and goals into manageable components; generate optimism and hope, provide autonomy, empower people by enhancing self-efficacy, encourage/support innovative behaviour and risk taking, be patient in accepting genuine mistakes, and act as role models to spur learning and innovation

Systems provide mechanisms to exchange ideas and reach quick and effective decisions. Thoughtful systems (for example, information systems infrastructure, systems for performance measurement, communication and human resource management) ensure that individuals are supported and guided in their efforts to deploy skills effectively. For example, specific systems can be strengthened as outlined below:

a) Performance measurement and review systems are designed to help identify problems and improvements, reward knowledge sharing, and use progress reviews to get to root causes of problems faced.
b) Communication systems help broadcast change priorities and results of successful change efforts to encourage people, and support collaboration between different parts of the organisation.

Building Change Capability

c) Human resource management systems identify and fill skill gaps, provide individuals greater exposure and greater variety of experiences by offering opportunities to work on challenging projects, give incentive for staff to commit time and effort to change priorities, bring people from different work areas together in regular dialogue and discussion, and reward development of new ideas and skills and innovations.

Thus interventions to build up systems would seek to achieve the following objectives:

- Search for and test new knowledge through on-going programmes and demonstration projects and utilise best practices or benchmarking/peer comparison studies for feedback and learning
- Transfer knowledge quickly and effectively through programmes for personnel rotation, reports, education and training, standardisation, knowledge management initiatives, incentives, etc.
- Institute diagnostic and action planning forums where individuals share their difficulties, decision-making levels have free and frank conversations with operational levels, priorities are worked out, different alternatives are critically examined, appropriate decisions made, and follow-up initiated

Structures channel attention to specific concerns and induce capacity for coordinated action. By providing the right behavioural framework, structures can get people into 'actor' (rather than 'spectator') mode—and thus favour learning. Interventions to enhance capability would include the following:

- Strengthen linkage and integration to bridge organisational 'boundaries'—for example, overcoming compartmentalisation of functions/roles through organisational arrangements like special task forces, cross-functional teams, personnel rotation, fair and equitable means of sorting out ownership and credit issues, etc.

- ➤ Design roles in a manner that enhances discretion and flexibility; Generate willingness among senior members to relinquish some autonomy of action so as to assure more reliable coordination
- ➤ Design activities to maximise learning and also assign specific responsibilities for learning initiatives
- ➤ Have forums for: (a) surfacing concerns from the front line and (b) discussing new initiatives

Strategies reflect the aspirations and so provide the rationale for capability building. Stretch goals provide the demand for generation of capability. Leadership in capable organisations do the following on a consistent basis:

- ➤ Set powerful vision to align people to important organisational challenges and link each unit's goals clearly with the larger strategic plan
- ➤ Focus employee energies and create strong need for new and innovative structures and systems through stretch goals
- ➤ Frame challenges in a manner that communicates excitement of achievement, progress and contribution inherent in the organisational challenges; Find ways of having dialogue about strategy with organisational members, as people support what they help create
- ➤ Clearly articulate the capabilities required to effectively execute strategies

Culture or mindset represents the bedrock or foundation for capability building efforts to survive and thrive. Without appropriate mindsets, structures and systems may lead to conformity, but not yield committed actions. For example, a context characterised by *discipline, support, trust, and stretch* is built when leaders commit to have meetings with employees on a regular basis, institute incentives—both symbolic and material—to encourage cross-functional collaboration or when staff members accept and embrace a more rapid pace of change.

Adler and associates state that among the five components (skills, systems, structure, strategy and culture), there is a hierarchical relation (Figure 6.2).

Figure 6.2: Components of Capability

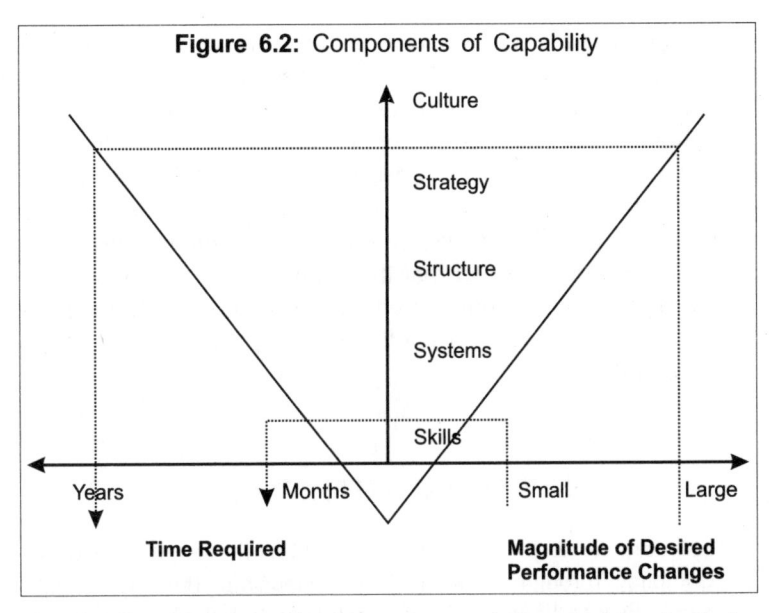

- Culture
- Strategy
- Structure
- Systems
- Skills

Time Required: Years ← → Months

Magnitude of Desired Performance Changes: Small → Large

Researchers found that though capability can be built by upgrading skills, advances tend to be modest without corresponding investments in systems. Changes in skills and systems would be limited unless organisational structures were also adapted. The 'higher level' transformation in strategies and culture yielded far greater enhancement of capability.

They also note that components of 'higher level' components like strategy and culture typically took far longer than those at 'lower levels' like skills and systems. They note:

> *The higher levels are more 'viscous' because they involve more numerous and more heterogeneous actors and because they rely on shared understandings that are both tacit (as distinct from explicit) and collective (as distinct from individual).*[58]

To sum up our discussions in this chapter, fast changing environments do not offer firms the luxury of taking time to initiate planned organisation-wide change. In such situation, organisational health and well-being requires building capability for change. This requires attention to learning mechanisms. There is a tendency to associate learning and knowledge with individuals. But as we have seen, learning capacity is embedded in habits, structures, systems, processes and culture. Leaders need to pay attention to all these aspects. They need to enhance aspirations of people, structure opportunities, create positive role models, design incentives, ensure support mechanisms, and engender feelings of hope and optimism. Most important, they need to help people perceive change as opportunity rather than threat. People need to feel that they can venture into new areas and come out on top. Thus self-efficacy represents the foundation of capability building, and leaders must be able to function as efficacy builders.

NOTES AND REFERENCES

1. Seshadri, D. V. R. & Tripathy, A. (2003). Re-inventing a Giant Company Through Corporate Entrepreneurship: The Case of Tata Steel. Proceedings of the Third International Conference on Entrepreneurial Innovation, Bangalore: 2003: pp. 360–389; Seshadri D V R & Tripathy Arabinda (2004). A Value-Based Approach for Sustainable Supplier-Customer Relationships: The Case of the Indian Steel Industry. Working Paper, IIM Ahmedabad; Mukherjee T., Bimlendra, Jha, Seshadri, D. V. R. & Tripathy, A. (2004). Innovation and Intrapreneurship through reinvention for sustainable competitive advantage: The Case of Tata Steel. International Engineering Management Conference 2004 (IEMC 2004), Singapore; D. V. R. Seshadri A. & Arabinda Tripathy (2004). Reinventing Tata Steel (A-E., IIM Ahmedabad Case Series on Tata Iron and Steel Company Limited.)
2. Tata Steel ranked World's Best Steel Producer, *The Hindu*, June 22, 2005.
3. www.dictionary.com
4. Williams, Monci J. (1997). Agility in Learning: An Essential for Evolving Organisations and People. *Harvard Management Update* May 1997; pp. 3–5.
5. Lombardo, M. & Eichinger, R. (2000). High Potentials as High Learners. *Human Resource Management*, 39(4): pp. 321–329.
6. Landry, M. (1995). A Note on the Concept of 'Problem'. *Organisation Studies*, 16(2): pp. 315–343.

7. Williams, Monci J. (1997). Agility in Learning: An Essential for Evolving Organisations and People. *Harvard Management Update*, May 1997; pp. 3–5.
8. Bandura, A. (1977). Self-efficacy: Toward a unifying theory of behavioural change. *Psychological Review*, 84: pp. 191–215.
9. Bandura, A. (1994). Self-efficacy. In V. S. Ramachandran (Ed.), *Encyclopaedia of Human Behavior* (Vol. 4: p. 71–81). New York: Academic Press.
10. Conger, Jay A. & Kanungo, Rabindra N. (1988). The Empowerment Process: Integrating Theory and Practice. *Academy of Management Review*, Vol. 13, No. 3: pp. 471–482.
11. Dorner, Dietrich (1996). *The Logic of Failure.* Perseus Books Group; Dorner, Dietrich (1996). On the difficulties of decision-making in complex and uncertain domains of reality. *The Journal of the European Society for Opinion and Marketing Research (ESOMAR)* 24 (1996), Nr. 1, S. 51-60; Ramnarayan, S. & Strohschneider, S. (1997). How organisations influence individual styles of thinking: A simulation study. *Journal of Euro-Asian Management,* 3: p. 1–29; Schaub, H. and Strohschneider, S. (1997). How Managers Deal with Strategic Complexities. In S. Ramnarayan & I. M. Pandey (Eds.). *Strategic Management of Public Enterprises in Developing Countries,* pp. 90–106. New Delhi: Vikas; Strohschneider, S. (2002). Cultural Factors in Complex Decision-making. In Lonner W. J., Dinnel D. L., Hayes S. A., & Sattler D. N. (Eds.), OnLine Readings in Psychology and Culture, Western Washington University, Department of Psychology, Center for Cross-Cultural Research Web site: http://www.wwu.edu/~culture; Dorner, D. & Schaub, H. (1994). Errors in Planning and Decision-making and the Nature of Human Information Processing. *Applied Psychology: An International Review*, 43(4): pp. 433–453; Dorner, D. & Wearing, A. J. (1994). Complex Problem Solving: Toward a Theory. In Frensch P. A. & Funke J. (Eds.), *Complex Problem Solving The European Perspective,* Hillsdale, N.J.: Lawrence Erlbaum Associates; Ramnarayan, S., Strohschneider, S. & Schaub, H. (1997). Trappings of Expertise and the Pursuit of Failure. *Simulation and Gaming,* 28: pp. 28–43.
12. Eisenhardt, K. M. (Spring 1990). Speed and Strategic Choice: How Managers Accelerate Decision-making. *California Management Review,* 32(3): pp. 39–54.
13. Garvin, David (2003). *Learning in Action: A Guide to Putting the Learning Organisation to Work,* Harvard Business School Press.

14. Bruch, H. & Ghoshal, S. (2004). *A Bias for Action: How Effective Managers Harness their Willpower, Achieve Results, and Stop Wasting Time.* Boston: Harvard University Press.
15. Ibid., p. 63.
16. *Delhi delighted with its new Metro,* in *International Herald Tribune.* March 12, 2005: http://www.iht.com/articles/2005/03/11/news/delhi.html
17. Ghosn, C. & Ries, P. (2005). *Shift: Inside Nissan's Historic Revival.* New York: Currency Doubleday, p. 115.
18. Ibid., p. 106.
19. Piramal, G. & Ghoshal, S. (March 17, 2005). The extraordinary story of Mittal Steel. *www.rediff.com (http://www.rediff.com/money/2005/mar/17mittal.htm)*
20. Ibid., p. 3.
21. Ibid., p. 6.
22. Tucker, A., Edmondson, A. & Spear, S. (2002). When Problem Solving Prevents Organisational Learning. *Journal of Change Management,* 15(2).
23. Hambrick, D. C. & Mason, P. A. (1984). Upper Echelons: The Organisation as a Reflection of its Top Managers. *Academy of Management Review,* 9(2): pp. 193–206.
24. Tucker, A., Edmondson, A. & Spear, S. (2002). When Problem Solving Prevents Organisational Learning. *Journal of Change Management,* 15(2).
25. Ibid.
26. Landry, M. (1995). A Note on the Concept of 'Problem'. *Organisation Studies,* 16(2): pp. 315–343.
27. French, W. L. & Bell, C. H. (1999). Organisation Development: Behavioral Science Interventions for Organisational Improvement, New Delhi: Prentice-Hall, pp. 146–147.
28. Ibid., pp. 147–148.
29. Ibid., pp. 149–150.
30. Finkelstein, S. (2003). *Why Smart Executives Fail.* New York: Penguin Putnam; Finkelstein, S. (2004). The seven habits of spectacularly unsuccessful executives. *Ivey Business Journal,* January/February.
31. Garvin, D. A. (1991). Building a learning organisation. *Harvard Business Review,* November-December: pp. 78–91.
32. Gary, Loren, (1997). What Makes for an Authentic Learning Organisation—An interview with David Garvin. *Harvard Management Update,* June, pp. 3–5.
33. Ibid., p. 5.

34. Ibid., p. 5.
35. Source: A Conversation with Steve Kerr, *Organisational Dynamics*, Spring, 1996, pp. 75–76.
36. Ibid.
37. Bennis, W. & Nanus, B. (1985). *Leaders: The Strategies for Taking Charge.* New York: Harper Perennial.
38. Bossidy, L. & Charan, R. (2004). *Confronting Reality: Doing What Matters to Get Things Right.* New York: Crown Business, p. 216.
39. Ibid., p. 218.
40. Ibid., pp. 218–219.
41. Williams, Monci J. (1997). Agility in Learning: An Essential for Evolving Organisations and People. *Harvard Management Update*, May 1997; p. 5.
42. Garvin, David, (2003). *Learning in Action: A Guide to Putting the Learning Organisation to Work,* Harvard Business School Press.
43. Finlayson, Andrew, (2001). *Questions that Work.* N.Y.: AMACOM.
44. Kim, C. W. & Mauborgne, R. A. (1992). Parables of Leadership. *Harvard Business Review,* July-August, p. 124.
45. Jick, T. D. (1993). *Managing Change: Cases and Concepts.* Boston, Mass.: Irwin.
46. Ibid.
47. Ibid.
48. Ibid.
49. Ibid., p. 332.
50. Bechler, Kimberly A., Marchand, Donald A., Kettinger, William J., & Segars, Albert H. (1996). *Bose Corporation: Middle Management's Push for Enterprise-wide Total Quality.* IMD, Lausanne, Switzerland, Distributed by the European Case Clearing House (ECCH) Reference No. 396-117-1.
51. For a more detailed account of the Konkan Railway Story, refer to E. Sreedharan's presentation on January 16, 2001 as part of the Department of Administrative Reforms and Public Grievances Lecture Series on '*Ideas That Have Worked*'; Menka Shivdasani & Raju Kane (1998). *A Dream Come True.* Konkan Railway Corporation Ltd.; S. V. Salelkar (1999). *A Treatise on Konkan Railway.* Konkan Railway Corporation Ltd.; Mario Cabral e Sa (2000). *Konkan-nama—A journey Across Time.* Konkan Railway Corporation Ltd.
52. Bartlett, Christopher A. & Ghoshal, Sumantra (1995). 'Rebuilding behavioural context: Turn process reengineering into people rejuvenation,' *Sloan Management Review*, Fall, pp. 11–23; Bartlett,

Christopher A. & Ghoshal, Sumantra, (1996). Rebuilding behavioural context: A blueprint for corporate renewal, *Sloan Management Review*, Winter, pp. 23–36.
53. Ibid., p. 15.
54. Ibid., p. 18.
55. Ibid., p. 18.
56. Mathias, F. & Brand, S. B. (1999). The Concept of the Learning Organisation" Applied to the Transformation of the Public Sector: Conceptual Contributions for Theory Development in *Organisational Learning and the Learning Organisation* (Eds.: Easterby-Smith, M., Burgoyne, J. & Araujo, L.). London: Sage Publications, pp. 130–156.
57. Adler, Paul S, Patricia Riley, Seok-Woo Kwon, Jordana Signer, Ben Lee. & Ram Satrasala. (2003). Performance Improvement Capability: Keys to Accelerating Performance Improvement in Hospitals. *California Management Review*, vol. 45(2): Winter, pp. 12–33.
58. Ibid., p. 28.

CHAPTER 7

Leadership and Change

OVERVIEW

In this concluding chapter, we discuss leadership issues in change management. We see the primary leadership task in change management as creating a positive behavioural context that facilitates inquiry, appreciation and change. Beginning with a discussion of Appreciative Inquiry—a popular change management technique—we follow it with a discussion on leadership. Our change management model identifies four core tasks. We argue that each task requires a specific leadership role. First, managers need to be *cognitive tuners* to appreciate change. Second, managers need to be *people catalysers* to mobilise support. Third, managers need to be *system architects* to execute change. Fourth, managers need to be *efficacy builders* to build change capability. We conclude with a set of simple rules to carry out these four roles.

APPRECIATIVE INQUIRY

In recent years, there is a growing realisation that organisations can become more productive and effective by accentuating the positive features of their culture and context. A new discipline called positive organisational scholarship has emerged in the United States to study positive phenomena in organisations.[1]

308 Change Management

We examine some aspects of this new discipline in the following section.

POSITIVE ORGANISATIONAL CHANGE

The central premise of positive organisational scholarship is that conventional research on organisations tends to over-emphasise aspects that are oriented to problems, deficits, errors, and dysfunctions. Management literature, in this tradition, concerns itself with competition, winning, control, self-interest and conflict. Change management, within this approach, focuses on what is wrong within an organisation. It seeks to identify the deficits or gaps. It seeks to overcome resistance to change. Employees are exhorted to change or face extinction.

Positive organisational scholarship seeks to correct this imbalance by focusing on what is good and positive in an organisation. Instead of solving problems or addressing weaknesses, it seeks to build on what is positive and good in an organisation. It argues that this approach leads to unanticipated positive results such as producing a positive spiral of development and growth that goes beyond financial results.

Positive organisational scholarship is the outcome of developments in other social science disciplines. For example, in the field of psychology, Martin Seligman initiated a new field of study called positive psychology that seeks to examine *positive experiences* such as happiness, joy, and pleasure; *positive human traits* such as character, talents and interests; and *positive institutions* such as family, school, business and community. Within this perspective, for instance, Fredrickson suggests a 'broaden-and-build' theory of positive emotions.[2] Based on empirical evidence from a variety of studies, she argues that positive emotions like joy, interest, pride, contentment and gratitude broaden people's habitual modes of thinking to make them more empathic, creative and flexible. Positive emotions also generate upward spirals toward optimal functioning.

Other researchers using positive organisational scholarship principles have suggested that organisational contexts that encourage acceptance of failure and dependence on others promote new knowledge creation by encouraging experimentation and help-seeking behaviours. However, the most significant contribution of positive organisational scholarship is in the area of organisational change. A new approach to positive organisational change called *Appreciative Inquiry* (AI) has emerged within this tradition. We discuss this approach in the following section.

BRIEF HISTORY OF AI

AI evolved out of the work of scholarly practitioners at the Department of Organisational Behaviour at Case Western Reserve University in the United States in the early 80s. Suresh Srivastva, a professor in the Department, and his doctoral student at that time, David Cooperrider, whose name is currently associated with this technique, jointly developed the basic ideas. Cooperrider noted that the prevailing way to study and analyse organisations was 'problem-focused.' Thus, the purpose of inquiry was to uncover the problems and deficits that plagued the organisation. It was as if the researcher was only interested in finding out what was 'wrong' with an organisation.

Cooperrider decided to adopt a radically opposite approach focusing on what is 'right' about an organisation. He applied these ideas in his study at the Cleveland Clinic, a highly advanced tertiary care medical centre in the United States. Cooperrider employed the term appreciative inquiry in his feedback report to the Board of the Clinic. The report created a huge impact on the Board and they decided to use this approach on the whole of the organisation.

The AI ideas continued to be developed by Srivastva, Cooperrider and their colleagues in the Department. In 1984, AI ideas were presented in conferences of the NTL Institute for Applied Behavioral Science and the Academy of Management. Cooperider's ideas were initially received with some scepticism at the Academy of Management conference. In 1987, Cooperrider and Srivastva published their first paper on AI titled *Appreciative Inquiry in Organisational Life*. In subsequent years, these ideas were presented in more conferences and published in papers and books. A significant event was the founding of the Taos Institute in New Mexico that became a significant catalyst in promoting AI as a strategy of change.

By the early 90s, AI had gained enough legitimacy to be considered seriously as a separate discipline of Organisation Development. The NTL Institute for Applied Behavioral Science started to offer professional development workshops in AI. Professional journals such as the *OD Practitioner* published special issues on AI. The watershed for AI was in 1999, when Cooperrider was invited to join a symposium at the conference of the Academy of Management. Titled 'The Past, Present, and Future of Organisation Development', this symposium featured Edgar Schein and Richard Beckhard—two of the greatest names in change management. According to Richard Beckhard, *'appreciative inquiry is creating a powerful and enduring change in the way OD will be conceptualised and practiced now and in the future... it is changing the way we think about change itself.'* In the last few years, AI has rapidly grown as a professional practice with a number of universities launching specialist degrees and programmes in AI.

BASIC IDEAS IN AI

The essence of AI is contained in the two words—*appreciative* and *inquiry*. This approach to change seeks to appreciate the positive and good aspects of an organisation. It seeks to identify the 'positive core' that lends vitality and energy to an organisation. This is the positive core that is valued by organisational members because it gives them a sense of purpose and meaning. The positive core is identified through a process of inquiry. In AI, inquiry consists of asking questions that lead to the creation of stories about how people inside the organisation experience the positive core. One of the premises underlying AI is that all organisations have a positive core that can be uncovered through a process of inquiry. Strengthening or amplifying the positive core brings about organisational transformation in AI.[3]

AI makes a number of assumptions about individuals and organisations[4]:

- ► The first assumption is that all organisations have something to value about their past. These are usually peak moments that energised the organisation towards collective action. Such moments unleash vitality and positive energy so that organisational members feel 'alive'
- ► The second assumption is that organisations move in the direction of questions they ask. This implies that if you focus on problems, you will find problems in an organisation. On the other hand, if you focus on what the organisation does best, you will discover positive aspects that can propel the organisation towards effectiveness and excellence
- ► The third assumption is that image and action are linked. Our behaviour is strongly shaped by our images of the future. In AI, this involves asking people to imagine the future and create a shared, collective image of the organisation in the future. Articulation of such images drives the organisation towards the future it imagined
- ► The fourth assumption is that organisations are not fixed. This implies that any organisation is open to change through a process of inquiry and dialogue

The four assumptions discussed above flow from the theoretical framework underlying AI. In particular, AI draws on the European philosophy termed post-modernism.[5] Within this perspective, organisations are viewed as social constructions. Language and discourse play a crucial role in constructing the organisations. Based on post-modern ideas of social constructionism, five propositions are advanced[6]:

1. *Constructionist principle:* Knowledge about an organisation and its future development are interlinked. In other words, the way we generate knowledge about an organisation creates its future.
2. *Simultaneity principle:* Inquiry and change are not separate discrete activities. Inquiry *is* change. The questions that people ask in trying to discover the positive core, lead to shifts in their cognitive frameworks so that they begin to see the organisation in newer ways.

3. *Poetic principle:* Organisational life is a narrative. Organisations are like open books; they are open to endless interpretation and re-interpretation. In post-modern terminology, organisations are stories co-authored by organisational members. The choice of topic for dialogue can lead to a new story, and therefore, a new organisation.
4. *Anticipatory principle:* Our images of the future transform us. Therefore, we can initiate change by changing our images of the future.
5. *Positive principle:* Positive images lead to positive actions. Positive emotions, positive thoughts and positive behaviour are the basis of enduring productive change.

While these principles may sound a little abstract, they have a number of practical implications for managing change in organisations. First, in the AI framework, change occurs at the individual and collective level when people undergo cognitive shifts leading to a change in their mental models. This is perhaps the single most important contribution of AI. In contrast to conventional change approaches, such as Organisation Development (OD), AI views organisational change as change in *people's thinking.*

Second, these cognitive shifts take place as people begin to inquire into their positive core. Thus, appreciative questioning leads to a rediscovery of the potential strengths and capabilities of the organisation.

Third, the potential of the organisation that was experienced in the past leads to collective envisioning of future possibilities. People feel confident in recreating the conditions that would lead the organisation to express everything that is positive and good about it.

Fourth, this positive image of the future acts as a catalyst for change. This is because the image rekindles energy and vitality that was experienced in the past when the organisation went through its peak moments.

Fifth, this change is largely brought about by people within the organisation as they jointly inquire, understand and co-create the future. Change in the AI framework is truly a collaborative effort that is genuinely participative and democratic.

Sixth, the process generates positive emotions, thinking and behaviour leading to an upwardly spiralling process of development and growth in the organisation's capability to manage change.

AI in Practice

In their original formulation of AI, Srivastva and Cooperrider[7] suggested four characteristics of an AI approach to change. First, the inquiry is about *appreciation* i.e. discovering what is good about the organisation. Second, the inquiry is *practical* i.e. it must be relevant and applicable. Third, the inquiry is *provocative* i.e. it asks questions that can transform people's thinking by giving them new insights. Fourth, the inquiry is *collaborative* i.e. people in an organisation collectively rediscover and change their thinking about the organisation.

While AI does not advocate a step-by-step approach to change, it suggests four phases for bringing about change.[8] This four-phase framework is called the 4-D cycle in AI literature. The first phase is called *discovery*. In this phase, organisational members engage in inquiry to appreciate what is good about their organisation. In order to do this, they agree on an *affirmative topic*.

Examples of affirmative topic include: best work experiences, best team experiences, best customer satisfaction experience and so on. Any problem or deficit can be reframed as an affirmative topic. For instance, in a large airline in the United States, the ground staff was very concerned about missing customer baggage. This was referred to as 'recovery.' Using the AI framework managers decided to reframe this problem as an affirmative topic: exceptional arrival experiences.[9] The key task in the discovery phase is to identify what is known as a '*generative metaphor*.' This is a sentence, quote or phrase that can provoke people to think in different ways.[10]

Generative metaphors not only lead to new thinking, but they can also alert people to new possibilities in terms of action. In the discovery phase, typically organisational members engage in inquiry using an interview guide. Table 7.1 shows a standard interview guide that can be used in appreciative interviews. Each interview is carefully recorded and summarised using a summary sheet (Table 7.2). What distinguishes AI from other change approaches is that organisational members collect 'stories' about their best experiences.

In the second phase called *dream*, organisational members collectively imagine new possibilities based on their stories from the discovery stage. They create images of the future that build on their positive experiences. In the third phase called *design*, organisational members collectively explore what is possible in light of their stories and dreams. In the final stage called *destiny*, organisational members set about to collectively create what they desire.

Does this unusual approach to change—based on a combination of post-modernism and values of participation and democracy—actually work? Surprisingly, AI is one of the fast growing and most popular approaches to change, which has been embraced by a variety of commercial, non-commercial and voluntary organisations around the world.[11] Organisations as diverse as the United States Navy and World Vision have successfully used AI to bring about change. Despite an almost exponential growth in its popularity, there are few studies that have systematically investigated the impact of AI in bringing about change.

Bushe and Khamisa conducted the only study that systematically attempted to assess AI as a strategy of change.[12] Their study examined 20 published cases of AI to assess whether transformation actually occurred. They found that only 35 per cent of the 20 cases showed a transformational outcome. In all these successful cases, transformation resulted in a change in the belief system of organisational members through the generation of new knowledge and a generative metaphor. In all the other cases, AI was used to change existing organisational practices. The seven successful organisations executed change through what the authors refer to as an *improvisational* process, which is contrasted with an *implementation* process in the other cases. Implementation is typically top-down driven by the pursuit of a specific goal that is agreed upon by key decision-makers. Improvisation involves a more emergent process of change resulting from a bottom-up process.

Table 7.1: AI Interview Guide

1. Times of change are full of both, uncertainty and opportunity. You have probably experienced many significant transitions in your life—at work, at home, or in your community. Some of those may have been difficult and some you may have come through very well. Think back to one of your most positive experiences of living through some major change at work—now, can you tell the story of that time? It would be a time when you felt energised, enthusiastic, positive and committed.
   a. What happened?
   b. Who was involved?
   c. How did you influence the outcome?
   d. What support did you have?
   e. What did you learn about yourself in this process?
2. What do you value most about your organisation? What is the 'core factor' that gives life to your organisation (without it the organisation would not be what it is)?
3. In any organisational change effort there are both highs and lows. If you allow yourself to do some positive whining, what hurdles, frictions or even frustrations have you experienced in your involvement with change in your organisation?
4. If you acknowledge that behind each whine there is a wish, what three wishes do you have to improve the way your organisation manages change?
5. Close your eyes and imagine that you had accepted an overseas assignment a few years ago and just returned to your organisation. It's 2007. When you report back for the first day, you notice a level of excitement amongst the staff—about their jobs and their personal development—that you have never seen among this or any other group of employees. The staff seems more customer-focused and energised. Customers are smiling. You feel compelled to ask your co-workers how all of this came to be. *What do they say were the keys to success? What was the smallest change that made the largest impact?*
6. What are you willing to do tomorrow to bring this new era (organisation of 2007) about?
7. What are the key steps that you can take right away? Your organisation?

Source: http://appreciativeinquiry.cwru.edu/

Table 7.2: AI Summary Sheet

INTERVIEW Summary Sheet	Date:
Interviewer:	Interviewee:
Organisation:	
What were the *best quotes* that came out of the interview?	
What were the *best stories* that came out?	
What were the *best wishes* that you heard?	
What were the *best practices* or *recommendations* that you heard reflected in your conversation?	

Source: http://appreciativeinquiry.cwru.edu/

Bushe and Khamisa conclude that a focus on changing how people think—instead of what they do—and a focus on supporting self-organising change processes that flow from new ideas—rather than leading implementation of centrally or consensually agreed upon changes, are the two distinguishing features of AI. Although their study has a number of limitations, it once again highlights the low success rates of organisational transformation efforts. However, their study suggests that the real contribution of AI may be in its ability to change people's mental models and, thereby, enhance the capability for change in the organisation. We believe that AI offers a simple, elegant and powerful way not only to build change capability but also to create a positive behavioural climate in an organisation.

The practice of AI promotes generative learning which is essential for creativity and innovation. In particular, as Barrett argues, it promotes four competencies that can significantly build change capability in an organisation.[13]

- First, it promotes *affirmative competence,* which is the ability to focus on past strengths and successes
- Second, it builds *expansive competence,* which is the ability to: set stretch goals, engage in experimentation, and envision new possibilities
- Third, it encourages *generative competence,* which enables organisational members to find a sense of purpose and meaning in their work
- Finally, it builds *collaborative competence,* which enables organisational members to value diversity and learn from one another

Affirmative competence is the capability to go beyond what is feasible in an organisation. For example, conventional strategic planning, with its emphasis on rational analysis, promotes conservatism by focusing on what is 'feasible.' In order to build capability, managers need to go beyond what is feasible and get in touch with their organisation's highest accomplishments. This is typically a feature of high performing organisations. As Barrett observes[14]:

This same focus on strength rather than 'feasibility' allowed other organisations to move into vanguard markets: Consider Sony's creation of the 8mm camcorder, Yamaha's digital piano, Casio's small-screen color LCD television, Apple's creation of the Newton. Similarly, 3M's competence with sticky tape allowed the company to imagine ventures into magnetic tape, film, coated abrasives, and Post-it notes. Canon's valuing of its core competence in optics and imaging led it to excel in copiers, laser printers, cameras, and image scanners.

Expansive competence stretches the organisation's ability by challenging organisational members to excel themselves. Generative competence builds the capacity to focus on critical issues such as quality, costs and customer satisfaction. It also builds the ability to transcend departmental boundaries and overcome the 'silo' mentality. Collaborative competence builds the ability to engage in dialogue that leads to deep learning. As Barrett notes[15]:

> And yet to say that organisations need to engage in continuous learning risks hiding an important distinction. It is not enough for organisations to respond, adapt, and cope with the pressures of change. The push for innovation requires a different kind of learning, one that goes beyond adapting to challenges and solving problems and instead focuses on imagining possibilities, on generating new ways of looking at the world. This is appreciative learning—the art of valuing and inquiring into possibility. Creating the radically new, not just adapting and responding to problems as they present themselves, innovative organisations go beyond the perceived constraints associated with adaptive learning. Appreciative learning cultures nurture innovative thinking by fostering an affirmative focus, expansive thinking, a generative sense of meaning, and creating collaborative systems.

To summarise, building a positive behavioural climate involves valuing employees so that they have a sense of efficacy. It involves valuing what is inherently good in the organisation and building on an organisation's positive core strengths. It involves engaging in dialogue to promote conversations that lead people to alter their thinking and see themselves, their work and the organisation in new ways. It involves promoting collaboration so that the organisation can leverage the diversity of thinking and perspectives that organisational members bring to their work. It involves valuing learning as a core activity.

Appreciative Inquiry offers a practical way to accomplish these in a way that is both challenging and affirming. AI offers change managers a practical and powerful tool to address the four critical tasks of our model. In particular, it requires a leadership style that is different from the heroic or charismatic type of leader often described in popular management articles. It requires a leadership style built on positive values such as integrity. In the following section, we examine this aspect of leadership in terms of conduct and character.

LEADERSHIP: CHARACTER AND CONDUCT

Leading an organisation in the current global environment is a tremendously challenging task. However, leadership qualities are necessary at all levels in an organisation. Whether you are a junior, middle or top-level manager, you will need to acquire and develop your leadership skills to be effective in your job. It is, therefore, not surprising that leadership has emerged as one of the most important areas for research and training in recent years.

LEADERSHIP AS ENVISIONING, ENGAGING AND ENACTING

Peter Cammock, a management scholar, youth leader and church activist in New Zealand has studied and researched leadership in management over the last 20 years. Based on a review of the leadership literature, he has identified three tasks of leadership[16]:

1. **Envisioning:** This, according to Cammock, involves seeing beyond the current constraints and developing an appreciative image or vision of what might be attempted or accomplished.
2. **Engaging:** This involves extending an invitation or call for involvement in a significant cause. According to Cammock, 'it is an invitation that may require great commitment and sacrifice and which often involves intense leader-follower relationships.'[17]
3. **Enacting:** This is about bringing the vision into action. It requires high levels of energy, effort and application over extended periods of time.

Based on his own research and a review of literature, Cammock identifies six personal characteristics of leadership. These are:

1. *Passion.* High level of ambition, drive, motivation, enthusiasm and work capacity. It helps the leader stick with difficult tasks by being persistent and disciplined.
2. *Courage.* This is the characteristic that enables fronting up to problems, tackling unpleasant tasks, taking tough decisions and assuming responsibility when things go wrong. Courage enables the leader to speak the truth when it may not be popular.
3. *Faith.* This is the characteristic that keeps leaders optimistic and hopeful. It also makes them resilient, i.e. they bounce back from failures.
4. *Concern for others.* This characteristic makes leaders approachable, sensitive, friendly and supportive.
5. *Sense of self.* This enables leaders be secure and confident. They feel secure in their position and develop presence.
6. *Integrity.* This enables leaders keep promises and be honest, open and straightforward in their dealings. They are willing to admit mistakes.

Integrity is probably the most important attribute of a change leader. Integrity means *consistency in thought, word and deed.* Change leaders have to be people who are consistent in their thoughts, words and behaviour. They must practise what they preach. They must live the values that they want their organisations to embrace. While qualities of character and integrity cannot be *taught*, they can be *acquired* by discipline and self-development. One needs to work on oneself to develop these qualities.

Mary Parker Follet, a well-known management thinker observes: '*The person who influences me most is not he who does great deeds but he who makes me feel I can do great deeds.*'[18] This, in fact, is the description of leadership that is most appropriate in organisational change. According to David Hurst, leaders create pathways that direct natural processes to flow along them. Leadership, according to him, is *the creation of conditions under which self-organisation or learning can occur.*[19] The purpose of leadership, according to Hurst, *is to build a large-scale loosely connected network of talented individuals who are held together by common values, a shared vision of the future, and a unique sense of who they are as a people. The two most important outputs of these activities are commitment and trust.*[20]

Creation and promotion of commitment and trust are central aspects of change leadership. It is the leader's task to create conditions for learning by stimulating meaningful conversations. Meaningful conversations can only take place when relationships are characterised by *trust, commitment and integrity*. Therefore, the challenge of change leadership is promoting trust, integrity and commitment in organisations. Obviously, leaders cannot promote these qualities unless they themselves display the qualities. The most important lesson from leadership research is that change leadership is rooted, *not in charisma, but in character*. Organisational change requires *value-based* leadership. The life and work of Mahatma Gandhi provides a powerful example of value-based leadership. Interestingly, he refers to the following as the seven deadly sins: (i) Wealth without work; (ii) Pleasure without conscience; (iii) Knowledge without character; (iv) Business without morality; (v) Science without humanity; (vi) Religion without sacrifice; and (vii) Politics without principle.

LEADERSHIP FRAMEWORKS

Organisational studies and experience indicate a strong correlation between leadership capability of an organisation and its sustained high performance. Leadership talent is therefore considered one of the most important assets of an organisation, and progressive organisations invest sustained efforts to build leadership at different levels. They consider leadership development too important to be left to chance.

When an organisation is keen to develop leadership across different levels, it finds it useful to develop a framework for leadership development. The framework would highlight the factors that are important for leadership effectiveness in the given context. It is then used for implementing a systematic approach for leadership development. In this section, we present short summaries of the leadership frameworks in a wide range of contexts: National Health Service, Infosys, Tata group, GE and Siemens.

NATIONAL HEALTH SERVICE (NHS) IN THE UNITED KINGDOM

The framework describes the key characteristics, attitudes and behaviours to which leaders in the NHS should aspire. It describes the qualities expected of NHS leaders.

There are fifteen attributes within the framework, arranged in three clusters:

- Personal Qualities
- Setting Direction and
- Delivering the Service

These attributes are defined at different levels of effectiveness, so that it is possible to define or diagnose the level of effectiveness at which an individual is operating at a given time.

Personal Qualities: Personal qualities and values are at the core of the framework. The scale and complexity of the change agenda facing leaders in the NHS means that they need to draw deeply upon their personal qualities to see them through the demands of the job. Key attributes are: personal integrity, drive for improvement, self-management, self-awareness and self-belief.

Setting Direction: Outstanding leaders set a vision for the future, drawing on their understanding of the organisations in which they work, and their political awareness of the context. This, combined with action-orientation and intellectual flexibility, allow them to move between big picture vision and local operational detail. This cluster includes certain attributes as indicated. Key attributes of setting direction are: intellectual flexibility, seizing the future, broad scanning and political astuteness.

Delivering the Service: High performing leaders work across the organisation and across the wider community to make things happen and deliver results. They use a range of styles that challenge traditional, organisational and professional boundaries and ways of working and emphasise empowerment and partnership. This cluster includes the key qualities of empowering others and collaborative working. Key attributes of delivering the service include: Leading change through people, ensuring accountability, empowering others and effective and strategic influencing.

INFOSYS LEADERSHIP FRAMEWORK

Infosys, the Indian Information Technology (IT) company, aspires to be at the forefront of the fast-changing industry in which it operates. The company therefore believes that its leaders require the spirit of learnability and commitment to continuous personal and professional development.

To be effective in their leadership role, individuals need continuous upgradation in specific areas of technology, management, leadership, cultural and communication skills, and other soft skills.

The Infosys framework highlights the following aspects.

- Setting Direction
- Performance Focus
- Relationship Building
- Customer Partnering
- Quality
- Technical/Functional Expertise
- Developing Leaders
- Interpersonal Effectiveness

TATA LEADERSHIP PRACTICES

The Tata Group has developed a common leadership framework for all its 91 businesses operating in different industries such as chemicals, engineering, power, software, steel, tele-services, and hotels. The framework has been defined in terms of Tata Leadership Practices (TLPs)—a set of behaviours that retain the key elements of the Tata leadership ethos, while taking on the world of tomorrow and the challenges it is likely to throw up. They are called 'practices' to focus on concrete behaviours and actions rather than abstract philosophy. The underlying assumption is that modifying actions is the more effective way to modify values and philosophies. Hence, TLPs, as they are commonly referred to, are aimed to help shape leaders. Tata group has three broad themes and TLPs under which leadership competencies are grouped:

1. *Delivering value—making money*
   - Drive for Results
   - Timely Decision Making
   - Customer Focus
   - Innovation Management
2. *Business leadership*
   - Managing Vision and Purpose
   - Strategic Capability
   - Dealing with Ambiguity
   - Business Acumen
   - Functional Excellence
3. *People and team leadership*
   - Taking Ownership
   - People Development
   - Interpersonal Effectiveness
   - Withstanding Pressure
   - Building Effective Teams

The Tata Leadership Practices cover different aspects of leadership. Leaders are expected to demonstrate leadership behaviours in each of these areas. TLPs help individuals identify their strengths and also the areas for improvement. They are used for making decisions pertaining to promotion and leadership development.

GE LEADERSHIP FRAMEWORK

General Electric (GE), in the United States, believes that leadership is critical for the success of any organisation, and it is leadership that takes the organisation forward or backward. The company has an elaborate system for developing leaders. Leadership competencies have been clearly defined, and GE

Leadership and Change

conducts 360-degree leadership assessment on these competencies to assess every leader.

The leadership competencies in the GE framework include:

- Vision
- Customer/Quality Focus
- Integrity
- Accountability/Commitment
- Communication/Influence
- Shared Ownership/Ability to work seamlessly across departmental, functional, hierarchical and geographical boundaries
- Team building/Empowerment
- Knowledge and Expertise/Intellect
- Initiative/Speed
- Global Mindset

Key GE Leadership Ingredients: GE believes that its leaders should possess 4Es:

- *Energy.* Enormous Personal Energy—Strong Bias for Action
- *Energizer.* Ability to Motivate and Energize Others; Infectious Enthusiasm to Maximise Organisation Potential
- *Edge.* Competitive Spirit; Instinctive Drive for Speed/Impact; Strong Convictions and Courageous Advocacy
- *Execution.* Deliver Results

SIEMENS LEADERSHIP FRAMEWORK

Siemens Leadership Framework specifies how it measures the performance of its managers and which personal capabilities managers at Siemens should possess. Measurement criteria have been spelt out clearly for excellent leadership at Siemens. These criteria play a key role in the staff dialogue, particularly for the managers.

Excellent leadership can mean different things in different cultures. The results achieved, however, are universal— outstanding financial results, satisfied customers, motivated employees and superior processes. For this reason, the company measures leadership performance in these four categories: financials, customers, employees and processes.

LEADERSHIP DEVELOPMENT

The leadership frameworks of the different organisations discussed above indicate certain commonalities. The Corporate Leadership Council, a highly regarded research agency has examined the leadership frameworks of these and a large number of other organisations operating in different sectors and in different countries. They have also carried out a very large and systematic survey of leadership attributes that make leaders effective. This survey conducted by the Corporate Leadership Council found that leaders consider people management skills as the most important attribute of effective leadership. This was followed by strategic management skills. Innate personal characteristics and skills in process management were considered to be important, but lower down in priority. Leaders across a wide range of organisations communicated that their organisations were weak in terms of both the numbers and quality of leaders. Many organisations may be adequately managed, but they are under led. With the environment becoming more demanding, leadership development has become even more critical for organisations.

KEY ELEMENTS OF LEADERSHIP DEVELOPMENT

The general experience appears to be that feedback and relationship based development programmes are highly effective for leadership development. In other words, people in key positions should have an opportunity to receive feedback from others (superiors, colleagues, subordinates and customers). Without this valuable feedback, the speed of development is greatly hampered. Individuals in key positions should also have opportunities to discuss their feedback and their development agenda and learning challenges with others.

That is why, in many progressive organisations, individuals in top positions allocate a certain amount of time for facilitating leadership development. One very interesting finding of the Corporate Leadership Council is with regard to the key role that autonomy plays in leadership development. The greater the decision-making authority given to managers, the faster would be their development as leaders.

STEPS FOR LEADERSHIP DEVELOPMENT

When we look at the leadership development approaches, we find some general and common trends. The OECD publication on leadership outlines the broad elements of the approach followed in OECD countries, which are briefly outlined thus:

1. *Define a competence profile for future leaders:* The first step taken to develop future leaders is to define the competence profile for future leaders. The competencies required for future leaders could be different from those required for present leaders in terms of their responsibility, capability and role. For this step, we should first make predictions of the future environment and the challenges that leaders are likely to face.
2. *Identify and select potential leaders:* This identification would be based on the competence framework for future leaders. A key choice would be whether we should select future leaders from outside or nurture them within our own organisations.
3. *Encourage mentoring and training:* There should be substantial efforts made to train future leaders. Progressive organisations have set up specialised institutions for leadership development, and others have established new leadership development courses for senior people within their existing training institutions.
4. *Keep leadership development sustainable:* We must remember that leadership development occurs over a period of time. To sustain the efforts over a long time, we must have a comprehensive programme for the whole of the organisation and ensure that senior people devote time to development programmes.

To sum up, we list the key stages that progressive organisations utilise to develop leadership skills:

- Adopt a leadership model
- Decide on who will receive leadership development
- Involve senior leaders in development process
- Define the results expected from leaders and link these to the larger strategy
- Use powerful learning and training methods to accelerate development
- Emphasise action learning projects
- Create a culture of feedback
- Make development a long term process, and not just an event

THE MINDSET FOR CHANGE MANAGEMENT

A myth about leadership is that it is all about communication and interpersonal effectiveness. As we have seen above, while these are highly desirable skills, there are specific enduring qualities that are crucial for effective leadership. Successful change leaders are ethical, honest and transparent. They are willing to take unpleasant decisions and are prepared to persist in the face of obstacles. They are emotionally secure, confident and have the ability to judge people and develop talent. They are adaptable but strongly focused on their goals.[21] More importantly, leadership is about *passion* and *compassion*. Passion gives the energy to drive change, face obstacles, stay focused, and remain confident. Compassion provides the energy to be sensitive, understanding and caring. It is the combination of passion and compassion that enables managers to judge people, identify talent and develop people.

Mindsets and attitudes are very important in managing change. If you want to become effective in managing change, you must cultivate the right mindset or attitudes. In the challenging environment facing most organisations, three qualities are particularly important. As a change manager, you have to be thoughtful, systematic and determined. The discipline of change management offers frameworks and models that can help managers become more thoughtful and systematic in their engagement with change. Determination is a quality that you need to cultivate yourself. Why are these qualities important?

Typically, managers are action-oriented. This is not surprising because they have been hired to achieve results. Faced with a problem or situation that needs resolution, the immediate tendency of most people is to *do something*. Under such conditions, usually, their actions will be based on what brought them success in the past. In a changing environment this can lead to problems. Solutions that worked in the past may not work in the present. Worse still, old solutions can create new problems. After a while, you will find yourself dealing with the problems that you created rather than dealing with change. Thus, thoughtless action can lead you to do things that can make your situation worse. When a whole team of managers act thoughtlessly, they can make serious strategic errors committing the organisation to a doomed course of action. The quality of thoughtfulness allows you to pause and reflect before you act. This will lead to better analysis and understanding of the change situation facing the organisations. It will also help you to look at a range of options for dealing with the situation.

Even if you are thoughtful, there are other ways in which you could mismanage change. One of them is by managing change in a haphazard and disorganised manner. This happens more frequently than you might imagine in most organisations. One of the reasons for this disorganised effort is that most change efforts are taken as an add-on, on top of one's normal, daily routines. Given that we have limited time and energy, most time and attention is likely to be spent on familiar, routine day-to-day activities rather than unfamiliar, new change tasks. When you add to this the proclivity to rush to meet deadlines, it is not surprising that many change efforts seem to follow a haphazard and messy trajectory. Again, the discipline of change management can give you tools and techniques to develop a systematic orientation to change.

In addition to being thoughtful and systematic, you need a third quality to succeed as a change manager: Determination. Most change efforts will throw up unanticipated problems. People around you will not always be motivated and cooperative.

Even before your change project is completed, there may be new challenges from the environment. Therefore, managing change effectively also requires you to be patient and persistent. Patience and persistence make up the quality of determination, which is the quality of not giving up easily in the face of obstacles. This is a leadership quality that you need to develop through constant practice and experience. However, the ideas and tools presented in this book will help you become more thoughtful and systematic in your approach to change.

REVIEW OF CHANGE MANAGEMENT MODEL

We began this chapter with a discussion of Appreciative Inquiry, and examined a key leadership challenge as creating a behavioural context that facilitates inquiry, appreciation and change. Now we briefly review our change management model, before concluding our inquiry with a section on core leadership roles in change management.

In our discussion of the core task of *appreciating change*, we had noted that the leadership should have processes in place for scanning and analysing the external context and examine the effect of three forces—competition, technology and institutional rules on their organisation. High rates of change in these three forces create uncertainty for managers and the challenge of change is coming to grips with this uncertainty and managing it. When the environment is hostile (e.g. during periods of economic downturn), managerial errors and incompetence are severely exposed. Conversely, during periods of growth, even poor decisions are masked.

An important challenge is to build flexibility, responsiveness and efficiency in organisations to build strength to cope with environmental changes. The importance of efficiency is well understood. Flexibility implies a firm's ability to adjust the scale of operations. Obviously higher flexibility helps lower risk. Responsiveness allows the firm to offer products and services that meet specific needs and also price those appropriately.

As we have seen, an important role of leadership is to shape the change agenda on the basis of a careful assessment of external environment, customers and markets, obstacles to growth, competition, etc. The leaders need to determine the best ways to grow their organisations profitably balancing the short term and long term interests. There should be clarity on the critical issues facing the organisation and how these would be addressed effectively. In the whole process, the leadership cannot lose sight of the internal capabilities and competencies required to execute the strategies.

In other words, in the first phase of appreciating change, the leadership should identify its business model and the underlying value proposition, and then examine whether the organisation needs a radical change or a refinement of their business model. But in the whole process, there has to be a great deal of sensitivity to one's own mental models. Faulty mental models can lead to strategic errors.

Inquiry into questions of what the organisation is passionate about or what drives our economic engine requires intense dialogue and meaningful conversations among managers. The objective of dialogue is to uncover the assumptions, values and beliefs that underlie the mental models in the organisations. These assumptions, values and beliefs need to be subjected to relentless scrutiny in light of changes in an organisation's external environment. By confronting the realities inside and outside the organisation, the leadership team can develop and refine the change agenda.

The next task of leadership is to take this change agenda to the rest of the organisation and *mobilise support*. Organisational change is most successful when there is participation, involvement and ownership of change in the organisation. Sometimes it is wrongly assumed that a powerful logic alone is quite adequate to get people convinced and obtain their support for change. But we must remember that organisational change is both cultural and political. It involves changing mindsets.

The process requires attention to several issues: building a critical mass with whose support the change can be launched; employing appropriate change management tactics based on sound principles of persuasion; putting in place an effective communication strategy that takes into account the audience, purpose, context and also credibility of communication; altering incentives; framing change agenda in a way that evokes support; engaging in one-on-one negotiation to get buy-in; and so on. In the whole process, it is important to relate the idea to realities of the employees with as much clarity as possible. When leadership pursues the ideas continuously and consistently with a sense of optimism, they gain acceptance for new ideas in the organisation.

No matter how well a change is appreciated and planned, and irrespective of how well it is supported by the organisation, if the change is not executed competently to produce results, the change effort would end up as a failure. In *executing change,* change leaders need to attend to certain critical tasks:

a) *Creating cross-functional linkages in the organisation:* Again this requires attention to mindsets apart from putting in place structure and mechanisms for collaborative working and development of cooperation/consensus building skills. Mindsets require attention to priorities and signals that leaders convey through their words and deeds.

b) *Aligning policies, procedures and removing structural impediments to change:* This includes ensuring that structure and policies reflect current priorities, and appropriate controls and incentives are in place.

c) *Creating new routines for continuous improvements and innovations:* The leadership should ensure that attention flows to generating and generalising ideas with impact. When clarity of purpose is high and effective processes are in place, people are able to add value.

d) *Attending to human aspects of executing change:* This requires deconstructing complex change so that priorities and objectives are clear, creating hope and optimism, and enhancing preparedness to manage the unexpected.

The fourth critical task in change management is one of building change capability. Self-efficacy, focus and energy are the key elements for building capability. Leadership builds capability when they: (a) set challenging goals; (b) create ownership; (c) structure activities to facilitate reflection and action; (d) initiate processes to accelerate unlearning and learning; and (e) foster a behavioural context that is positive and learning oriented. The basic leadership task is to develop people's confidence by demonstrating faith in their capabilities. More specifically, they would attend to the following: Developing inquiry skills and building mindsets of systematic problem solving; building systems to identify improvement opportunities, rewarding knowledge generation and sharing; strengthening linkage and integration mechanisms in structures and building in greater discretion and flexibility; articulating stretch goals and capabilities required to achieve those goals in a manner that communicates excitement of achievement and progress; and creating a culture that values free and frank conversations, risk taking and seeks to be the best.

Thus, our model suggests that change management requires multiple leadership roles. Each core task in change management demands specific leadership capabilities. We now discuss these four roles in the final section of this book.

CORE LEADERSHIP ROLES IN CHANGE MANAGEMENT

COGNITIVE TUNER

The first core task of appreciating change requires a manager to tune into both the external business environment and the internal organisational setting. First, the manager needs to attend to changes that are taking place in the external environment. These may arise from competitor actions, shifts in customer preferences, technological changes and changes in institutional rules. These changes may be subtle and may require the manager to attend to and amplify weak signals. Second, the manager needs to assess the organisational capabilities and competencies to address the external changes. This may require evaluating the organisation's readiness to change and weighing up its ability to develop the required skills and competencies. Both these tasks face a formidable barrier. The barrier is the manager's own mental model. In a complex, dynamic environment the manager's mental model can prevent him or her from accurately perceiving the reality. In fact, their mental models can make them blind. Therefore, in order to be effective cognitive tuners, managers need to first become aware of their own mental models. Mere awareness is not sufficient. They must also be willing to shed their mental models. Here are some simple rules for becoming an effective cognitive tuner:

1. *Expose yourself to variety.* Cognitive tuning requires openness to multiple perspectives. Attending industry conferences and seminars, participation in training programmes, conversations with industry analysts and experts and paying attention to competitor actions are some ways of acquiring multiple perspectives on the external environment. Conversations with suppliers, distributors and employees can enlarge a manager's understanding of the internal context. Openness to multiple perspectives requires a manager to cultivate curiosity. Always be aware that your knowledge and understanding is limited. Seek knowledge like a curious child in order to become more effective in your role.
2. *Introspect and reflect on your mental models.* Cognitive tuning requires awareness of one's own mental models. Managers need to spend time on introspection and reflection to become aware of their assumptions, values and beliefs. You need to interrogate your mental model. Write down your assumptions about your organisation, your customers, your competitors and your external environment. What do you value? What do you consider important? What do you believe to be true? Talk about your values, assumptions and beliefs to a close associate or friend. Ask them to play the role of a devil's advocate and challenge your assumptions and beliefs.
3. *Bust your mental models periodically.* Cognitive tuning requires the ability to forego one's mental models. Expose your thinking to scrutiny by your close associates. Test your assumptions against their beliefs and assumptions. Compare your values to their values. Which of your assumptions are you willing to let go? What values seem inappropriate or

irrelevant? It is important that you do not derive your identity from your mental models. Treat your mental models as if they are the clothes that you wear. Just as you discard clothes when they are worn out and old, you need to cast off old mental models.
4. *Expose yourself to dissent and negative feedback.* The best way to bust one's mental models is through disconfirmation. Listen to people who disagree with you. What are they saying? Separate their message from their personality. Does the message make sense? Welcome negative feedback on your ideas and behaviour because it gives you the opportunity to improve yourself. Don't feel defensive or threatened when others challenge your ideas and thinking. These are valuable moments for learning and change and such opportunities are rare.

PEOPLE CATALYSER

The second core task of mobilising support requires managers to be catalysts for change. They need to catalyse people by building support, manufacturing consent and facilitating cognitive shifts in organisational members. Managers need to be communicators, persuaders and negotiators. This is a crucial step in change management and many managers and organisations fail to execute change because they either ignore this task or do not pay sufficient attention to it. The following simple rules are intended to help managers become effective people catalysers:

1. *Prepare yourself before engaging people.* It is not a good idea to jump into the task of mobilising support without careful preparation. Mobilising support represents the political aspect of change. Who you talk to first, what words you use and how you sequence your mobilisation efforts can significantly shape the outcome of your efforts. Therefore, analyse your context before you begin any action. Who are the people whose support you need? What are their self-interests and values? What are the common areas of agreement that you can count on? What are your options for influencing them? What is the specific type of support

that you require from key individuals? You need to address all these questions and—when you are satisfied that you have the answers—you are ready to initiate action.
2. *Use all forums and media for influencing people.* Mobilising support requires relentless and repetitive communication of your change agenda. Use formal meetings, informal gatherings, newsletters, e-mails, one-on-one conversations, training sessions and speeches to reinforce your message. Your message must be direct, simple and compelling.
3. *Don't run away from tough decisions.* Change management may occasionally involve making decisions that are unpopular and unpleasant. If you are convinced that they are right for your organisation, you need to build up the courage to stick to your decisions regardless of the consequences. This may involve confronting people in the organisation. Ensure that you follow a transparent, fair and inclusive process for decision-making. Provide resources generously to implement tough decisions. Trust yourself and instil faith in yourself.
4. *Develop credibility, trust and respect.* Your chances of influencing people are significantly higher if people around you respect you as a credible and trust-worthy professional. You can enhance trust and credibility by being good at your job and being benevolent and generous. If you are transparent, fair, inclusive and competent in your job, your credibility and respect in the organisation is likely to be high.

SYSTEMS ARCHITECT

The third core task of executing change requires managers to be systems architects. They need to create the systems, processes and routines to execute the change plan or agenda. This involves setting explicit goals, establishing cross-functional teams and monitoring progress. The following simple rules are intended to help managers play this role effectively:

1. *Clarify individual roles and contribution:* Each member of the organisation should have goals that are SMART (Specific,

Measurable, Achievable, Relevant, Time bound). SMART goals ensure focus, direction and teamwork, and help the unit achieve high performance. Clear expectations contribute to greater role effectiveness. Clarify your expectations from units and teams.
2. *Select/recruit team leaders carefully.* Quality of team leaders is crucial for effective execution of change. Team leader selection for cross-functional teams is an important task that should not be taken lightly. Select individuals with high levels of focus, energy and self-efficacy. They should be committed to the organisation and its change agenda. Jim Collins refers to this as 'getting the right people on the bus.'
3. *Create mechanisms for sharing best practices.* Coordination of activities and continuous improvement are essential ingredients for effective execution of change. Change managers can foster coordination and improvement by establishing processes and routines for sharing best practices among the departments and units. This promotes learning from each other and fosters appreciation of each other's contribution.
4. *Eliminate routines that are barriers to change.* Organisational past practices, procedures and policies can frequently slow down and derail change. Change managers need to vigorously identify such past routines and eliminate them. This may entail structural reorganisation, establishing new policies and developing new routines.

EFFICACY BUILDER

The fourth core task of building change capability requires a manager to build efficacy for change in the organisation. As an efficacy builder, managers need to make organisational members have faith in their ability to learn, overcome obstacles and engage in change. In his popular bestseller, *Good to Great*, Jim Collins argues that effective leaders don't motivate people. They help people motivate themselves. Based on their research on willpower among European managers, Bruch and Ghoshal suggest six strategies for capability building[22]:

1. *Help managers visualise their intentions.* As leaders, you can help your managers formulate vivid and clear pictures of what they want to achieve.
2. *Prepare managers for obstacles*: Ensure that your managers fully understand the potential costs and benefits of a project before they commit to it. They should ask themselves three questions: (a) What would it cost me personally to undertake this project? (b) What must I stop doing? (c) What else would I do if I did not take up this project?
3. *Encourage managers to confront their ambivalence.* Your managers need to confront their emotions when they feel unsure and reflect on their commitment to the project.
4. *Develop a climate of choice.* Offer your managers choices and encourage them to use those choices. Without compromising on the goals and performance standards, provide your managers with enough space to act on their choices.
5. *Build a self-regulating system.* This involves making any manager who initiates a project also responsible for deactivating it. Insist that managers define their own stopping rules.
6. *Create a desire for the sea.* This involves providing managers with difficult and stretching tasks. The goals and objectives of such task must be personally meaningful to managers. Challenges need to be emotionally captivating.

The role of efficacy builder involves structuring opportunities for people to learn and grow together. The following simple rules are intended to help you become an effective efficacy builder:

1. *Demonstrate faith in people.* Focus, energy and self-efficacy are the three important attributes of change capability. The most effective way to enhance self-efficacy in others is to show faith in their abilities. Setting demanding goals, communicating positive expectations in their ability to achieve these goals and supporting them in the achievement of the goals can do this.
2. *Select and develop individuals for leadership positions.* An important part of building change capability is to select

and groom future leaders for the organisation. According to Janice Klein, author of *True Change*, effective change managers are 'outsider-insiders.' These are managers who understand the company's capabilities and culture but can bring in new perspectives and break out of existing mental models. An organisation can create outsider-insiders by selecting promising insiders and structuring opportunities for their professional growth. This would involve assigning these insiders challenging tasks and projects and sending them outside for education and training.
3. *Establish processes for storing and sharing organisational knowledge.* A significant aspect of building change capability is to build a repository of organisational knowledge that captures insights from people's tacit experiences. This includes best practices developed by different units, teams and departments, templates and routines for carrying out similar projects and information on potential pitfalls and obstacles in specific areas of work. For instance, the Capability Maturity Model (CMM) developed by the Software Engineering Institute (SEI), Carnegie Mellon University in the United States, is an effective way for knowledge management in software companies. According to current statistics, India has over 89 companies at the SEI CMM Level 5, which is the highest level of assessment. Six Sigma is another quality initiative that can be used to build and share organisational knowledge.
4. *Promote resilience.* Resilience is the ability to anticipate and adjust to changes that threaten an organisation's business model. This part of building change capability is closely related to the core task of appreciating change. In their article titled 'The Quest for Resilience' in the *Harvard Business Review*, Gary Hamel and Lisa Valikangas argue that four challenges need to be mastered for creating resilience in an organisation. The first challenge is cognitive. Change managers must be alert to the dysfunctional consequences of arrogance, nostalgia and denial. Often, these three are related. Organisational members must be exposed to variety and subjected to feedback and disconfirmation

to prevent them from being stuck in the past or the present. The second challenge is strategic. This involves encouraging the organisational members to experiment to generate new options. The third challenge is political. Experiments that are successful and projects that show promise need resources and support. Often these resources need to be diverted from existing products and projects. This will require managing the politics of resource allocation. The fourth challenge is ideological and related to changing mindsets about continuous renewal and transformation. Renewal must become as important as cash flow or profit maximisation.

The four leadership roles in change management that we have discussed above are perhaps more prosaic than the qualities and attributes discussed in the leadership literature. However, these roles and the associated rules facilitate the task of change management.

We finish this book with a sobering observation. Change management is not just about creating business models, making profits and acquiring market share: fundamentally, it is about creating enduring institutions. It is about ensuring that our legacy of competence, capabilities and values is carried forward for future generations. It is about human emancipation and progress mediated through our organisations and institutions.

NOTES AND REFERENCES

1. Cameron, K. S., Dutton, J. E., & Quinn, R. E. (Eds.). (2003). *Positive Organisational Scholarship: Foundations of a New Discipline*. San Francisco: Berrett-Koehler.
2. Fredrickson, B. L. (2003). Positive emotions and upward spirals in organisations. In K. S. Cameron, J. E. Dutton & R. E. Quinn (Eds.), *Positive Organisational Change: Foundations of a New Discipline* (pp. 163–175). San Francisco: Berrett-Koehler.
3. See http://appreciativeinquiry.cwru.edu/ for a comprehensive account of AI. This excellent site lists articles, tools and links to researchers and communities practicing AI. Classic works in AI include: Cooperrider, D.L. & Srivastva, S. (1987). Appreciative inquiry in organisational life. In Woodman, R. W. & Pasmore, W.A.

(Eds.). *Research In Organisational Change And Development*, Vol. 1: (pp. 129–169). Stamford, CT: JAI Press; Cooperrider, D. L., Barrett, F., Srivastva, S. (1995). Social construction and appreciative inquiry: A journey in organisational theory. In Hosking, D., Dachler, P. & Gergen, K. (Eds.). *Management and Organisation: Relational Alternatives to Individualism* (pp. 157–200). Aldershot, UK: Avebury; Cooperrider, D., Srivastva, S. (2000). Appreciative Inquiry in Organisational Life. *Appreciative Inquiry: Rethinking Human Organisation Toward a Positive Theory of Change*. Cooperrider, D. L. (2000). Positive Image, Positive Action: The Affirmative Basis of Organising. *Appreciative Inquiry: Rethinking Human Organisation Toward a Positive Theory of Change*, pp. 29–53; Cooperrider, D. L., Whitney, D. (1999). *Collaborating for Change: Appreciative Inquiry*. Berrett-Koehler Publishers Bushe, G.R. (1995). Advances in appreciative inquiry as an organisation development intervention. *Organisation Development Journal*, 13: pp. 14–22. Bushe, G.R. (1998). Appreciative inquiry in teams, *Organisation Development Journal*, 16: pp. 41–50. Bushe, G.R. (2001a). Five theories of change embedded in appreciative inquiry. In Cooperrider, D. Sorenson, P., Whitney, D. & Yeager, T. (Eds.), *Appreciative Inquiry: An Emerging Direction for Organisation Development* (pp. 117–127). Champaign, IL: Stipes.

4. Leibler, C. J. Getting Comfortable with Appreciative Inquiry. *http://appreciativeinquiry.cwru.edu/*
5. Cooperrider, D. L., Barrett, F., & Srivastva, S. (1995). Social construction and appreciative inquiry: A journey in organisational theory. *http://appreciativeinquiry.cwru.edu/*
6. Barrett, F., & Fry, R. E. (2002). Appreciative Inquiry in action: The unfolding of a provocative proposition. In R. E. Fry, F. Barrett, J. Seiling & D. Whitney (Eds.). *Appreciative Inquiry and Organisational Transformation: Reports from the Field* (pp. 1–23). Westport, CT: Quorum.
7. Cooperrider, D. L. & Srivastva, S. (1987). Appreciative inquiry in organisational life. In Woodman, R. W. & Pasmore, W.A. (Eds.). *Research In Organisational Change And Development*, vol. 1 (pp. 129–169). Stamford, CT: JAI Press.
8. Cooperrider, D. L., & Whitney, D.A. Positive revolution in change: Appreciative Inquiry. *http://appreciativeinquiry.cwru.edu/*.
9. Bushe, G. R., & Khamisa, A. (January 2004). When is Appreciative Inquiry Transformational? A Meta-Case Analysis. *http://www.gervasebushe.ca/aimeta.htm*

10. Barrett, F. J. & Cooperrider, D. L. (1990). Generative metaphor intervention: A new approach for working with systems divided by conflict and caught in defensive perception. *Journal of Applied Behavioral Science*, 26: pp. 219–239.
11. Ludema, J. D. Whitney, D., Mohr, B. J. & Griffen, T.J. (2003). *The Appreciative Inquiry Summit*. San Francisco: Berret-Koehler.
12. Bushe, G. R., & Khamisa, A. (January 2004). When is Appreciative Inquiry Transformational? A Meta-Case Analysis. *http://www.gervasebushe.ca/aimeta.htm*
13. Barrett, F. J. (1995). Creating Appreciative Learning Cultures. *Organisational Dynamics*, 24: pp. 36–49.
14. Ibid., p. 42.
15. Ibid., p. 48.
16. Cammock, Peter (2003). *The Dance of Leadership: The Call for Soul in 21st Century Leadership*. Auckland: Prentice-Hall.
17. Ibid., p. 42.
18. Follett, M. P. (1918). *The New State*. New York: Longmans, Green & Company.
19. Hurst, David K. (1995). *Crisis & Renewal: Meeting the Challenge of Organisational Change*. Boston, Mass.: Harvard University Press, p. 148.
20. Ibid., pp. 148–149.
21. *Economist*. (October 25, 2003). How to run a company well.
22. Bruch, Heike & Ghoshal, Sumantra (2004). *A Bias for Action: How Effective Managers Harness Their Willpower, Achieve Results, and Stop Wasting Time*. Boston, MA: Harvard Business School Press.

Index

Abrahamson, Eric, 193–94
accomplishment, 207, 220, 239, 255, 275, 317
accountability, 89, 207, 230, 277, 297, 323, 325
acquisition, 231
action, actions, 117, 282, 285, 289, 300; effects, relationship, 242; plan, 236; and reflection, 112, 248, 252, 332; research and dialogue, 27–28
advertising, 79, 111, 195
Air France, 86
airline industry, 85–86
AirTran, 86, 121
alternative, perceptions of, 172–74
ambiguity, 253–54, 268, 270, 284, 288
American Airlines, 85–86, 121
American Revolution, 145
anticipatory change, 99–100, 312
anxiety and stress, 141, 258, 276
Apple, 81–82, 101, 123, 124
Apple/Macintosh, 76

appreciating change, 30, 31–38, 52, 285, 313, 330; a framework, 99–103
appreciative inquiry (AI), 307–13, 330; four phase framework, 313–14; in practice, 313–19
Argyris, Chris, 110, 112, 114–17
arousal, 241
aspirations, 33, 99
Aspirational Initiatives to Retain Excellence (ASPIRE), 249–50
attentiveness, 284
attitudes, 282, 285–87, 328
attribution, 116
audience involvement, 159
authority boundary, principle, 151, 155, 206, 208, 226
automobile industry, 72, 73, 75–76, 85, 213
autonomy, 22, 228, 229, 256, 289, 298, 300
AVT Natural Products, 176
awareness, 103, 277, 285, 334
Axelrod, four approaches to change, 135–37

balancing, 200, 214, 288
Bandura, Albert, 255
bandwagon effect, 154
banking industry, 90
bankruptcy, 59
bar-codes, 79
BATNA (Best Alternative To a Negotiational Agreement), 179, 180
beauty industry, 73
Beckhard, Richard, 310
Beetle, 106
behaviour, behavioural context, 107, 114, 208, 209, 265, 280, 282, 286–87, 299, 330, 333; barriers, 182; positive, role, 289–95, 307
beliefs and assumptions, *See* mental models, mindsets
benchmarking, 172, 231, 237, 280, 299
beneficiary, unlearning mindset of, 222
BMW, 126
body language, 28
Bose Corporation, 290
brand image, 213
British Airport Authority (BAA), 91
British Airways, 86, 91
bureaucracy, 137, 227, 228, 234, 256, 290
business acumen, 324
business cycle, 61–62, 64, 68; predictability, 65, 68–69
business models: identifying, 126–27; and value propositions, 120–27
Business Process Reengineering, 44
business savvy leadership, 283
BusinessLand, 124

capability, capabilities: and competencies, 46–48, 93; components, 295–301; *See also* change capability, building
Capability Maturity Model (CMM), 339
car industry, 85
cause-effect relationship, 111, 112, 195
CDMA, 84
Centre for Creative Leadership, 254
C-Flex system, 69
change: agenda, 94–95, 98, 150, 170, 172, 273, 331–32;—refining, 129–31; capability building, 46, 92, 191, 264, 307, 337; challenges, 17–19; consent for, 39, 40; consequences, 31; content, 35–36, 192; failure, 195–200; human aspect, 212, 234; implementation, implementers, 39, 41, 186, 189, 192, 314; management, 100–1, 108–9, 135–36, 148, 173, 190, 251, 308;—model, 30–31, 330–33; need analysis tool, 33–34; packages, 44; planned, 39; recipients, 39; change-related chaos, 193, 194; scope, 42; size, 192; strategists, 39; styles, 43–44; types of, 42–43
Cialdini, Robert, 150–57
civil society, 27
coalitions, 167
codes, internal and external, 25
coercion and threat, 155
coercive persuasion, 27
cognition, cognitive, 120, 255–56, 334; frameworks, 311; role in

Index 345

appreciating change, 98; habits, 119; limitations, 118; and organisational change, 103–5; processing, 260; shifts, 312; turning, turners, 45, 307, 333–35; *See also* leadership
coherence and collective purpose, 217–18
collaboration, collaborative function, 216, 244; factors contributing non-collaboration, 216–18
collective intuition, 259
commercial focus, 221
commitment, 48, 136, 140–41, 144, 148, 155, 164, 167–68, 185, 199, 229, 238, 255, 260, 273, 295, 321, 325
Commodore, 123
communication, communication skills, 18, 28, 48, 50, 59, 134, 152, 165, 176–78, 200, 215, 218, 273, 277, 298, 325, 328; campaign, 228, 291; context and credibility, 332; to influence the people, 157, 159–65; plan, 236; strategy, 331
community expectations, 25
Compaq, 123–24
compartmentalisation, 213, 215, 290, 299
compassion, 328
compensation system, 169
competency, competencies, 118–19, 168, 244, 256–57, 276, 317–18, 324–25, 327, 331, 333; destroying innovations, 77–78, 80; enhancing innovations, 77
competition, competitors, competitiveness, 17, 18, 33, 56–57, 71–76, 87, 90, 100–1, 130, 140, 199, 216, 219, 249, 269, 282, 330, 331
competitive advantage, 47, 82, 93
complexity, 201, 209, 253, 256
compliance, 294
comprehension, 103
compromise, 289
computer industry, 82, 121
ComputerLand, 124
concentration, 70, 71, 85
confidence, 253, 258, 260, 333
conflict of interest, 89
confrontation, 277
consciousness, 29, 216
consensus, 259, 332
conservatism, 101, 120, 317
consistency, 151, 154–55, 164, 178, 320
consolidation, 74, 190
Constitution of Society, by Anthony Giddens, 23
constructionist principle, 311
consumer electronics industry, 81–82
consumer focus, preferences, 74, 83
context analysis, 163–65, 166–69
contingency planning, 241
continuous improvement, 231–32, 244
contractual relationship, 294
control, control systems, 208, 230, 244, 257, 273
convergence, 46
conversations, 29, 331
cooperation, 135, 151, 159, 178, 211, 289, 332
Cooperrider, David, 309–10, 313
coordination mechanisms, 50, 191, 201, 226, 233, 243, 273, 300, 337

Corporate Leadership Council, 326
Cortes, Hernando, 173
cost, costs, 317; efficiency, 124; the target for change, 36; rationalisation, 252
counselling, 288
CR3, 72
crafting the message, 185–86
Craik, Kenneth, 105
creative destruction, 193
creativity, 29
credibility, 93, 142, 144, 152, 159, 162–63, 178, 336
crisis and credibility, 163
critical mass, concept of, 148–49, 154, 165, 331
cross-functional linkage, teams (CFTs), 45, 50, 189, 208, 212, 216–26, 238, 240, 266, 268, 282, 299, 300, 332, 336; credibility, 223; effectiveness, 223; for execution excellence, 218–22
culture, cultural, 25, 41, 44, 58, 300–2; transformation, 176
customer focus, orientation, 36, 57, 126, 213, 228–29, 233, 270, 325, 333
customer satisfaction, 313, 317, 325
Cyert, Richard, 31
cynicism, 102, 136, 152, 193, 194, 262

Daimler, Chrysler, 69, 76
decision-making, power, process, 37, 44, 104, 137, 149, 174, 177, 204, 208, 210, 215, 224, 226, 228, 233, 241, 258, 274, 294, 324, 327, 336
deconstruction of complex change, 240–41

defensive routines, 115–17, 129
Delhi Metro Rail Corporation (DMRC), 149, 155–57, 159–60, 172, 174, 227–29, 263
Dell and Walmart, 101
Dell Computer Corporation, 121–22, 124–25
Dell, Michael, 122, 124–25
Delta Airlines, 86, 121
democracy and participation, 27, 141, 216, 314
departmentalisation, 24, 226
deregulation, 90–91
design function, 227
design incentives, 302
despair, 262
difference of opinion, 235
Digital Equipment Corporation (DEC), 123
digital imaging, 81
digital music and iPod phenomena, 82–83
Digital Video Discs (DVDs), 80
Dikshit, Sheila, 174
direct marketing model, 122, 125–26
discipline, 294, 295, 297, 300
discretion, 47, 256, 300, 333
disenchantment, 286
disengagement, 262
dissent, 204
dissonance, 184
distinctiveness, 38
distrust, 276
diversity, 317
dogmatism, 243
Domino's Pizzas, 126
dot-com companies, 120–21
Dr. Reddy's Laboratories (DRL), 218–21
Drucker, Peter, 284
dynamic complexity, 194–95

dysfunctional constraints, 243, 259, 290

EasyJet, 86, 121
economies of scale, 74
economy, 57, 61, 64, 68
effectiveness, 114, 140, 210, 220, 234, 256, 276, 289, 311; interpersonal, 328
efficiency, 68
EISA, 124
emotional, emotions, 28, 105, 107, 144, 147, 185, 241, 255, 259; negative, 286, 288; positive, 308
employee: cynicism, 102, 136, 152, 193, 194, 262; performance assessment, 115; *See also* participation
empowerment, 190, 267, 298, 325
entanglement principle, 164
equity and fairness, 174–75
Ericsson, 237
errors, 98, 102
espoused theory, 114
evolutionary change, 192
exchange, 87
executing change, 30, 41–42, 45; challenges, 190–95; framework for, 209–12; human aspects, 239–42, 332
expansion, 61
experience, 28, 118–19
experimental learning model, 31, 99
experimentation, 231, 279, 309, 317, 340
exploration, 119
external environment, as driver of change, 57–61

Exxon, 124

failure tolerance and acceptance, 282–83, 308
faith, 320
fast food chains, 73
feedback, feedback loops, 110–11, 115, 116, 194, 205, 207–8, 231, 257, 272, 274, 277, 282, 299, 326, 328, 335, 340
fermentation, 75
flexibility, 47, 300, 330, 333
fluctuations, 64
focus of change, 44, 48, 177, 239, 248, 274, 295; and energy, 260–64
foot-in-the-door approach, 164–65, 169, 185
forces of change, 61–70
Ford, 70, 106
formal constraints, 87
frame-breaking change, 42–43, 46–47
frame-living change, 42
framing change, 169–71
framing of challenges, 268–70
free choice, 27–28, 29
free will, 28
freedom, 141
frustration, 205, 241
Fujitsu, 123
full time equivalent employees (FTEs), 59–60
fund-management, 65, 68

Gandhi, M.K., 113, 321
Garvin, David, 278, 279, 280, 284
Gates, Bill, 58
General Electronics (GE), 234, 237, 281–82; leadership framework, 324–25

General Motors (GM), 68, 69, 72, 106
Ghoshal, Sumantra, 260–61
Ghosn, Carlos, 175, 212–15, 224–26, 263, 264, 265
Giddens, Anthony, 22–23; *Constitution of Society*, 23
Gillette, 79
Gladwell, Malcolm, 167; *The Tipping Point*, 144–48
Glidewell, John, 142
global recession, 266
global terrorism, 18
globalisation, 17, 18, 64
goal, goals, 32–33, 47–48, 58, 114, 176; change, 25, 42–43; oriented systems, 32; and processes, conflicting interpretations, 199; role, 264–70
Google, 126
government agencies, 57
growth rate, 57
GSM, 84

habits and traditions, 25
Halberstam, David, 106
helplessness, 215, 241, 243
Henry Ford, 72
heuristics, 104
Hewlett-Packard (HP), 123
hierarchy, 24, 197, 203, 206, 214, 226, 233, 274, 300, 325
hostility, 45
Hrebiniak, Lawrence, 192, 229–30
human relations workshops, 28
human resource management systems, 299
human resource practices, 37
human system, 27

IBM, 76, 123, 124, 279, 283

identity, 167–68, 184, 185, 214; boundaries, 206, 207
Imexsa, 237–38, 266–67
immorality, 232
improvisation process, improvement projects, 237, 314
incentive systems, 229–30, 244
inconsistencies, 116
incremental change, 100, 111, 129, 193
Industrial Technology Research Institute, Taipei, 80
industry cycle, dynamics, 70–94
industry evolution and concentration, 85–87
inflation, 57, 64
influence networks, 167, 183
influencing perceptions of alternatives, 172–74
information revolution, 18
information sharing, 273
information systems, technology, 221, 296
Infosys, 92, 322; leadership framework, 323
initiative overload, 193, 194
innovations and improvements, 274, 275, 298; developing new routines for, 231–39
inquiry skills, inquiry orientation, 47, 109, 111–12, 307; *See also* appreciative inquiry (AI)
Institute on Governance (IOG), 216, 218
institutional rules, 56, 70, 74, 87–94
integration and coordination, 47, 126, 191, 206, 211, 239, 243, 282, 296
integrity, 293, 318, 320–21
interactions, 24, 277

inter-connectedness, 18, 25
interdependence, 244
Internet, 78–79
interpersonal barriers, 182
interpretations, 118
investment risk, 69
involvement and participation, 27–28, 134–36, 140–41, 150, 185, 238, 277, 314, 331
iPod, 82–83, 101
Ispat, 266, 268
iTunes, 82, 83

J&J, 278
Jaju, Sanjay, 221, 222
Janus and Putnam, 67
JetBlue, 85, 121
Jick, Todd, 191
job design, 256

K-strategies, 72, 85
knowledge, 277, 301, 334; creation and diffusion, 47, 309; management initiatives, 231, 244, 299; sharing, 43, 234, 239, 279, 298, 333; transfer, 280–81, 299
Knowledge Integration Programme (KIP), 239
Koeda, Itaru, 224
Konkan Railway Corporation (KRC), 291–94
Konkan Railway project, 290–94
Kotter, John, 190–91

labour division, 226
lag effects, 111 (why changed to large)
Langer, Ellen, 107–9
leader, leadership, 30–31, 48–53, 152, 156, 165, 170, 217, 220, 270, 296, 298, 300, 330–32; character and conduct, 319–21; charismatic, 49, 318, 321; development, 326–28;—key elements, 326–27; driven approach to change, 135; education, 281; and follower relationship, 319; frameworks, 321–26; role in change management, 17, 278, 307, 333–40; skills/qualities, 170, 283, 322
lean production, 44
learning, learning process, 26, 47, 98, 220, 223, 244, 251, 253, 275, 277, 281, 295–96, 298–302, 320, 335; anxiety, 26–27, 48; for capability building, 278–89; and change, 109–20; by doing, 118, 205, 243; from experience and history, 279–80; from failures, 280; frame, 269; to learn, 282; promoting, 278–89; structuring activities for, 274–77; workshops, 268
legitimacy, 88
Lewin, Kurt, 17, 19–29
LG, 83
liberalisation, 249
liking, 151, 152
Lincoln Navigator, 70
linear thinking, 111
linkage and integration, 47, 204, 206, 299, 333
Linux, a Unix-based system, 76
liquidation, 59
listening, 176, 270, 284–85, 296, 298
low-cost carriers (LCCs), 86, 121

Manthan, 231–32, 234, 235

March, James, 31, 110, 117–20
market, marketing, 18, 207; development, 74, 93; knowledge as source of responsiveness and pricing power, 70; shift, 106; the target for change, 36–37
maturity, 71
mavens, 146
McDonald, 73, 126
McKinsey and Company, 92
medium of message, 177–78
Mendoza, Rafael, 237
mental models or mindset, 20–26, 46, 47, 49–50, 95, 98, 109, 110, 112–13, 129, 131, 134, 159, 162, 205, 242, 244, 272, 278–79, 287, 300, 331, 333–35; and change, 105–9; changing, 26–27, 166, 169, 174, 220, 253; for change management, 328–30; and culture and values, 218; role, 37–38
merger and acquisition, 59, 73, 214
Metallocenes, 80
Michelin, 213
Microsoft, 76, 123, 124
middle managers, 262
mindfulness, 108–9
mindlessness, 107–8
mindset, See mental models
mistrust, 102
Mittal Steel, 237, 263, 265
Mittal, Lakshmi Niwas, 263, 266–67
Mobil, 124
mobile phone industry, 82; strategic changes, 83–84
Moffet Studios, 180, 181
monopoly restriction, 87
morality and fairness, 162
Morgan Stanley, 68
motivation, 43, 114, 135–36, 149, 190–91, 255, 275, 320
Motorola, 83
MS-DOS, 75
Murphy, Franklin, 106

Nakamura, Shiro, 227
NEC, 123
need for change, 31–36, 39
negativity, 45–46
negative consequences, 168
negotiating for change, 178–83
negotiations, 50, 289
Network Walkman, 83
new product development, 202–3, 214
New Zealand: small and medium enterprise (SME), 59
newspaper industry, 78–79
Nissan, 106, 175, 226–27, 241, 263, 268; experience with cross-functional teams (CFTs), 224–26; turnaround, 212–16
Nokia, 82, 83–84
non-linearity, 111, 194, 195, 242
norms and conventions, 21–22, 24, 41, 44–45, 57, 296
NTL Institute for Applied Behavioural Science, 309–10

objectivity, 288
obsolescence, 119
Okubo, Nobuo, 224
Olivetti, 123
ontological security, 22
openness, 208, 223, 296, 334
optimism, 51, 148, 187, 241, 244, 273, 277, 302, 332
organisation, organisational: architecture, 20–21, 289;—role

in change execution, 214–16; behaviour, 18; concept of, 19–20; factors, 256, 289; limitations, 118; structures, policies and rules, 262
Organisation Development (OD), 274–77, 310, 312
original design manufacturers (ODMs), 84
Osterholm, Mike, 163
outcome orientation, 108
outsourcing, 123
ownership and involvement, 134, 136, 140–42, 248, 251, 270–74, 299, 332

paperwork, 293
parallel organisation, 137, 140
participation, *See* involvement and participation
passion, 320
patience and persistence, 238, 330
pattern of activities, change, 25
PC-DOS, 123
people catalyser, 49–50
perceptions, 102–3, 117, 185, 205; and cognitions, 28
performance, 32–34, 57–60, 62, 67, 93, 102, 115, 118–19, 142, 156, 189, 215–16, 221, 231, 238, 250, 264–65, 267, 276, 289, 298; appraisal system, 169; and aspirations/targets, gap, 99, 118–19, 217; criteria, 230; evaluation, 116, 119; frame, 269; improvement, 249, 252, 296
Perkins, George, 180–81
persistence, 144
personal computer (PC) industry, 76, 122

personal mastery, 112–13
persuasion, 144, 166–67, 331; indirectly, 177–78; psychology of, 150–57
pharmaceutical industry, 74
photography industry, 80–81
physical transformation, 74
plastics industry, 80
poetic principle, 312
Pohang Iron and Steel Company (POSCO), Korea, 250
policies, aligning and removing structural impediments to change, 226–31, 332
political aspect of organisational change, 149–50
political boundaries, 206, 207
political dynamics, 118
politics and Indian public systems, 263
politics of change, 40–41
Popular Electronics, 122
population ecology theory, 56, 57–60, 70–71, 85
pornography industry, 78
positive organisational change, 308–9, 312
post-modernism, 311, 314
premature cognitive commitment, 108
preparedness, 241–42
price and market-share, relationship, 111
pricing power, 69, 70
problem-focus, 309
problem-solving process, skills, 45, 111, 180, 235, 236, 256–57, 271–72, 274, 277, 279, 293, 308, 333; time-based, 232
process, processes, 44, 45, 101, 234, 302; driven approach to change, 135–36

procrastination, 258, 261-62
product innovation, 101
product life cycle, 84
product planning, 227
professional conduct, 25
profitability, 32, 59, 65, 94
programmatic change, 44-45
Programme on Negotiation (PON), 179
promotions, 274
property prices, 65
Proust, Marcel, 254
psychological and organisational strain, 276
psychological safety, 27, 241
psychological transition, 45
public opinion, 155
public policy formulation, 216
purposefulness, purpose, sense of, 240, 261-62; among top managers, 262-63
push strategy, 145

quality, 46, 317; of action, 281; evaluation, 209; management, 210; of relationship, 256; the target for change, 36
Quality Circles (QC), 136
quasi-stationary equilibrium, 19
questioning, 298; seven elements, 284-85

radical change, 100, 129
Radio-Electronics, 122
Radio Frequency Identification (RFID), 79
rates of interest, 57
reactive change, 99-100
reasoning, 103, 105, 116
reciprocity, 151, 153
recruitment policy, 209

Reddy, Mahendar, 153, 164-65
relevance, 276
reliability, 118
Renault, 212-13, 227, 264
repetitive change syndrome, 193-94
reporting relationships, 44
Reports, Approvals, Meetings, Measures, Policies and Practices (RAMMPP), 235-36
resentment and frustration, 144
resilience, 339
resistance to change, 26, 45, 137, 251, 280, 288
resource, resourcefulness, 72, 205; allocation for change, 42; partitioning, 85; struggle for, 58; sharing, 74
response to change, managing, 45
responsiveness, 67, 69, 330
retailing, 79
retention, 58, 280
revenue management, 70
reward systems, 216-17, 256
rigid work routines, 256
risk-taking, 48, 218, 274, 287, 289, 297, 298, 333
role models, 51, 267, 302
Roosevelt, Theodore, 181
routines, 117, 209-11, 262; identification of dysfunctional, 210-11; and mental models, 20-26, 31
r-strategies, 72, 85
rules, rule structure, 87, 256; written and unwritten, 22-23, 209, 280
rural e-Governance, 222

Sabena, 86
salesmen, 147-48

Samsung, 83, 84
Santayana, George, 279
scarcity principle, 151, 156, 158
scenario planning, 259
Schein, Edgar, 26–28, 32, 310
Sebenius, James, 181
selection process, 58
self, sense of, 320
self-confidence, 284
self-development, 320
self-discipline, regulation, 208, 236, 295, 338
self-efficacy, 48, 50–51, 248, 295, 298, 332, 338; focus and energy for capability building, 253–60
self-esteem, 214
self-interest, 149–50
self-regulation, 208, 236, 338
Seligman, Martin, 308
Senge, Peter, 110–17; five disciplines, 112–13
shared ownership, 325
shared purposes, 234
shared vision, 113
Siemens leadership framework, 325
Simon, David, 221, 265, 270
Simon, Herbert, 31
simultaneity principle, 311
Six Sigma, 44, 136
skills, 43, 111–12, 218, 296, 299, 301
small scale industry (SSI), 64
SMART (Specific, Measurable, Achievable, Relevant, Time bound) goals, 336–37
smart labels, 79–80
social architecture, 50
social constructionism, 311
social networks, 183

social proof principle, 151, 153–54
socio-cultural norms, 277
Software Engineering Institute (SEI), Carnegie Mellon University, 339
software services, 91–92
Sony, 83, 101
Sony-Ericsson, 83
Sony Walkman, 101
Southwest, 86, 121
specialisation, 24
spectator orientation, 254
Sreedharan, E., 155–56, 174, 227, 263, 290–94
Srivastava, Suresh, 309, 313
stability, 26, 29, 46
standardisation of operations and products, 74
status quo, 19, 26, 29, 31, 141, 157, 168, 206, 274
step-by-step sequential approach, 52, 147, 313
stock market, 68
strategies, 296, 300–1
stress, 184; management, 288
structure vs. process, 44, 45, 58
structuring of activities, 23, 264
superstitions, 119
supply chain management, 232
support mobilisation, 30, 38–46, 50, 134, 294, 297, 300–2, 307, 331, 335–36
survival anxiety, 26
sustaining the momentum, 186
Swissair, 86
systems approach, 47, 110–17
systems architect, 50, 211–12, 242–44, 336–37

tacit (unwritten) rules, *See* rules, written and unwritten

Tandy Radio Shack, 123
target orientation, 117
Tata Chemicals, 154, 231–32
Tata Consultancy Services (TCS), 92
Tata Leadership Practices (TLPs), 323–24
Tata Steel, 249–50, 251–52, 256, 268, 270
team building, 325
team-based approach to change, teamwork, 135–36, 234–35
team effectiveness, 275
team-based incentives, 230
team learning, 113
technology, technological, 56, 70, 93, 99, 122, 330; change, 17, 59, 74–82, 91, 333; discontinuity, 75, 77, 81; general purpose, 74–75, 78; industry-specific, 75; and strategy change, 82–87; the target for change, 36
telecommunication industry, 90, 91
Texas Instruments, 123
theory-in-use, 114–16
thoughtfulness, thought process, 28–29, 329
timing, timeliness, 35–36, 186, 260
The Tipping Point, by Malcolm Gladwell, 144–48
tolerance, 288
top management, top managers, 208, 215; commitment and support for change, 48; perceptions, 32; purposefulness, 262–63; role in executing change, 211
top-down control, 295

Toshiba, 123
Total Operational Performance (TOP), 249
Total Quality Management (TQM), 44, 136
transformation, 251, 265, 301
transition management team, 45
transparent, 169, 175, 228, 328
trial and error experimentation, learning, 118
Truman, Harry, 284
trust, 147, 182, 184, 208, 289, 294, 297, 300, 321

uncertainty, 18, 57, 68, 72, 90–91, 94, 99–100, 141, 168, 173, 201, 202, 242, 253–54, 256, 271, 315, 330; self-efficacy in, 258–60
under-utilisation, 234
Union Chemical Laboratories, 80
United Kingdom: Britain: automobile industry, 73; National Health Service (NHS), 322–23
United States of America: airline industry, 86; automobile industry, 72, 75–76, 106; Conference Board and Economic Cycle Research Institute, 65; corporate scandals, 89; Gross Domestic Product, 61, 62; National Bureau of Economic Research, 61; personal computer (PC) industry, 122–24; Public Company Accounting Oversight Board, 89; recession, 62, 64; Sarbanes-Oxley Act, 2002, 89–90; stock market, 68; telecommunication industry, 91; attack of 9/11, 86

unlearning and learning, 248, 286–89, 333

value, values and beliefs, 25, 29, 45, 47, 127, 152, 185, 214, 298, 322, 334–35; based leadership, 321; propositions, 37, 98, 120–27
variation process, 58
vision, 319, 325
vision statement, 149
Vodafone, 91
volatility, 64, 68
Volkswagen, 106

Walmart, 126
Watson, Tom, 283
Westinghouse, 294
Wipro, 92
working conditions, 18
workout methodology, 234
World Bank, 92
World Steel Dynamics (WSD), 250

Xerox, 123

Zenith, 123

About the Authors

V. Nilakant is Associate Professor, Department of Management, College of Business and Economics, and Associate Dean, Faculty of Commerce at the University of Canterbury, Christchurch, New Zealand.

S. Ramnarayan is a Professor at the Indian School of Business, and Director, Change Management, at the Centre for Good Governance.

Both the authors have extensive management consulting experience in India and overseas. They have worked together at Tata Management Training Centre in Pune, India, and have been involved in change management programmes in the Tata group of companies, other private and public sector organisations and for the government in India. They have also consulted with companies overseas on issues relating to change. Their previous book *Managing Organisational Change,* published by Response Books in 1998, received the prestigious Best Book Award in the National Book Competition held by the Indian Society for Training and Development.